FORTRAN IV PROGRAMMING AND APPLICATIONS

HOLDEN-DAY COMPUTER
AND INFORMATION SCIENCES SERIES

S. D. Conte, Editor

FORTRAN IV PROGRAMMING AND APPLICATIONS

C. Joseph Sass

Department of Operations Research
University of Toledo

Holden-Day, Inc.
San Francisco

Düsseldorf   Johannesburg   London
Panama   Singapore   Sydney

FORTRAN IV PROGRAMMING AND APPLICATIONS

Copyright © 1974 by Holden-Day, Inc.
4432 Telegraph Avenue, Oakland, CA 94609

All rights reserved.

No part of this book may be reproduced, stored in a retrieval system, or transmitted, in any form or by any means, electronic, mechanical, photocopying, recording, or otherwise, without permission in writing from the publisher.

Library of Congress Catalog Card Number: 72-93537
ISBN: 0-8162-7473-8

Printed in the United States of America

0 HA

PREFACE

The FORTRAN programming language, which was first introduced in the mid-1950s, continues to be one of the most widely used languages. It is employed by businessmen, engineers, mathematicians, social scientists, educators, professional and nonprofessional programmers, and students. This book is designed for their use in learning the language FORTRAN. It can be used in a formal course with instructional aid, as a self-teaching manual for readers who are learning FORTRAN on their own initiative, or as a reference source for persons using FORTRAN currently. The groups mentioned will find the text appropriate, with problems and questions applicable to each group.

The text incorporates three concepts that will prove helpful to the readers, especially to introductory programmers. First, a large number of complete computer programs are illustrated throughout the text. The accompanying data and actual computer output are shown with each program, as is a flowchart. Each sample illustrates a particular use or programming concept. To ensure continuity from one chapter to the next, the same two program samples, one concerning a sales tax and the other statistics, are employed throughout most of the text. Also, a number of relatively simple mathematical problems are included. The programs are expanded as new material is introduced, thereby providing the reader the opportunity of following small program solutions upward to more complicated applications.

The second concept involves a series of figures that are an integral part of the discussion of each FORTRAN statement. The figures (1) describe and list examples of the use of each instruction; (2) portray and describe the common errors that the novice usually incurs; and (3) present a correct statement in place of the erroneous instruction. The purpose of these figures is to limit the number of "trial and error" approaches to programming by indicating what can and cannot be done.

The third helpful factor included in the text is that each chapter is subdivided into sections; each section is concerned with one main topic, followed by a set of exercises pertaining only to that topic. Answers to many of the questions are at the back of the book, thus accommodating the readers who wish to check their progress. Additional problems of a general nature are included at the end of each chapter, with selected answers available at the back of the book also.

Although many versions of FORTRAN exist, the content here is based on USAS Basic FORTRAN IV, with many of the options and extensions of standard FORTRAN IV included either as separate sections or as appendixes. The extensions are footnoted where used, and the end result is intended to give the student familiarity with a language that he will be able to use on any of several computer systems.

A brief introduction to computers and programming is contained in Chapter 1, with the language being covered in detail in the remaining chapters. Flowcharting techniques are also emphasized throughout the text. In the quarter system, Chapters 8 and 9 may be omitted. However, the entire text can be covered adequately in a semester. In some cases, the instructor may choose to cover Chapter 7 along with Chapter 3. For schools using WATFOR or WATFIV compilers, Appendix A should be covered with Chapters 2, 4, and 5 while delaying Chapter 3.

I am indebted to many persons who have made this book possible, especially Kenneth Knoke, Julia Gormley, and Jean Schaefer. Use of the computer facilities at The University of Toledo is also greatly appreciated.

C. J. S.

CONTENTS

1 INTRODUCTION TO PROGRAMMING AND FORTRAN, 1

- 1-1 Introduction, 1
- 1-2 Programs and Programming Tasks, 3
- 1-3 Flowcharting, 5
- 1-4 Types of FORTRAN IV Statements, 7
- 1-5 FORTRAN IV Example, 8
- 1-6 Constants, 11
- 1-7 Variable Names, 15
- 1-8 Mathematical Operators, 16
- 1-9 Summary, 18

2 BEGINNING FORTRAN STATEMENTS, 21

- 2-1 Arithmetic Assignments, 21
- 2-2 The WRITE Statement, 27
- 2-3 END and STOP Statements, 30
- 2-4 Program Sample—SALES TAX, 31
- 2-5 Program Sample—STATISTICS, 34
- 2-6 Miscellaneous Mathematical Sample, 36
- 2-7 Summary, 37

3 COMMENTS, FORMAT, AND CONTINUATION STATEMENTS, 41

- 3-1 Comments, 41
- 3-2 FORMAT Statement, 43

3-3 Continuation Statements, 50
3-4 Program Sample—SALES TAX, 51
3-5 Program Sample—STATISTICS, 53
3-6 FORMAT Extensions, 56
3-7 Program Sample—SALES TAX, 60
3-8 Miscellaneous Mathematical Samples, 62
3-9 Summary, 64

4 ADDITIONAL I/O COMMANDS, 67

4-1 The READ Statement, 67
4-2 Program Sample—SALES TAX, 74
4-3 Program Sample—STATISTICS, 77
4-4 Extensions to the Basic I/O Commands, 80
4-5 Program Sample—SALES TAX, 85
4-6 The DATA Statement, 87
4-7 Program Sample—STATISTICS, 90
4-8 Miscellaneous Mathematical Sample, 91
4-9 Summary, 94

5 THE TRANSFER COMMANDS, 97

5-1 The GO TO Statement, 97
5-2 Program Sample—SALES TAX, 102
5-3 Program Sample—STATISTICS, 105
5-4 The IF Statements, 108
5-5 Program Sample—SALES TAX, 115
5-6 Program Sample—STATISTICS, 120
5-7 The Computed GO TO Statement, 123
5-8 Program Sample—SALES TAX, 126
5-9 Miscellaneous Business Sample, 129
5-10 Summary, 132

6 THE DO, CONTINUE, AND DIMENSION STATEMENTS, 135

6-1 The DO and CONTINUE Statements, 135
6-2 Program Sample—SALES TAX, 143
6-3 Program Sample—STATISTICS, 146
6-4 The DIMENSION Statement, 150
6-5 Program Sample—SALES TAX, 159
6-6 Program Sample—STATISTICS, 160
6-7 Miscellaneous DIMENSION Samples, 166
6-8 Implied DO Loops in I/O, 173
6-9 Program Sample—STATISTICS, 177

CONTENTS ix

6-10   Miscellaneous Implied DO Samples, 178
6-11   Summary, 182

7 SPECIFICATION STATEMENTS, 185

7-1   INTEGER-type Specification, 185
7-2   REAL-type Specification, 186
7-3   DOUBLE PRECISION Specification, 189
7-4   Program Sample—SALES TAX, 193
7-5   Program Sample—STATISTICS, 197
7-6   The COMMON Statement, 202
7-7   The EQUIVALENCE Statement, 203
7-8   Program Sample—SALES TAX, 209
7-9   Program Sample—STATISTICS, 210
7-10   Summary, 212

8 FUNCTIONS AND SUBPROGRAMS, 217

8-1   FORTRAN-supplied Subprograms, 217
8-2   Program Sample—STATISTICS, 222
8-3   Miscellaneous Samples with Trigonometric Functions, 226
8-4   Statement Functions, 231
8-5   Program Sample—STATISTICS, 236
8-6   Miscellaneous Program Sample, 239
8-7   FUNCTION Subprograms, 242
8-8   Program Sample—STATISTICS, 249
8-9   Miscellaneous Program Sample, 253
8-10   Summary, 255

9 SUBROUTINE SUBPROGRAMS, 259

9-1   Subroutines with Arguments, 259
9-2   Program Sample—STATISTICS, 269
9-3   Miscellaneous Program Sample, 271
9-4   Subroutines with COMMON Statements, 280
9-5   Miscellaneous Student Sorting Sample, 288
9-6   Miscellaneous Payroll Sample, 290
9-7   Summary, 295

A WATFOR AND WATFIV EXTENSIONS TO FORTRAN IV, 299

B USING THE CARD PUNCH TO PREPARE PROGRAM AND DATA CARDS, 309

FORTRAN-SUPPLIED MATHEMATICAL SUBPROGRAMS, 319   **C**

ERROR MESSAGES, 323   **D**

MORE ON LOGICAL OPERATIONS, 325   **E**

ANSWERS TO SELECTED EXERCISES AND QUESTIONS, 331   **F**

INDEX, 347

FORTRAN IV PROGRAMMING AND APPLICATIONS

INTRODUCTION TO PROGRAMMING AND FORTRAN 1

Computers are being used throughout our society to solve a number of diverse problems in the areas of engineering, research projects, and business operations, as well as in such new fields as educational methodology, ecological studies, flight-control systems, crime prevention, and other social studies.

1-1 Introduction

To utilize the capabilities of a computer system, it is necessary to provide a set of instructions or a *program* to allow the user to control the operation of the system. This book will furnish the reader with the elementary knowledge required to program computers in the FORTRAN IV programming language. Before proceeding to this main task, it is worthwhile and essential to understand the primary components and functions of a computer system. This minimum background will aid the reader in understanding the programming material in the following chapters.

A computer system is composed of five separate components (Fig. 1-1): the *input, output, control, memory*, and *processor* or arithmetic units. Each unit serves a distinct purpose. To begin using a computer, information consisting of data values or program statements must be entered. The input function satisfies this basic need. Various types of input devices can be used to transmit data into the computer. One of the most common

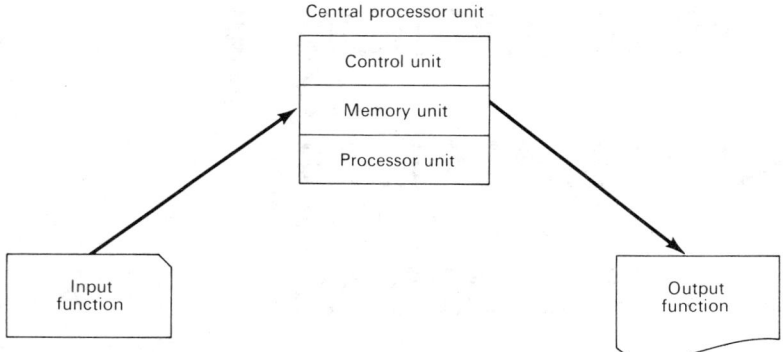

Figure 1-1 Components of a typical computer system.

devices used is the card reader, which normally processes 80-column punched cards. The punched card input method will be assumed in the program samples shown in this text.

As the input component serves to pass information to the computer, the output function serves to transmit data from the computer to the user. A high-speed line printer is the common output device for providing the answers generated by a program. The line printer will be assumed as the output device in later program samples.

The last three components of a computer system, the memory unit, the control unit, and the processor unit, form together the *central processor unit* (CPU). The three components are often physically housed in the same unit and hence are classified singularly as the CPU. However, each performs different operations. The memory unit serves the purpose of retaining or storing for later use program statements or data that has been transmitted to the computer by the input function. The memory unit thus serves as a retention device. The control unit performs the necessary function of coordination among the five components. It monitors and supervises the activities and operations of the entire computer system and ensures that the processing steps are executed in the order dictated by the user program. The final component is the processor unit, or, as it is often called, the arithmetic unit. Mathematical and logical operations—addition, subtraction, multiplication, division, and also logical or decision tests—are made within the processor unit. Data is manipulated arithmetically only within this unit.

INTRODUCTION TO PROGRAMMING AND FORTRAN

These five physical components form a computer system (Fig. 1-2). When combined with a set of instructions or computer program, they can be operated to advantage in solving many different types of problems. The computer can be viewed in this regard as a sophisticated tool.

1-2 Programs and Programming Tasks

A program is necessary to use the computer as a sophisticated tool. But what is a program? A computer program is a specific set of directions or instructions that, when performed in a logical sequence, leads to the solution of a particular computer problem. Usually the set of instructions is written in a high-level programming language such as *FORTRAN IV*. A trait of computer programs is that they must be precisely written in the selected programming language. This trait is critical because the computer does exactly what it is instructed to do by the program and nothing else. Unfortunately, it does not do what is sometimes *intended* by the programmer but only what is specified by the statement he writes.

A minimum of five steps is usually necessary to write a program. The first step is *problem definition*. Before it is possible to begin

Figure 1-2 A typical large computer system. (*Reprinted by permission of IBM Corporation.*)

writing a program to solve a problem, a clear understanding of what is needed is a prerequisite to the second step. An analysis of the type of input, the mathematical procedures that must be performed to obtain the desired answers, and the format of the output are necessary parts of writing a program. The second step is formulating a *method of solution* or an *algorithm* that will lead to the desired answers. A method of solution or algorithm is a set of procedures or logical steps necessary to calculate and modify the input data values to obtain the answers. It is the development of a logical approach to a problem, which is often the most difficult part of writing a program. Once the sequence of steps is established, the remaining requirements follow easily.

The third step is the establishment of a *logical flow* of directions or instructions necessary to solve the defined problem. A logical flow or *flowchart* is the representation in pictorial form of the procedures outlined in the method of solution. A flowchart will accompany most of the programming examples in this text; therefore, a further discussion of flowcharting will be included in Sec. 1-3.

The fourth step involves translating the flowchart into FORTRAN IV program statements. This fourth step is called *coding the program*. When the first three steps have been executed precisely, the coding is a relatively easy task, provided the established rules of the programming language are followed. The fifth step includes running the program, testing for logic errors, and documentation of the program. Testing is essential to ensure that the correct answers are produced as output from the program. Often it is necessary to make minor revisions to the original program in order to correct a logic error. Testing is required at the beginning, but *documentation* is required once the program is ready for productive use. Documentation identifies exactly the purpose of the program, the type of input needed to run the program, the methodology used to obtain the output, and any other helpful comments or remarks that explain the program and its function.

Some programs may require more than the five steps outlined here. However, a good working program is the result of an evaluation and understanding of each of the five steps identified.

INTRODUCTION TO PROGRAMMING AND FORTRAN

The primary purpose of a program flowchart is to portray in graphic form the various arithmetic and logical procedures required to solve a particular problem. A flowchart can be identified as an abbreviated set of instructions that are placed in special symbols. Each symbol (Fig. 1-3) has an implied standard meaning. The symbols are usually connected by directional arrows that indicate the sequential flow of operations as they are to be performed by the computer. Within each symbol, a written note in verbal terms specifies the procedure or activity

1-3 Flowcharting

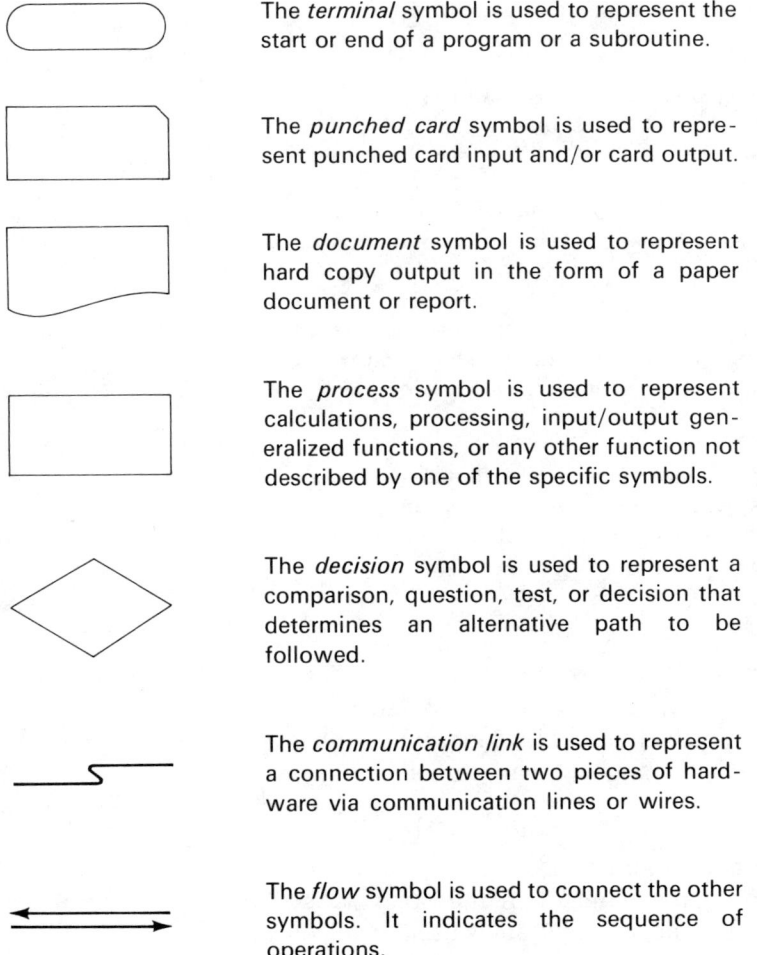

The *terminal* symbol is used to represent the start or end of a program or a subroutine.

The *punched card* symbol is used to represent punched card input and/or card output.

The *document* symbol is used to represent hard copy output in the form of a paper document or report.

The *process* symbol is used to represent calculations, processing, input/output generalized functions, or any other function not described by one of the specific symbols.

The *decision* symbol is used to represent a comparison, question, test, or decision that determines an alternative path to be followed.

The *communication link* is used to represent a connection between two pieces of hardware via communication lines or wires.

The *flow* symbol is used to connect the other symbols. It indicates the sequence of operations.

Figure 1-3 Standard flowcharting symbols.

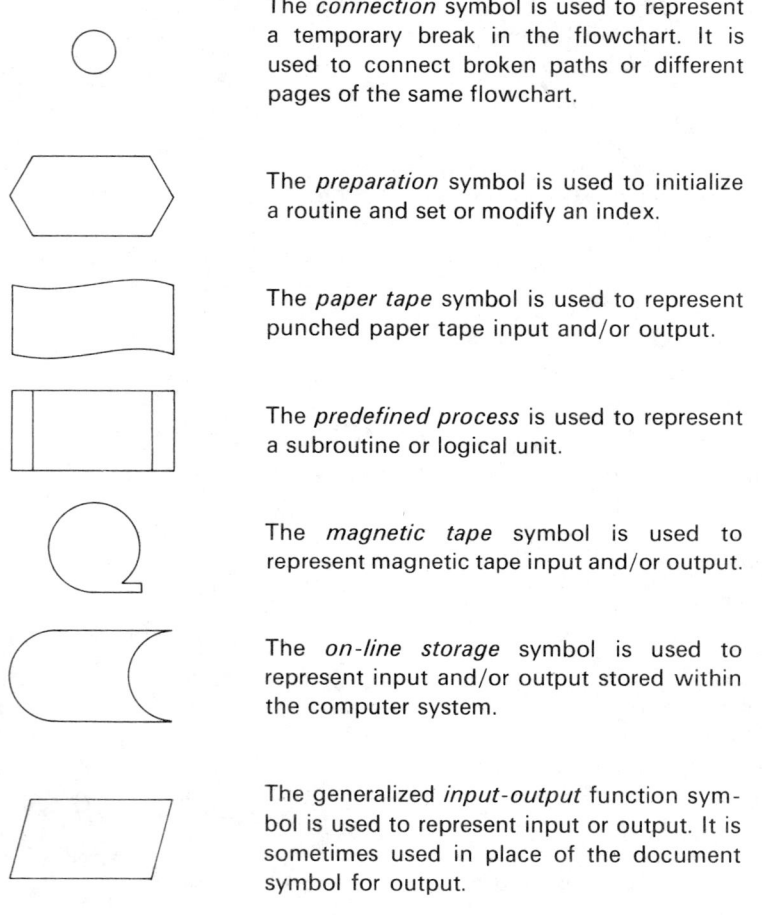

The *connection* symbol is used to represent a temporary break in the flowchart. It is used to connect broken paths or different pages of the same flowchart.

The *preparation* symbol is used to initialize a routine and set or modify an index.

The *paper tape* symbol is used to represent punched paper tape input and/or output.

The *predefined process* is used to represent a subroutine or logical unit.

The *magnetic tape* symbol is used to represent magnetic tape input and/or output.

The *on-line storage* symbol is used to represent input and/or output stored within the computer system.

The generalized *input-output* function symbol is used to represent input or output. It is sometimes used in place of the document symbol for output.

Figure 1-3 Standard flowcharting symbols (*cont'd*).

represented by the symbol. The flowchart can be used to trace the flow of operations from step to step. Thus, flowcharting provides the programmer with the means of visualizing a problem solution as it is constructed from beginning to end.

There are four reasons for flowcharting. First, it facilitates the definition of the problem and program development. Second, each of the individual segments required in the solution is identified; the source of input data, the logic steps used to solve the problem, and the specific output are designated. Third, the flowchart is a guide to the programmer as he writes the FORTRAN IV programming statements. Finally, it is a vital part of the documentation or organized information relating to a specific computer application.

A few standard guidelines are suggested when drawing a flowchart. First, whenever possible isolate each operation or group of procedures that must be performed to arrive at the solution. Begin drawing the flowchart by starting the flow of information in the upper left-hand corner of the page and work down and to the right. Use the standard symbols to convey the primary purpose of each step. Within each of these symbols, write simple but concise messages to explain each process that must be performed. Once the complete flowchart has been developed, the actual program statements can be written. The statements for this book will be written in FORTRAN IV. The different types of statements available are included in Sec. 1-4.

1-4 Types of FORTRAN IV Statements

The acronym FORTRAN is formed from the words FORmula TRANslation. FORTRAN was originally developed in the mid-1950s as a scientifically oriented language designed primarily to speed up the programming process. Although it is still used primarily in scientific fields, its usage has expanded to both business and social applications. The language has continually been updated and improved so that now the most recent version is called FORTRAN IV. FORTRAN is available for use on almost all the systems produced by the various computer manufacturers.

FORTRAN statements consist of certain key words used together with the basic elements of the language. The basic elements include constants, variables, and expressions or mathematical formulas that will be defined later. The different types of statements available are

1. *Arithmetic statements:* Values are assigned to variables by the arithmetic assignment statement. The values may be constants or the result of mathematical calculations.

2. *Input/output statements:* For user analysis, data is transferred from an external source to the computer or from the computer to an output medium by input/output statements.

3. *FORMAT statement:* The layout design, or the form in which data is transmitted to or from the computer, is specified by the FORMAT statement.

4 *Control statements:* The sequential flow of the program statements, the logic, and the termination of the program is directed by various control statements.

5 *Specification statements:* Properties of variables, arrays, and subprograms are designated by various specification statements.

6 *SUBPROGRAM and FUNCTION statements:* Separate, commonly used routines or procedures and functions can be established or defined by SUBPROGRAM and FUNCTION statements.

1-5 FORTRAN IV Example

The program statements must be written in a form acceptable to the computer. To simplify this task, the statements should be written or "coded" on a FORTRAN coding form (Fig. 1-4). To transmit the program information to the computer, a special machine called a *keypunch* (Fig. 1-5) is normally used. The keypunch is used to generate punched cards, identical to the statements contained on the coding form; the cards are then used as input to the computer. The cards (Fig. 1-6) are punched according to the following restrictions[1]:

1 A comment designation may appear in column 1, or a statement number may be placed in the first five columns.
2 A continuation character may appear in column 6.
3 The program statement is punched beginning in column 7.
4 Program identification may appear in columns 73 to 80.

Within the program statements, spaces may be inserted wherever they make the card more readable.

The next step is to feed the cards to the computer. The program cards plus special control[2] cards are input to the computer. Provided the statements are correct, output from the program will be generated according to the logic supplied. On the next page is a sample program and its output illustrating the various types of statements:

[1] Further keypunch details will be discussed in Chap. 2. Also, the phrases "comment designator" and "continuation character" that follow will be defined in detail as they are introduced later.

[2] In most installations, the special control cards are distributed by the computer center's operating personnel. The programmer need not be concerned with them.

INTRODUCTION TO PROGRAMMING AND FORTRAN 9

```
// STAT      JOB @CJ SASS@,@       ROOM 416 UH        @,MSGLEVEL=)0,0*  ⎫
// EXEC FORTGCLG,PARM=NOMAP                                             ⎬ 1
//FORT.SYSIN DD *                                                       ⎭
      VAL1 = 75.          ⎫
      VAL2 = 89.          ⎪
      VAL3 = 73.          ⎬ 2
      SUM = VAL1 + VAL2 + VAL3 ⎪
      AVG = SUM/3.        ⎭
      WRITE(6,300)VAL1,VAL2,VAL3,SUM,AVG } 3
300   FORMAT(5F10.0) } 4
      STOP ⎫
      END  ⎬ 5
           ⎭
/*
//GO.SYSIN DD * } 1
/*
```

        75.   89.   73.   237.   79. } 6

1 to 5 indicate input cards. (1) Special control cards (variable from computer to computer); (2) arithmetic statements; (3) input/output statement; (4) FORMAT statement; (5) control statements. (6) Computer output (output listing or printer).

The same program will now be repeated using a different set of control cards. Notice that the output is exactly the same.

```
//WATFIV   JOB 0001,COMPCENTER,MSGLEVEL=)0,0*                           ⎫
//JOBLIB DD DSN=WATFIV.JOBLIB,VOL=SER=TOLEDO,UNIT=2314,DISP=SHR          ⎬ 1
// EXEC WATFIVS                                                         ⎭
//WATS1.SYSIN DD *
$JOB STAT        WATFIV,PAGES=10,LINES=50
      VAL1 = 75.          ⎫
      VAL2 = 89.          ⎪
      VAL3 = 73.          ⎬ 2
      SUM = VAL1 + VAL2 + VAL3 ⎪
      AVG = SUM/3.        ⎭
      WRITE(6,300)VAL1,VAL2,VAL3,SUM,AVG } 3
300   FORMAT(5F10.0) } 4
      STOP ⎫
      END  ⎬ 5
$ENTRY     ⎭  } 1
/*
```

        75.   89.   73.   237.   79. } 6

1 to 5 indicate input cards. (1) Special control cards (variable from computer to computer); (2) arithmetic statements; (3) input/output statement; (4) FORMAT statement; (5) control statements. (6) Computer output (output listing or printer).

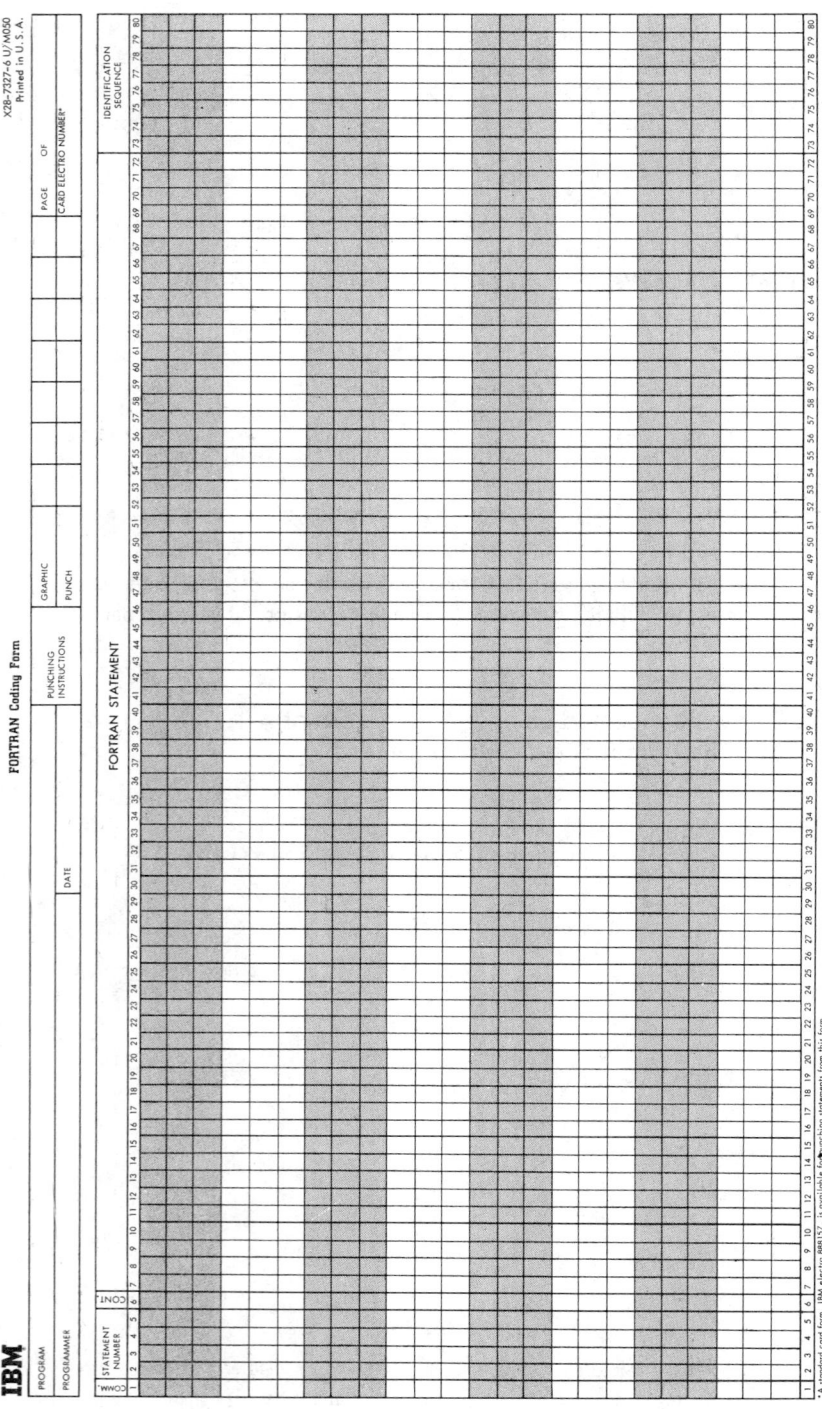

Figure 1-4 A FORTRAN coding form. (*Reprinted by permission of IBM Corporation.*)

INTRODUCTION TO PROGRAMMING AND FORTRAN 11

Figure 1-5 The IBM Model 029 keypunch. (*Reprinted by permission of IBM Corporation.*)

This example is only an illustration; the reader should not be concerned with the detailed analysis because it will be discussed further in Chap. 2. However, to begin, examination of the first three statements in the sample reveals constants (underlined below).

```
VAL1 = 75.
VAL2 = 89.
VAL3 = 73.
```

What are valid types of constants or numbers permitted in the FORTRAN language?

As mentioned previously, a trait of computer programs is that they must be precisely written in the selected programming language. In FORTRAN, three types of numeric constants are

**1-6
Constants**

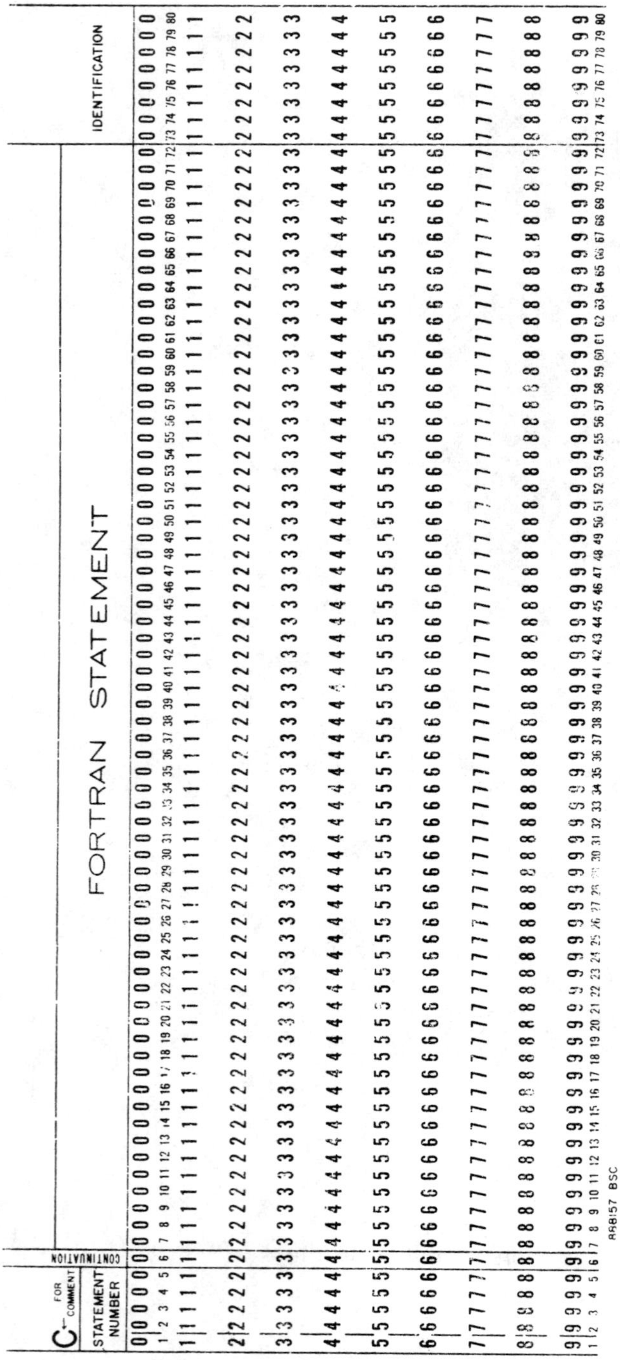

Figure 1-6 FORTRAN card layout.

INTRODUCTION TO PROGRAMMING AND FORTRAN 13

permitted: *integer, real,* and *double-precision.* Integer constants are simply whole numbers written without a decimal point. It may be of positive, zero, or negative value but must lie in the range of ± 2147483647.* Examples of valid integer constants are

$$2 \quad -73 \quad +8282828 \quad -6000600$$

Examples of invalid integer constants are

FORTRAN Constant	Error Description
5,800	Commas are not permitted as part of integer constants.
2.0	Decimal points must be excluded in integer constants.
9200000000	The integer value exceeds the maximum range.
$200	The dollar sign ($) is an invalid numeric character.

The difference between integer and real or double-precision constants is that the first does not contain a decimal point but the latter two do. *Real constants can be expressed in decimal notation or in scientific notation (exponential form)* and must lie in the approximate range of 10^{-78} to 10^{75}. Sample real constants are

$$62.5 \quad 8. \quad 2186.03 \quad 786.882$$

Real constants are also called single-precision[1] constants. Seven significant digits, or ± 9999999, is the maximum range for single-precision constants. How, then, is a number like 123456789.012 represented as a real constant? For the moment excluding double-precision, the number can be represented in scientific notation with a one- or two-digit exponent such as 123456.8E+03. Note that the least significant digits are lost, but the decimal point location is retained. The E notation

---

*This range applies to the IBM 360 computer series. Refer to the particular system reference manual being used for limits on other models.
[1] In simple terms, single- and double-precision refer to the number of locations reserved for a value in the computer's memory. Double-precision constants are able to retain approximately twice as many significant digits as single-precision constants.

can be interpreted as raising 10 to the power indicated after the E and multiplying the constant by this result. For example, valid real constants in exponential form are

REAL constant	is the	mathematical equivalent of:	or
25.1E2		25.1×10^2	2510.
878.33E03		878.33×10^3	878330.
40.77E−02		40.77×10^{-2}	.4077
1.23E+05		1.23×10^5	123000.

Some examples of invalid real constants, expressed in either decimal or scientific notation, are

REAL Constant	Error Description
10	The decimal point is omitted.
8,678.23	The comma is an invalid character.
66.67E+99	The value exceeds the allowable range of 10^{75}.
$66.67E−99	The dollar sign is invalid and the value is outside the allowable range of 10^{-78}.
.012E+100	Only two-digit integer constants are permitted after the E.
123456789.	The value contains too many positions for a single-precision constant.

The third category of constants is double-precision. Although single-precision constants may contain seven digits, double-precision constants may contain 16 digits. However, the value must still lie within the range of 10^{-78} to 10^{75}. In scientific notation, an E represents a single-precision constant while a D is used as the exponent in double-precision constants. Valid double-precision constants are

Double-precision constant	is the	mathematical equivalent of:	or
216.667D+03		216.667×10^3	216667.
4561234567890123.		4561234567890123.	4561234567890123.
10.D+00		$10. \times 10^0$	10.
5.1234567D−03		5.1234567×10^{-3}	.0051234567

INTRODUCTION TO PROGRAMMING AND FORTRAN

The errors identified earlier for integer and single-precision constants apply also to double-precision constants and are therefore omitted here. The examples of valid and invalid constants are intended to familiarize the reader with the basic rules governing their use in FORTRAN programs.

1-7 Variable Names

In the sample program shown, the first three statements include both constants and variables. The different types of constants were discussed above, but what are variables? A FORTRAN variable[1] is a name or symbolic representation of a quantity that is stored within the computer's memory unit. The value of a variable may be changed within a program, and only the most current value is retained; all previous values are lost. A variable name may contain from one to six characters. The first character must be alphabetic, and the remaining five may be either letters or numbers. Variable names have an implied mode of either integer or real. Variables that begin with the letters I to N are integer mode by default. All other variables beginning with A to H and O to Z are real mode by default. (Naming the mode of a variable by using the first character is known as default declaration or implicit declaration.)

As just implied, only integer constants can be assigned to integer variable names. However, either real single- or double-precision constants may be assigned to real variable names. Some examples of valid variable names are

FORTRAN Variable	Mode of Variable
I	Integer
X	Real
KOUNTR	Integer
SUMSQR	Real
M2N4	Integer
XBAR28	Real

Examples of invalid variable names are

---

[1] Two types of variables, unsubscripted and subscripted, are used in FORTRAN. The first, unsubscripted, is discussed here; the second, subscripted, is discussed in Chap. 6.

FORTRAN Variable	Error Description
1SUM	The first character is not alphabetic.
B B	The two spaces between the letters are not permitted, and only letters or numbers can be used.
SUMMARY	The name contains more than six characters.
AB.C	The decimal point is an invalid character.

By avoiding the common errors identified in these samples, the programmer can prevent delays in receiving answers to his problems. Referring back to the sample program, note that all the variables used are real mode.

1-8 Mathematical Operators

The right-hand side of the fourth statement contains a real-valued expression, or real expression, or real mathematical formula. Expressions may be either integer or real mode, depending upon the constants and variables used. To designate specific calculations in FORTRAN expressions, a set of operators is used. These operators are

Operator Symbol	Operation	Example in FORTRAN with Variables X and Y	Mathematical Equivalent
**	Exponentiation	X**Y	X^Y
*	Multiplication	X*Y	$X \times Y$
/	Division	X/Y	$X \div Y$
+	Addition	X+Y	$X+Y$
−	Subtraction	X−Y	$X-Y$

Expressions, whether they are integer or real mode, are evaluated within a program from left to right and according to the rules of precedence or the priority of the operators. The highest priority is exponentiation. Multiplication and division share the second highest priority, and addition and subtraction share the third highest priority. Thus, the rule for evaluating expressions is to proceed from left to right unless the priority of the operators specifies differently. However, there are two exceptions to the rule. One, parentheses can be inserted to ensure the proper sequence of evaluation. When a set of parentheses is used,

INTRODUCTION TO PROGRAMMING AND FORTRAN   17

calculations within the set are evaluated first. Two, when exponentiation operators appear consecutively, the evaluation is from right to left. A few examples will illustrate:

Example 1: 2+3*4 — The expression is evaluated according to the hierarchy stated above; thus, multiplication takes precedence over addition.

2+12 — The second step is addition; hence, the result is 14 not 20 as might be assumed.

Answer = 14

Example 2: (2.+3.)*4. — The calculation within parentheses is evaluated first.

5. *4. — The second step is multiplication since the parentheses have priority.

Answer = 20.

Example 3: 4./4.**2 — Exponentiation (**) has the highest priority and is evaluated first.

4./ 16. — Division is carried out after the exponentiation, resulting in the answer 0.25.

Answer = .25

Example 4: 5./10.*2. — Because division and multiplication have equal precedence, the computer works from left to right. Note that a different result occurs by evaluating from right to left. If the answer is intended to be 0.25, parentheses would have to be inserted.

.5 *2.

Answer = 1.

Example 5: 2.**2.**3. — The second exception to the general rule involves consecutive exponentiation. In this case, the computer works from right to left in evaluating the expression. As with the prior example, parentheses could be used to change the sequence of evaluation.

2.** 8.

Answer = 256.

These examples illustrate how the computer evaluates expressions or formulas within the guidelines established for the programming language. The following table summarizes the hierarchy explained.

Priority of Operations

Evaluate parentheses
Exponentiation (from right to left for consecutive exponents)
Multiplication and division
Addition and subtraction

An understanding of these samples will help alleviate future problems when writing program statements.

1-9 Summary

This text is intended to provide the reader with a working knowledge of FORTRAN IV. To do this, it is useful to understand the basic components of a computer system—the input and output operations, the memory unit, the control unit, and the processor unit—and the purpose of each. To employ the components effectively, a computer program containing specific instructions is required.

A program is made up of a number of different types of statements, each serving different objectives. Five steps were identified as necessary prerequisites to writing an effective program. Of these five, flowcharting contributes greatly.

Also, in this chapter constants, variables, and mathematical operators and their roles in program statements were identified. The next chapter will discuss the first group of program statements and the development of sample programs. At the beginning, the sample programs will be elementary in nature, becoming more sophisticated in later chapters.

Questions

1 Define the following terms or concepts:
   (a) The purpose of each of the five components of a computer system
   (b) Program
   (c) Real mode
   (d) Integer mode
   (e) Single-precision constant
   (f) Double-precision constant
   (g) The purpose of each of the five steps in writing a program

2 Identify each of the following constants as either (a) real, (b) integer, or (c) double-precision:

      123   0.0   8722.5E+01
      1.23   80000   423456.7891011
      1.23D+00   4.87E−02   67867

3 Convert the following values to scientific notation, i.e., exponential form:
   (a) 423.   (b) −649.825
   (c) 1124.78   (d) 100.
   (e) −10000.1   (f) 87632156789

INTRODUCTION TO PROGRAMMING AND FORTRAN

4. Convert the following values to their decimal equivalent:
    - (a) 12.05E+01
    - (b) 12.05E−01
    - (c) 1.2E+00
    - (d) 1869.0D1
    - (e) 763.333E9
    - (f) 55.5E−4

5. Identify and correct any of the following items that are *not valid real variables*:
    - (a) SXUM
    - (b) XSUMMARY
    - (c) 1AVG
    - (d) Y-BAR
    - (e) AB20
    - (f) RHOSUMS
    - (g) INTO1
    - (h) 18.2

6. Identify and correct any of the following items that are *not valid integer variables*:
    - (a) I
    - (b) INTEGER
    - (c) 5
    - (d) MN-MN
    - (e) L55L
    - (f) ABSOL
    - (g) KOUNTER
    - (h) 15K K

7. Identify and correct any of the following items that are *not valid constants*:
    - (a) 2,156.5
    - (b) 18.*6.
    - (c) 42.03
    - (d) 15(7)
    - (e) $400.22
    - (f) −200
    - (g) 2P
    - (h) −8.2B+01

8. Evaluate formulas (a) to (f) according to the priority scale. Assume that the variable VAR has a value of 3.5.
    - (a) IANS = 7**2+6*8
    - (b) ANS = 7./VAR*2.5
    - (c) ANS = (5.+2.)**2
    - (d) ANS = (3.+5.)/(2.+2.)*(3.**2)
    - (e) ANS = 2.**3**2
    - (f) ANS = VAR*(8./.5)/3.−VAR*6.5

BEGINNING FORTRAN STATEMENTS 2

A computer program normally contains a number of different programming statements. Three types or classes of statements will be discussed in this chapter. One class involves an assignment process; a second pertains to the output process. The third class terminates the execution of the program. The arithmetic assignment, WRITE, STOP, and END statements, referring to these three classes, are included in this chapter.

2-1 Arithmetic Assignments

The class of statements involving assignments and mathematical calculations in FORTRAN is called the *arithmetic assignment* process. The general form of the arithmetic assignment statement is

sl   [variable] = [expression]

where sl represents an optional statement label.[1] The label[2] may be placed anywhere within the first five columns[3] or may be omitted entirely. The variable on the left side of the equals

---

[1] In the general form of each statement, the sl will be used to represent "statement label." In the program examples, actual statement labels will be specified when required.
[2] The label must be integer mode with a value between 1 and 99999.
[3] Refer once again to Fig. 1-4, the FORTRAN coding form.

sign may be placed anywhere after column 6 while the balance of the statement can be entered in the remaining columns up to but excluding columns 73 to 80.

The statement is used to assign values, expressed on the right side of the equals sign, to variables. The values may be constants, expressions or formulas, or other variables. Although the form contains an equals sign, the statement does not represent an algebraic equation. Note that the term *assigns values* has been specified. Thus, the statement should be interpreted as "assign the value of the expression on the right-hand side of the equals sign to the variable on the left-hand side of the equals sign." It is a replacement statement, which means that the *expression on the right side is evaluated and the result replaces the current value of the variable on the left.*

The statement serves three basic purposes. First, it can be used to assign the value of a constant to a variable. Second, because it evaluates formulas, it is the principal computational statement in FORTRAN. In this use, note that only *defined* variables, that is, variables that have previously been assigned some value, may be inserted on the right side of the equals sign. And third, the statement can be used to store the value of other variables. A few simple examples are

```
100     M = 1
102     A = 2.3
103     B = A*2.61
```

where M is assigned a value of 1, A a value of 2.3, and B a value of 6.003.

In Chap. 1, real and integer modes were identified. When integer and real variables or constants are combined in the same arithmetic expression, the statements are referred to as *mixed-mode* expressions. Usually, real-mode variables should be assigned real values, and, likewise, integer-mode variables should be assigned integer values.

Consider two examples that illustrate the potential problems which occur as a result of using different modes in one statement. When two integer values are divided (for example, 5 ÷ 2), an integer value (2) is the quotient. Thus, if the statement

A = 5/2

were evaluated, A would be assigned the value 2.0, not 2.5. Likewise, if two real values are divided (for example, 5.0 ÷ 2.0), a real value (2.5) is the quotient. However, assigning the result to an integer variable, as in the statement

IN = 5.0/2.0

causes the value of IN to become 2, not 2.5. As shown here, because subtle errors can occur when mixing the mode of variables in an assignment statement, the practice should be avoided wherever possible. There are exceptions, though. One occurs when raising a number to a power. For example,

X = A**2

is a valid expression since the integer 2 is used as an exponent. A second exception occurs when using the form

XN = N

In this example, assigning an integer variable to a real variable, no loss of accuracy or error occurs. In the same light, the form

N = XN

is often used. However, a loss of accuracy could occur if XN contains a fraction, such as 3.67. In this case, N would be assigned the integer value 3. A form to be avoided in all cases is

A = 2*3.5

because integer (2) and real (3.5) values are mixed on the right side of the equation. This represents an inefficient use of the computer and should be listed as

A = 2.*3.5

Figure 2-1 lists examples of the common purposes of the arithmetic assignment statement along with a description of the use. Figure 2-2 lists the common errors that occur when using the arithmetic assignment statement. An accompanying description indicates the type of error.[1]

A summary of the arithmetic statement indicates that it is an

---

[1] Along with the valid examples that are permitted in FORTRAN statements, a listing of the common errors that are often made will be included with each discussion of the individual statements.

Figure 2-1 Examples of arithmetic expressions.

	Program Statements	Description
10	I = 0	The statement is identified with label 10, and the integer variable I is assigned an integer value of zero.
	J = 3 * 11	The integer variable J is assigned the integer value of 33 as a result of the calculation.
	KNTR = KNTR + 1	The integer variable KNTR is assigned a value based on the previous value of KNTR. If the previous value of KNTR were 7, for example, the new value would be 8. To be a valid statement, KNTR must have a previous value.
20	MON = NOB + NOT	The integer variable MON is assigned the sum of the two integer variables NOB and NOT. Note that label 20, identifying the statement, may be placed anywhere within columns 1 to 5. Here it is placed in columns 4 and 5.
30	ALPHA = 10.	The statement is labeled 30, and the real variable ALPHA is assigned a real constant value of 10.
	POWER1 = 2.13E2	The real variable POWER1 is assigned a real constant value of 213, determined by the constant 2.13E2, expressed in scientific form.
	POWER2 = 2.13E2 * 8.01	The real variable POWER2 is assigned a real value of 1706.13 as a result of the calculation.
	AREA = BASE * HGT	The real variable AREA is assigned the product of the multiplication of the two real variables BASE and HGT.

BEGINNING FORTRAN STATEMENTS

	Program Statements	Description
40	AREA1 = AREA	The current value of AREA1 is simply replaced by the value of the variable AREA.
	XNT = NT	The integer value of NT is converted to real mode and assigned to XNT.

Note: In the samples illustrated in these and all the remaining figures, it is assumed that the P in the heading Program Statements corresponds to column 7 of the FORTRAN card layout.

Figure 2-2 Common errors that occur with arithmetic expressions.

	Program Statements	Description
10	1A = 0.	The variable name 1A is not permitted. Variable names must begin with an alphabetic character. A correct entry would be 10 A1 = 0.
	TOOLONG = 7. * A + B	The variable name TOOLONG is not permitted because it contains seven characters; only six are permitted. A correct entry would be TOOLON = 7. * A + B
A5	ITEM = 2,100	Two errors are evident in this statement. One, the label must be integer mode between 1 and 99999. Two, commas are not permitted as part of integer or real constants. Thus, a correct entry would be 15 ITEM = 2100
	DOLLAR = $75.00	The dollar sign ($) is not permitted as part of an arithmetic expression. The two zeros are permitted although not necessary. A correct entry would be DOLLAR = 75.00

Figure 2-2 Common errors that occur with arithmetic expressions (*cont'd*).

	Program Statements	Description
20	INT = 68.535 * ALP	The variable INT is integer mode; however, the calculation involves two real values. Thus, a mixed mode results and a loss of accuracy occurs. The fraction is lost in the assignment. Arithmetic expressions should contain like modes throughout. A correct entry preventing any loss of significant digits would be 20 XINT = 68.535 * ALP
25	RATE * HOURS = PAY	The format of the statement is incorrect. The calculation must be placed to the right of the equals sign and the variable to the left. A correct entry would be 25 PAY = RATE * HOURS

assignment or a replacement process, not an algebraic equation. Numeric real or integer constants can be assigned to valid variable names. Calculations or formulas can also be evaluated within the statement. And finally, the statement can be considered as one of three methods for entering data, via a constant assignment, into a program.

Arithmetic Assignment Exercises

1. What value would the computer assign to the variables listed in statements (*a*) to (*f*)?
   - (*a*) A = 5.
   - (*b*) BUB = 3.5/2.5+1.
   - (*c*) DELTA = 3.5/(2.5+1.)
   - (*d*) ISUM = 3**(2+1)+6*7
   - (*e*) DIFØ1 = 8.2−.5*.7+2.
   - (*f*) KTAB = 81/(6+2*1+1)

2. Write the arithmetic statements that are equivalent to the following verbal descriptions:
   - (*a*) Sales equal $125,000.
   - (*b*) Net sales equal sales minus 5 percent of sales.

BEGINNING FORTRAN STATEMENTS

(c) Inventory equals 66.67 percent of net sales.
(d) Sales tax equals 4.5 percent of net sales.
(e) Gross profit equals 85.5 percent of net sales minus $2,000.

3 Explain potential errors that arise as a result of an evaluation of the following statements:
(a) I = 3/2.0
(b) IDIV = 5*(1/2)
(c) AB = 3/6*3

4 With the variables AA, BB, II, and JJ, assigned values of 5.5, 11.0, 3, and 4, respectively, evaluate statements (a) to (e):
(a) X = 3./(AA/BB)
(b) Y = (AA/BB)/3
(c) EXP1 = AA**II
(d) KNT = JJ−II*(II+JJ)
(e) EXPS = AA**JJ−BB**(II−1)

5 Identify and correct errors contained in the following statements:
(a) X = 5(3)
(b) I = 8.3*2.1
(c) SUM+BASE=Y
(d) SALES = $100.00
(e) MAK = 2,100·1,400

2-2 The WRITE Statement

The purpose of the WRITE statement, which serves as the output instruction in FORTRAN programs, is to transmit data from the computer's memory unit to a designated output device. There are two general forms of the statement, the first of which is

sl   WRITE(ia,b)

The sl, as in the arithmetic assignment statements, refers to an optional statement label. The ia is an unsigned integer constant or variable specifying a particular output device. The different output devices available are assigned specific numbers by each computer center. The actual number in use in each installation must be obtained to use the computer system. A standard device assignment for the line printer is 6; hence, all the samples in this text will refer to output device number 6. The b in the instruction refers to a specific FORMAT statement: a separate statement that must be used to structure or specify the layout design of the output when using the WRITE instruction.

This first general form of the WRITE statement generates as output only the information contained in the referenced FORMAT statement. The second general form of the statement causes data values to be generated on the specified output device

sl   WRITE(ia,b) [list of variables, separated by commas]

The sl, ia, and b have the same definition as in the earlier form. Additionally, the values of the variables in the list are written on the designated output device in the manner dictated by the contents of the FORMAT statement. (The FORMAT statement will be covered in detail in Chap. 3.)

When using the second form, only defined variables may appear in the WRITE statement. Also, calculations or expressions can not be included as part of the statement. Figures 2-3 and 2-4 contain valid examples and the common errors that occur in the use of the WRITE instruction.

Figure 2-3 Examples of the WRITE statement.

	Program Statements	Description
400	WRITE(1,100)	Statement 400 causes the literal data contained in the FORMAT* statement 100 to be transmitted to the output device specified by the integer 1.
	WRITE(6,101)A	The value of the variable A is transmitted to the output device specified by the integer 6. The output generated is determined by FORMAT statement 101 and the value of A.
500	WRITE(6,102)I, HOURS, PAY	The statement is identified by label 500. Three values, one integer and two real, are written to the output device specified by the integer 6. The output structure is determined by FORMAT statement 102.
	WRITE(LP,200) SALE	The value of the variable SALE is written to the output device specified by the integer value of the variable LP. The data written is controlled by FORMAT statement 200.

*The FORMAT statement is discussed in the next chapter; however, it is enough to say here that its purpose is to control the structure of the output from a FORTRAN program.

BEGINNING FORTRAN STATEMENTS

Figure 2-4 Common errors that occur with the WRITE statement.

Program Statements	Description
600 WRITE(1.5, 4.5) X, Y	Only integer constants or variables are permitted within the parentheses in the WRITE statement. Thus, the real constants 1.5 and 4.5 are incorrect. A correct entry would be 600 WRITE (1,4) X, Y

WRITE(6,200) A + B*C	The expression A + B*C is not valid as part of the WRITE statement. Two statements are required to perform the operation indicated here:
	      X = A + B*C
	      WRITE (6,200) X

WRITE(6,188) HOURS PAY	The two variables HOURS and PAY must be separated by commas; otherwise the computer assumes that there is only one variable name, HOURSPAY. By itself, HOURSPAY is not a valid variable name because it contains eight characters. A correct entry would be WRITE (6,188) HOURS, PAY
7.0B WRITE HOURS, PAY	Two errors are evident in the sample. First, the label must be integer mode. Label 7.0B contains two invalid characters, the decimal point and the B. Second, the device and format references have been omitted along with the parentheses. A correct entry would be 70 WRITE (6,188) HOURS, PAY Note that the label 70 may be placed anywhere within the first five columns.

As stated, the WRITE statement is an output instruction that generates information from a FORMAT statement and/or the values of the variables listed in the statement.

WRITE Exercises

1. Assuming the output device is number 6 and the label of the FORMAT statement is 1, list the output instruction required to generate the
   - (a) Contents of FORMAT label 1 only
   - (b) Integer values for the variables IJ and JK
   - (c) Real values for X, XSUM, and XSUMSQ
   - (d) Values of the variables A, B, KNT, BASE, IAREA, and SA

2. Assuming the output device is identified by the variable IPRT and the label of the FORMAT statement is 3000, list the output instruction required to generate the
   (a) Contents of FORMAT label only
   (b) Integer values for LM, LP, and LX
   (c) The values of the variables TOTAL and ITOTAL
   (d) Real values for X, Y, Z, R, S, and T

3. Assuming that the label of the FORMAT statement is identified by the variable[1] FMT and the output device by variable LPD, list the output instruction required to generate the
   (a) Value of the variables GAME and NAME
   (b) Contents of the FORMAT statement only
   (c) Integer values for four arbitrary variables
   (d) Real values for four arbitrary variables

4. Identify and correct errors, if any, in the following WRITE statements:
   (a)   WRITE 6,10 SUM
   (b)   1WRITE(6,200)X,Y
   (c)   AB   WRITE(6,3000)M,N,NOB
   (d)   1.5   WRITE(5.1,5)TOTALS, AVG,GRADE
   (e)   20   WRITE(1,20)MAY,BE,SUMMER,DAI
   (f)   WRITE(I,25), HOME MORT MON
   (g)   10000 WRITE(−5,99980)

2-3 END and STOP Statements

Every program written in FORTRAN must be concluded with the END statement to signify the physical end of the program card deck. It is a signal to the computer to begin compilation[2] of the program into machine-usable form. This is the only purpose served by the instruction, which implies that it is a *nonexecutable* statement. Its form is simply

END

As noted, it must be the last program statement in a card deck and can not have a statement label.

The STOP statement serves a different purpose, although the two statements are often confused. The STOP instruction

---

[1] This use of the variable FMT is an example of an advanced programming technique. At this point, the reader need be concerned only with how the WRITE statement is written using this form.

[2] Simply stated, "compilation of the program" is a sequence of events that leads to the execution or processing of a program in order for the user to obtain the output.

BEGINNING FORTRAN STATEMENTS

causes the computer to terminate the execution of a program, or in other words, to stop processing. The STOP statement may be placed anywhere within the program to indicate the logical end of a program. Multiple STOP instructions may be included in the same program if more than one logical end exists. The form of the statement is

sl   STOP

where sl again represents an optional statement label.

Thus, the difference between the two statements is that the END instruction denotes the physical end of the program; the STOP instruction terminates processing. Consequently, every FORTRAN program must have at least one END and one STOP statement.

2-4 Program Sample SALES TAX

Throughout the text, the important programming segments will be summarized by their use and application in sample problems. Initially, the problems are relatively simple and would not require the use of a computer. However, it is intended to state simple tasks so that the reader can concentrate on the FORTRAN statements rather than creating the program logic. The problems at the end of each chapter permit the reader to test his logic capability.

Discussed thus far have been four statements, encompassing arithmetic assignments, WRITE, STOP, and END operations. How can these statements be incorporated into a program?

To start with a small problem, consider the purchase of any taxable item. Can a FORTRAN program be written that will calculate the sales tax based on a purchase price of $1,000 and a sales tax rate of 4 percent? Recall from Chap. 1 that there are five steps involved in writing a program. The first includes problem definition, which has already been stated in the question above. The second is determining a method of solution. One solution to the problem is simply

$$\text{Sales tax dollars} = \$1{,}000 \text{ times } 4 \text{ percent}$$

The third step is to establish a logical flow of information. Quite readily, the only requirements in this task involve (1) calculate the sales tax dollars; (2) write the output; and (3) terminate

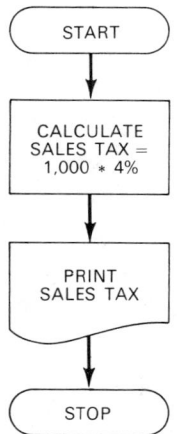

Flowchart 2-1 SALES TAX—Assignment and WRITE statements.

the program. Therefore, the logical flow of Flowchart 2-1 outlines the necessary steps.

The fourth step is to write the FORTRAN statements. In recalling the various statements identified, it is possible to make calculations only in the arithmetic assignment statement. Since the sales purchase price could involve dollars *and* cents while the tax rate already includes a decimal point, only real values and variables should be used in the assignment. Thus, the first statement needed in program SALES-1 to solve the problem is an arithmetic assignment using the real variable SALETX. The next statement is a WRITE that generates the output. The next statement is a FORMAT, whose purpose is to dictate how the output will be generated (discussed in detail in the next chapter). The final two statements, STOP and END, are needed to terminate compilation and execution of the program.

The actual program statements and the output illustrating the answers to the problem are

```
        SALETX = 1000. * .04
        WRITE(6,400)SALETX
400     FORMAT(F10.0)
        STOP
        END


        40.
```

BEGINNING FORTRAN STATEMENTS

There are other possible solutions. For example, it might be meaningful to print out not only the sales tax in dollars but also the purchase price and the tax rate. The steps needed to solve this approach include:

1 Defining values for purchase price and tax rate

2 Calculating sales tax dollars

3 Printing the answers

Flowchart 2-2 reflects these steps. As before, the fourth step involves writing the FORTRAN statements. A second variation

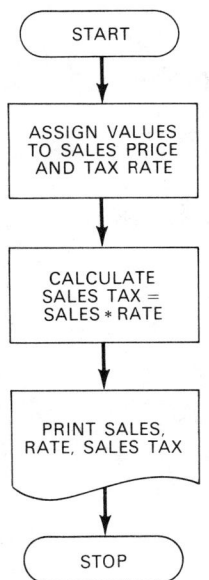

Flowchart 2-2   SALES TAX—Assignment and WRITE statements.

of the arithmetic assignment statement permits constants to be assigned to variables. Therefore, the first two statements assign values to the variables SALES and TAXRAT; the third calculates the tax dollars. The WRITE and FORMAT statements are modified slightly to generate three values in this solution. As usual, the last two statements are STOP and END. Program SALES-2 and the actual output are shown on the next page.

```
      SALES = 1000.
      TAXRAT = .04
      SALETX = SALES * TAXRAT
      WRITE(6,400) SALES,TAXRAT,SALETX
  400 FORMAT(3F10.2)
      STOP
      END
```

```
   1000.00        0.04        40.00
```

The reader will soon learn that many different solutions to the same problem exist, all of which may be correct as evidenced by the two programs shown here.

To continue with another sample, the second problem concerns the calculation of the average of three values. Assuming that the average of the three numbers 75, 89, and 73 is needed, what steps must be performed? First, the values must be defined, the average calculated (by summing and dividing by 3), and the answer printed. Flowchart 2-3 shows these steps; program STATISTICS-1 and the output follow:

2-5 Program Sample STATISTICS

```
      VAL1 = 75.
      VAL2 = 89.
      VAL3 = 73.
      AVG = (VAL1 + VAL2 + VAL3)/3.
      WRITE(6,300) VAL1,VAL2,VAL3,AVG
  300 FORMAT(4F10.0)
      STOP
      END
```

```
     75.       89.       73.       79.
```

In examining the program and the output, observe that real variables were employed. In this sample, integer variables could have been inserted as well, but in the next chapter the reason for using real variables will become apparent. Also, what would happen if the parentheses were omitted from the calculation of the average? Additionally, the three numbers were printed along with the average because it is normally good programming practice to print all pertinent information as output.

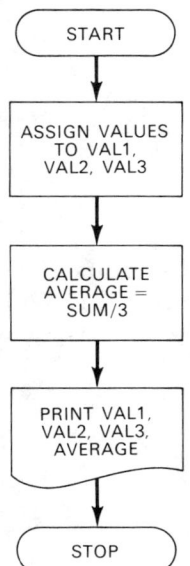

Flowchart 2-3 STATISTICS—Assignment and WRITE statements.

What changes to the program are necessary if the sum is required as one of the answers? In the prior example, the sum was included only as part of the formula for computing the average. If it is to be one of the answers, it must be assigned to a variable. Hence, the necessary changes required to print the sum are listed in STATISTICS-2. The program and the output are

```
      VAL1 = 75.
      VAL2 = 89.
      VAL3 = 73.
      SUM = VAL1 + VAL2 + VAL3
      AVG = SUM/3.
      WRITE(6,300)VAL1,VAL2,VAL3,SUM,AVG
300   FORMAT(5F10.0)
      STOP
      END
```

    75.   89.   73.   237.   79.

In both the SALES and STATISTICS programs, one major limitation exists. In the first, is the program effective if the purchase price is $500 or the tax rate 4.5 percent? In the second, what if more than three values are to be averaged? The programs work only for specific data and hence are of limited value. However, Chap. 4 introduces FORTRAN statements that enable the programmer to build a flexible program which will handle any data.

2-6 Miscellaneous Mathematical Sample

If two points on a straight line are given by their x and y coordinates, for example, (x_1, y_1) and (x_2, y_2), the slope of the line can be computed by using the formula

$$\text{Slope} = \frac{y_2 - y_1}{x_2 - x_1}$$

For example, the slope of the straight line that passes through the points $(1,1)$ and $(4,3)$ is

$$\frac{3-1}{4-1} = \frac{2}{3}$$

To write a program to compute the slope of a line, Flowchart 2-4 identifies the necessary steps. The statements needed are

```
        SLOPE = (3.-1.)/(4.-1.)
        WRITE(6,1) SLOPE
1       FORMAT(F10.2)
        STOP
        END
```

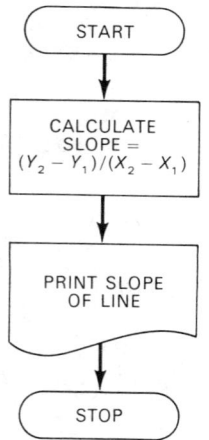

Flowchart 2-4 Slope of a line—Assignment and WRITE statements.

BEGINNING FORTRAN STATEMENTS

Note that real variables and constants were used in the calculation of SLOPE. Why? If integers were inserted, a loss of accuracy and an incorrect answer would result. Also, is the set of parentheses needed in the computation of SLOPE? Output from this small sample is

0.67

2-7 Summary

In this chapter, four FORTRAN statements have been covered, including arithmetic assignment, WRITE, STOP, and END instructions. The arithmetic assignment instruction is used to assign constants or the results of formula evaluations to variables. The constants and variables may be integer or real mode, but mixed-mode expressions should be avoided. The WRITE statement is used by the programmer to direct the answers or output to be written to a specific device. The STOP and END statements are used to indicate the logical and physical ends of each program.

Questions

1 Draw a flowchart that identifies the program logic used to write program STATISTICS-2.

2 There is $580 in a bank account on deposit. If the interest rate is 3.5 percent compounded annually, write a FORTRAN program to compute and print (a) the interest payment at the end of 1 year, and (b) the new bank balance. The interest payment is equal to the deposit multiplied by the interest rate; the new bank balance is equal to the interest payment plus the bank balance at the beginning of the year. Use as the FORMAT statement for the WRITE
   100   FORMAT(2F10.2)

3 The number of students enrolled at SMC College last year was 6,128. The number has increased at the rate of 4.2 percent for the last 3 years. Write a FORTRAN program that will print the year and the forecasted enrollment for each of the next 3 years. The output should appear as
   19XX   6128.
   19XX   XXXX.
   19XX   XXXX.
   19XX   XXXX.
   Use as the FORMAT statement for the WRITE:
   3   FORMAT(I6,F10.0)

4 Write a FORTRAN program that will compute and print the radius of a circle using the formula

$$r = (x^2 + y^2)^{1/2}$$

when x and y are equal to 4.2 and 6.2, respectively. As the FORMAT statement, use

    4   FORMAT(F10.3)

5 In the geometric progression represented by

$$a, ar, ar^2, \ldots, ar^{x-1}$$

write a program that will compute and print the values for the first and last terms when a is 6, r is 5, and x is 4. Besides printing the values for the first and last terms, print also the values for r and x. As the FORMAT statement, use

    5   FORMAT(4F10.0)

6 In an inventory control environment, the best order quantity or economic order quantity (EOQ) can be found by using the formula

$$EOQ = \sqrt{\frac{2(\text{demand})(\text{cost/order})}{\text{cost/unit}(\text{carrying cost})}}$$

Write a program that will compute and print the value of EOQ when demand is 1,000, cost/order is $2.50, cost/unit is $12.45, and carrying cost is 12 percent of the cost/unit. Print also the values for each of these items. Use as the FORMAT statement:

    6   FORMAT(5F12.2)

7 An often-used statistic, the coefficient of correlation (r), can be computed using the equation

$$r = \frac{a\Sigma XY - (\Sigma X)(\Sigma Y)}{\sqrt{\{[a\Sigma X^2 - (\Sigma X)^2][a\Sigma Y^2 - (\Sigma Y)^2]\}}}$$

Supply your own values for a, ΣXY, ΣX, ΣY, ΣX^2, and ΣY^2, and then write a program that will compute and print the value of r. Select one of the above FORMAT statements to use in your program.

8 Write a program to evaluate and print Z when

$$Z = \frac{AX^2 + BX + C}{X - 2} \quad \text{and} \quad A = 2, B = 3, C = 4, X = 3$$

Using the same values for A, B, and C, change X to 2 and evaluate the results by running the program on the computer. Select one of the above FORMAT statements for use in your program.

9 Write a program to compute and print the volume of a cylinder, where the volume is

$$V = \pi r^2 h \qquad \pi = 3.1416, r = 3.5, h = 61.178$$

Select one of the preceding FORMAT statements.

COMMENTS FORMAT AND CONTINUATION STATEMENTS 3

In Chap. 2 the FORMAT statement was listed in the program samples without explanation. This chapter will present a detailed discussion of the options and functions of the statement. However, the first topic concerns a method for providing internal program documentation.

3-1 Comments

The COMMENTS statement, created by placing a C in column 1, is not a FORTRAN instruction but merely a statement used for in-program documentation or identification purposes. The statement is ignored by the computer but can be inserted by the programmer for his own benefit in recognizing particular segments of a problem. When the letter C is placed in column 1 of a card, the remaining columns may be filled with programmer notes and information. The comment card is printed in sequence along with the other statements but has no effect on the computer run. Its use permits explanatory remarks, directions for running the program, identification of segments of a large program, or other worthwhile messages to be included within a program listing. Comment cards may be placed anywhere within the program.

The following list is an example of a group of comment cards containing general information that might appear at the beginning of a Monte Carlo marketing program.

```
C      THIS IS A FORTRAN MONTE CARLO SIMULATION
C      PROGRAM.
C      THE AUTHOR OF THE PROGRAM IS GERALD H.
C      DAVIS.
C      WRITTEN 3-15-72.
```

The SALES and STATISTICS programs from the earlier chapters are repeated here with appropriate comments inserted.

```
C PROGRAM SALES-1
C THIS PROGRAM COMPUTES THE SALES TAX FOR 1 ITEM, AT A RATE OF 4 PERCENT
C
       SALETX = 1000. * .04
       WRITE(6,400)SALETX
400    FORMAT(F10.0)
       STOP
       END


C PROGRAM SALES-2
C THIS PROGRAM COMPUTES THE SALES TAX FOR 1 ITEM, AT A RATE OF 4 PERCENT
C
       SALES = 1000.
       TAXRAT = .04
       SALETX = SALES * TAXRAT
       WRITE(6,400) SALES,TAXRAT,SALETX
400    FORMAT(3F10.2)
       STOP
       END


C PROGRAM STATISTICS-1
C THIS PROGRAM COMPUTES THE AVERAGE OF THREE VALUES
C
       VAL1 = 75.
       VAL2 = 89.
       VAL3 = 73.
       AVG = (VAL1 + VAL2 + VAL3)/3.
       WRITE(6,300)VAL1,VAL2,VAL3,AVG
300    FORMAT(4F10.0)
       STOP
       END


C PROGRAM STATISTICS-2
C THIS PROGRAM COMPUTES THE AVERAGE OF THREE VALUES
C
       VAL1 = 75.
       VAL2 = 89.
       VAL3 = 73.
       SUM = VAL1 + VAL2 + VAL3
       AVG = SUM/3.
       WRITE(6,300)VAL1,VAL2,VAL3,SUM,AVG
300    FORMAT(5F10.0)
       STOP
       END
```

COMMENTS, FORMAT, AND CONTINUATION STATEMENTS   43

Often, delimiter cards (i.e., a comment card with only a C in column 1 and the remaining columns blank) are placed before and after the cards containing detail comments. This procedure emphasizes the notes inserted in the program. Because comment cards have no effect on the length of the run time for any program, they should be used liberally.

3-2 FORMAT Statement

The FORMAT statement provides the programmer with the facility to control in a precise manner the results to be printed as answers from a program. It is also used to process input data (discussed in Chap. 4) that is punched in a particular form. The general form of the statement is

sl   FORMAT($f_1, f_2, f_3, \ldots, f_n$)

where sl in this case represents a *mandatory* statement label and $f_1, f_2, f_3, \ldots, f_n$ are specific codes. The various format codes include provisions for processing integer values, real values, scientific notation numbers, double-precision data, Hollerith or literal fields, alphanumeric or character fields, and blank fields.

The first format code to be discussed concerns integer values. The general form for representing integer data within a FORMAT statement is

Iw

where I designates an integer field and w is the number of positions or digits (including one for the sign) in the field. In the code, w must be an unsigned integer constant as it must be in all the following designations. The number of digits specified in the Iw form must be equal to or greater than the number of digits to be processed. For example, I5 defines a five-position integer field capable of processing a number such as −1234 or 12345. However, an I6 code is necessary to process a number such as −12345 because when counting the minus sign as position one, the field is six positions long.

A second form for representing integer data is

aIw

where I and w are the same as above. However, a indicates the number of fields specified as Iw in length; for example, 2I3 indicates that there are two successive fields, each three integer positions long. When the integer form is listed in a FORMAT statement, the variable in the referencing WRITE or READ statement (see Chap. 4) must also be integer mode. Figures 3-1 and 3-2 contain descriptions of various Iw format codes along with other types of format codes that follow.

Figure 3-1 Examples of FORMAT statements.

	Program Statements	Description
100	FORMAT(I3)	The FORMAT statement labeled 100 describes a three-digit integer data field as designated by the specification I3.
101	FORMAT(I3,I4)	The FORMAT statement labeled 101 describes two data fields. Both fields are designated as integer mode, the first three digits and the second four digits in length.
102	FORMAT(2I5)	Two five-digit integer data fields are specified by the FORMAT statement labeled 102.
120	FORMAT(F10.2)	The statement labeled 120 describes a 10-digit real data field, where two decimal places are indicated by the 2 following the decimal point. The 10 digits include one for the sign ($+$ or $-$) and one for the decimal point (.). When writing output using label 120, the value would be rounded to two places.
121	FORMAT(E13.6)	Statement number 121 describes a 13-digit real data field, where the output is formatted in scientific notation. Six significant digits (rounded first) are printed as dictated by the 6 following the decimal point. Note also that seven print spaces are required to print the sign ($+$ or $-$), the zero (0), the decimal point (.), plus the exponent ($E \pm nn$), as in the example $-0.123456E-02$
130	FORMAT(I3, 5X, I3)	Three fields are identified in statement number 130. The first and third are three-digit integer fields. The second indicates a five-digit field that, when used for output, supplies five blanks (spaces).
131	WRITE(6,131) II, AA, EE FORMAT(I4,5X,F8.2,6X,E14.7)	The three variables II, AA, and EE are written on the specified output device according to the codes contained in statement 131. The first four digits of the output are integer mode followed by five blanks; the next eight positions are real mode followed by six blanks; and the last field is 14 positions long in exponential form.

Figure 3-2 Common errors that occur with FORMAT statements.

Program Statements		Description
100	FORMAT(3I)	The I and 3 in the statement are reversed. To designate an integer field, the specification must be of the form: Iw. A correct entry would be 100 FORMAT(I3)
	FROMAT(F10.2)	The statement is misspelled and the label has been omitted. Each FORMAT statement must have a numeric label. A correct entry would be 102 FORMAT(F10.2)
103	FORMAT(F6.7)	The FORMAT statement attempts to designate more decimal places (7) than are designated for the entire field (6). The number of decimal places must be one less than the field size. A correct entry would be 103 FORMAT(F8.7)
104	FORMAT(I3, X5, F10.0)	The order of the characters in the X5 specification is reversed. The form must be wX. A correct entry would be 104 FORMAT(I3, 5X, F10.0)
1000	FORMAT(E12.7)	For output purposes, the length of the E field must be seven or more digits larger than the number of decimal places indicated. A correct entry for output use would be 1000 FORMAT(E14.7)

1001	WRITE(6,1001) II, AA
	FORMAT(F10.0,I5)
		The type of variable listed in the WRITE statement must agree with the type of code appearing in the FORMAT statement. Thus, II must be written with an I code and AA with an F code. A correct set of entries would be
		    WRITE(6,1001) II, AA
		1001 FORMAT(I5, F10.0)
		    or
		    WRITE(6,1001) AA, II
		1001 FORMAT(F10.0, I5)

1002	KI = 6672 WRITE(6,1002) KI FORMAT(I3)	Because the variable KI contains four significant digits, an integer field of I5 or greater must be specified in label 1002. The value of KI would not be printed as a result of the FORMAT statement listed. A correct entry would be 1002 FORMAT(I8)

The second type of format code to be discussed pertains to real variables. The two general forms for representing real data are

Fw.d

and

aFw.d

where a and w have the same values as expressed earlier. The F is used to designate floating-point values; the d designates the number of places to the right of the decimal. For example, F5.1 denotes a five-position field with, as part of the five positions, a decimal point and one decimal place. It can be used to process numbers five positions in length, such as 123.5 or −12.5. However, an F6.1 code is required to process −123.5 because, counting the minus sign and the decimal point, the field is six positions long. Refer again to Figs. 3-1 and 3-2 for more examples.

The third type of format code also pertains to real variables. The two general forms for representing real data in exponential form or scientific notation are

Ew.d

and

aEw.d

where a and w are the same as before. The E denotes that the data value is to be processed in scientific notation form, and the d refers to the number of significant decimal digits. A format code of E12.5 defines a field of 12 positions, 7 of which are required for the scientific form; 5 represent the number of significant decimal places. The value $+0.12345E+02$ is an example of an E12.5 code; $-0.111116E+03$ and $+0.7777777E-04$ are examples of E13.6 and E14.7 codes, respectively. When writing values in E format, observe that the sign ($\pm$), the 0., and the E$\pm$00 form are always reserved. Thus, the value of w in the Ew.d code should always be seven or more digits greater in value than d.

The fourth type of format code permits spaces to be generated in output records or fields to be skipped in input records. The general form is

wX

where w defines the number of characters to be skipped. When creating output, if five blanks are desired between two data values, the form 5X serves this purpose. The form 4X generates four blanks, and 33X supplies 33 blank columns.

Each of the previous codes, with the exception of the wX code, is used with variables. However, it is sometimes desirable to supply as output alphabetic information such as column headings, titles, messages, or labels providing identification. The H or Hollerith notation is used to specify alphanumeric output. The general form is

wH character string

where w is an integer constant defining the field width, H is the Hollerith notation form, and a user character string follows. As an example, to create a column heading containing the string of 12 characters HOURS WORKED, a Hollerith format would be: 12HHOURS WORKED. If spaces are required before and after the column heading, the format would be: 14H HOURS WORKED . The count for w must reflect the exact number of places in the character string, including spaces and special characters.

As Figs. 3-3 and 3-4 show, commas are used to separate various format codes. However, the commas can be omitted when the omission does not result in ambiguity. The two specific needs for commas occur when X and H specifications follow numeric formats. For example, the two codes I5 and 5X can be misinterpreted when placed together as I55X. Or the two codes I5 and 3HSUM, when placed together as I53HSUM, are ambiguous. In these cases, the X and H forms must be preceded by a comma. However, the use of commas throughout the format specification alleviates any potential errors.

Two additional characteristics can be illustrated before continuing. With repeating fields such as

(I5,I3,I5,I3,I5,I3)

a shortcut method for writing the equivalent is

(3(I5,I3))

where the 3 indicates that the group of fields within the inner parentheses is repeated three successive times.

The second characteristic concerns a special character, the slash (/). Assume that two successive WRITE statements refer to the two format codes

Figure 3-3 More examples of FORMAT statements.

	Program Statements	Description
140	FORMAT(5HTITLE)	A five-character literal field is identified in statement 140. The literal TITLE is transmitted to an output device when specified by the execution of a WRITE statement containing FORMAT label 140.
151	FORMAT(8HCOLUMN 1, 5X,8HCOLUMN 2)	Two eight-character Hollerith fields containing the literals COLUMN 1 and COLUMN 2 are designated in the statement. The two fields are separated by five blanks as the result of the 5X designation.
160	FORMAT(4(F10.2, 5X))	The two fields F10.2 and 5X identified within the inner set of parentheses are designated as repeating fields. They are repeated four times as a result of the 4 preceding the inner parenthesis.
170	FORMAT(I3/F10.5)	The first field, a three-digit integer, is outputted on one line. The slash (/) causes the next 10-digit real data field to be outputted on the following line. If two slashes (//) are indicated, the 10-digit field is outputted on the second line following.
180	WRITE(6,180) X FORMAT(4HX IS, F8.2)	The value of variable X is printed, preceded by the label X IS, according to the F8.2 code. The output from both statements would be on one line.
190	WRITE(6,190) XOBA WRITE(6,190) XOBB FORMAT(6HXOB IS, F11.1)	As shown, one FORMAT statement may be referenced by multiple WRITE statements. Each WRITE statement causes one line of output, with the label XOB IS followed by the value of XOBA. On the second line, the label is followed by the value of XOBB.

COMMENTS, FORMAT, AND CONTINUATION STATEMENTS   49

Figure 3-4 More common errors that occur with FORMAT statements.

	Program Statements	Description
105	FORMAT(16HCOLUMN HEADINGS)	The literal denoted contains 15 characters including the space. The character count indicates 16; therefore, the ending parenthesis is taken as part of the literal causing an error. A correct entry would be 105 FORMAT(15HCOLUMN HEADINGS)
106	FORMAT(3(F10.2,5X)I5)	A field separator is required between specifications. The parenthesis following 5X must be separated from the I5 field by a comma. A correct entry would be 106 FORMAT(3(F10.2,5X),I5)
107	FORMAT(I8/ ,F10.5)	When using the slash for line spacing within the statement, it can not be followed by a comma. A correct entry would be 107 FORMAT(I8/F10.5)

108
108
	WRITE(6,108) A, B, I, J
	FORMAT(2(F7.1,I3))
		Two errors occur in this sample. First, duplicate labels are not permitted. Second, the grouping of codes in the FORMAT statement does not align with the variable names in the WRITE statement. Correct entries are
		   109 WRITE(6,108) A, B, I, J
		   108 FORMAT(2F7.1,2I3)

F6.0

and

F8.3

The two WRITEs and the format codes can be combined into one by writing

(F6.0/F8.3)

where / dictates that the second format F8.3 is to be printed on a second line of output. Two consecutive slashes cause the output to be double-spaced. More than two slashes can be used with corresponding results.

Thus far, basic USAS FORTRAN IV format codes have been discussed. Later on in the chapter additional format codes will be presented.

FORMAT Exercises

1 Evaluate samples (a) to (f) and detail the column-by-column output. Assume that the variables A, B, and I have the values 10.5, 12.226, and 5, respectively.
   (a)   WRITE(6,100)I
       100 FORMAT(I5)
   (b)   WRITE(6,101)A
       101 FORMAT(F10.1)
   (c)   WRITE(6,102)A,B
       102 FORMAT(2F10.2)
   (d)   WRITE(6,103)A
       103 FORMAT(E13.6)
   (e)   WRITE(6,104)A,B,I
       104 FORMAT(3H A=, F6.2, 5X, 3H B=,F6.2,3X,I6)
   (f)   WRITE(6,105)A,B,I
       105 FORMAT(F8.2/6X,F8.2/12X,I5)

2 Supply the WRITE and FORMAT statements needed to fulfill the requirements:
   (a) Create a heading for a report that will print BONDS, beginning in column 1; ISSUE DATE, beginning in column 20; and YIELD TO MATURITY, beginning in column 40.
   (b) On one print line, output the variables AN, with a maximum of four characters; I, with up to seven places; Z, with five whole numbers and two decimal places; and ZOB, in scientific notation with six significant digits.
   (c) Generate on one line the label THE VALUE OF SUMXS IS and the value of the variable SXS, which is a maximum of seven whole and two decimal places.
   (d) On one line print the label AVERAGE and the variable AVER plus the label STANDARD DEVIATION and the variable STD.

3 Supply FORMAT statements that will process the following records:
   (a) A five-position integer field and a ten-position real field that contains two decimals
   (b) Three integer fields, each six digits in length. Separate each of the fields with five blank characters
   (c) Four scientific notation fields, with six significant places each

3-3 Continuation Statements

Before proceeding to the program samples, one additional topic will be discussed. A *continuation card* or continuation statement is a FORTRAN statement that is too long to be placed on one card. When a statement can not be punched within columns 7 to 72 of one card, it may be continued on successive cards by placing any of the FORTRAN characters

COMMENTS, FORMAT, AND CONTINUATION STATEMENTS

other than a blank or zero in column 6 of another continuation card. Normally a 1 is placed in column 6 of the first continuation card, a 2 in column 6 of the second continuation card, and so forth. The need for continuation cards arises because punched cards can contain only 66 characters (columns 7 to 72, inclusive), although output devices such as the line printer may contain as many as 132 positions. For example, a 78-position header label requires the use of a continuation card as shown:

```
100    FORMAT(78H THIS HEADER LINE REQUIRES TWO
      1FORTRAN CARDS TO PLACE IT ON ONE LINE OF
      2OUTPUT)
```

Also, continuation cards are sometimes needed for WRITE and arithmetic expression statements

```
2010   WRITE(6,400) NOB, TOTAL, AVERAG, SUMSQS,
      1NOB1, TOTAL1, AVERA1, SUMSQ1
510    PROFIT = FIXED + 0.83326*VARIAB*UNITS +HOU
      1RLY
```

The program samples following will illustrate use of continuation statements.

3-4 Program Sample SALES TAX

To continue with the pattern established in Chap. 2, the discussion of the program statements will be concluded with two sample problems. The first problem referred to the purchase of a taxable item. Assuming a purchase price of $1,000 and a tax rate of 4 percent, a program was written to calculate the sales tax. The sample program is expanded here to illustrate the use of three format codes, the F, X, and H codes plus use of the slash (/). The problem analysis is exactly the same as in the earlier section. However, Flowchart 3-1 is modified slightly to reflect the use of column headings in the output, the purpose of which is to identify the answers printed. The program statements conforming to the flowchart are listed in the following printout:

```
C PROGRAM SALES-3
C THIS PROGRAM COMPUTES THE SALES TAX FOR 1 ITEM, AT A RATE OF 4 PERCENT
       SALES = 1000.
       TAXRAT = .04
       SALETX = SALES * TAXRAT
       WRITE(6,401)
       WRITE(6,402)SALES,TAXRAT,SALETX
```

```
401    FORMAT(6H SALES,5X,8HTAX RATE,5X,9HSALES TAX/)
402    FORMAT(1X,F6.0,3X,F8.3,5X,F8.0)
       STOP
       END
```

Appropriate COMMENTS statements have been inserted at the beginning to denote the name and intent of the program. The first WRITE statement provides column headings according to FORMAT statement 401; the second WRITE generates the values of the three variables according to FORMAT 402. In the FORMAT statements, the F codes are used to generate data values; the H codes supply the labels. The X codes supply the proper spacing between fields, and / as the last character in label 401 provides a line feed so that the output below appears in double-spaced form.

```
SALES      TAX RATE      SALES TAX

1000.      0.040         40.
```

Using the same program logic, the output can be printed on one line by revising the WRITE and FORMAT statements. This requires the use of the continuation function. Column headings

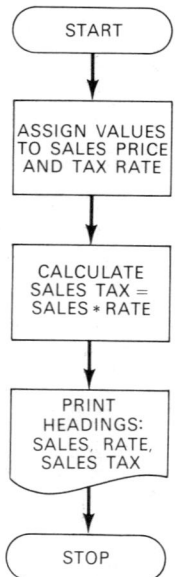

Flowchart 3-1   SALES TAX—FORMAT statement.

COMMENTS, FORMAT, AND CONTINUATION STATEMENTS

may be omitted when there is limited output, as in this case. The revised program statements and the output illustrating these ideas are

```
C  PROGRAM SALES-4
C  THIS PROGRAM COMPUTES THE SALES TAX FOR 1 ITEM, AT A RATE OF 4 PERCENT
       SALES = 1000.
       TAXRAT = .04
       SALETX = SALES * TAXRAT
       WRITE(6,401)SALES,TAXRAT,SALETX
401    FORMAT(13H SALES EQUALS ,F6.0,17H TAX RATE EQUALS ,F6.3,
      118H SALES TAX EQUALS ,F8.0)
       STOP
       END


SALES EQUALS 1000.  TAX RATE EQUALS   0.040 SALES TAX EQUALS        40.
```

In this sample, only the H and F codes are used. However, note that each of the Hollerith strings is terminated by a blank character to ensure that there is at least one space between the label and the data value. The X code could have been used for this purpose, but the method shown is much simpler. Finally, a continuation statement is indicated by the presence of a 1 in column 6 of the card immediately preceding the STOP statement.

3-5 Program Sample STATISTICS

In this section the use of the I and E codes will be shown in the program samples. The problem requires the calculation of the average of three values. In the first program, only the number of values and the average will be printed. The logic needed to calculate the average remains the same; however, the output format will be improved by identifying the data. Hence, Flowchart 3-2 is revised slightly to reflect the differences. The program statements, including new comment cards, an assignment card indicating the number of values, and revised WRITE and FORMAT statements provide for the output on one line.

```
C  PROGRAM STATISTICS-3
C  THIS PROGRAM COMPUTES THE AVERAGE OF THREE VALUES
       NOB = 3
       VAL1 = 75.
       VAL2 = 89.
       VAL3 = 73.
```

```
      AVG = (VAL1 + VAL2 + VAL3)/3.
      WRITE(6,300)NOB,AVG
300   FORMAT(4H FOR,I3,24H VALUES, THE AVERAGE IS ,F7.0)
      STOP
      END
```

```
FOR  3 VALUES, THE AVERAGE IS      79.
```

The use of the I code is introduced here to print the number of values averaged. As shown, the decimal point is not printed for integer values but is printed when the F code is used.

The same basic program can be modified once again to show (1) the use of the E format in printing the output; (2) column headings for the data; (3) another continuation card; and (4) double spacing of the output. In this sample, each of the values plus the sum and the average will be part of the output. Flowchart 3-3 details the logic changes; the actual statements needed are

```
C PROGRAM STATISTICS-4
C THIS PROGRAM COMPUTES THE AVERAGE OF THREE VALUES
```

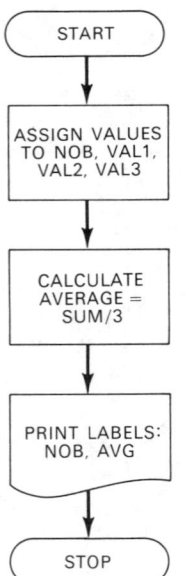

Flowchart 3-2 STATISTICS—FORMAT statement.

COMMENTS, FORMAT, AND CONTINUATION STATEMENTS

```
      VAL1 = 75.
      VAL2 = 89.
      VAL3 = 73.
      SUM = VAL1 + VAL2 + VAL3
      AVG = SUM/3.
      WRITE(6,300)VAL1,VAL2,VAL3,SUM,AVG
300   FORMAT(10H 1ST VALUE,6X,9H2ND VALUE,6X,9H3RD VALUE,6X,3HSUM,6X,7HA
     1VERAGE//E10.3,5X,E10.3,5X,E10.3,1X,E10.3,3X,E10.3)
      STOP
      END
```

The important points in this sample are contained in the FORMAT statement. The first part of the card up to the double slashes creates column headings. The two slashes provide for double spacing between the heading and the detail output. Following the slashes, the E codes are present to dictate the form of the answers printed.

1ST VALUE	2ND VALUE	3RD VALUE	SUM	AVERAGE
0.750E 02	0.890E 02	0.730E 02	0.237E 03	0.790E 02

This sample shows how the E codes generate output in scientific notation. It is much easier to read F-code output, but in

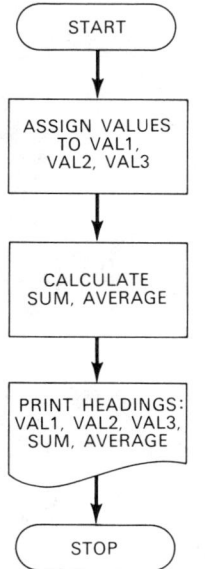

Flowchart 3-3 STATISTICS—FORMAT statement.

advanced problems often the E notation is mandatory when dealing with extremely large or small numbers.

The second half of the FORMAT statement in this program could be shortened slightly by grouping the first four codes as

1VERAGE//2(E10.3,5X),E10.3,1X,E10.3,3X,E10.3)

The output would appear exactly as before if this change were included.

3-6 FORMAT Extensions

Basic USAS FORTRAN IV format codes have been discussed previously. However, two extensions[1] to the basic set provide additional capability. The first extension involves alphanumeric data. An H format can be used to generate character data output. But to print character data stored in variables, the A format is required. The general forms are

Aw

and

aAw

where the A designates an alphanumeric field w characters in length. The a denotes the number of repeating fields such that 5A4 would represent five alphanumeric fields, each four characters in length. Refer to Figs. 3-5 and 3-6, which contain examples of its use.

Two comments are pertinent to the use of the A format. First, if the number of alpha characters in the variable is less than the field size indicated by the w, the rightmost part of the output field is filled with blanks; however, if the number of characters in the variable is greater than the size of the output field, the rightmost characters exceeding the size of the field are truncated, i.e., not printed. Consider the variable X with a value of ABC. When a format of A4 is used, ABC plus one blank is generated as output. When a format of A2 is used, only AB is generated as output.

Second, in most advanced FORTRAN compilers A data is

---

[1] Most advanced FORTRAN compilers provide the capability discussed in this section, so they will be used throughout the text. However, it may be necessary for the reader to refer to the particular systems manual being used for clarification purposes.

COMMENTS, FORMAT, AND CONTINUATION STATEMENTS

Figure 3-5 More examples of FORMAT statements.

	Program Statements	Description
110	FORMAT(A4)	The statement labeled 110 describes a four-character data field. The field may contain alphabetic characters, numeric digits, or special characters.
120	FORMAT('TITLE')	A five-character literal field is identified in statement labeled 120. The literal TITLE is transmitted to an output device.
130	WRITE(6,130) A, B FORMAT('A= ',E14.7,' NAM ',A3)	The two variables A (assumed to be a single-precision value) and B (assumed to be an alphanumeric value) are printed on output device numbered 6. Each of the variables is preceded by an accompanying Hollerith label.

Figure 3-6 More common errors that occur with FORMAT statements.

	Program Statements	Description
101	FORMAT(4A,5X,4A)	The order of the characters in the A specifications is reversed. The form must be Aw. A correct entry would be 101 FORMAT(A4,5X,A4)
102	FORMAT(TITLE OF REPORT)	The Hollerith string TITLE OF REPORT must be either preceded by the H code and the character count or bracketed with quotes. A correct entry would be 102 FORMAT('TITLE OF REPORT')
103	WRITE(6,103) MON FORMAT(A5)	Assuming that the variable MON contains alphanumeric data, there is no syntax error in the statements. However, if it is the programmer's intention with the A5 format to print five characters, a different form is required because MON contains a maximum of four. A correct entry for printing five characters would be WRITE(6,103) MON1, MON2 103 FORMAT(A4,A1)

stored in groups of four characters.[1] One variable, therefore, can store only four characters; two variables are required to store five to eight characters; and so forth. Thus, if A6 is used

---

[1] However, it may be necessary to refer to the particular systems manual being used to clarify the number of characters permitted.

Figure 3-7 More examples of FORMAT statements.

	Program Statements	Description
100	FORMAT(1H+,2I3)	The first character in the FORMAT statement is used for control of vertical spacing. No advance in vertical spacing is indicated by the plus (+) sign in statement 100. Either of the two forms can be used to dictate no advance. The 2I3 designates that a three-digit integer data field is repeated twice.
100	or FORMAT('+',2I3)	
101	FORMAT(1H ,F10.0)	A vertical advance of one line space is designated by the blank appearing as the first character in the FORMAT statement. The F10.0 designates a 10-digit real field, with no decimal places.
101	or FORMAT(1X,F10.0)	
101	or FORMAT(' ', F10.0)	
102	FORMAT(1H0,2A4)	Vertical spacing is advanced two lines as directed by the zero (0) contained in the literal field. An eight-character field is specified by the 2A4 parameter.
102	or FORMAT('0', 2A4)	
103	FORMAT(6H1TITLE)	The 1 in the six-position literal field causes an advance to the next page before the literal TITLE is generated as output. Note that the carriage-control character can be combined with another literal within the same statement.
103	or FORMAT('1TITLE')	
	WRITE(6,104)	The WRITE and FORMAT statements shown here produce two lines of output. The first appears at the top of a new page; the second is double-spaced below.
104	FORMAT('1HEADING−1'/'0HEADING−2')	

to store a string in one variable location, only four characters are retained. If A4 is used to store two characters in one variable location, the data is stored and blanks are inserted on the right side of the field.

A second method of representing Hollerith fields is to use quotes.[1] The set of characters desired as output is inserted within quotes in a FORMAT statement in place of using the H designation. For example, the Hollerith field, 12HHOURS

---

[1] Single quotes are used for the IBM 360 and 370 series; other manufacturers may require asterisks, for example, CDC 3600 and 6600, or double quotes, as for GE635 time-sharing. Refer to the particular systems manual being used for clarification.

COMMENTS, FORMAT, AND CONTINUATION STATEMENTS   59

WORKED, can be replaced by 'HOURS WORKED'. Quotes are convenient because the number of characters within the field does not have to be counted.

The final format option controls line spacing for the printer. A control character, appearing as the first entry in the format list, dictates different spacing of the computer output. When the control digit is equal to a,

Control Character	Line Spacing Action
Blank	Single spacing occurs.
0	Double spacing occurs.
1	Skip to the top of the next page occurs.
+	No spacing occurs.

The control character is required only when printing output and should be included in either an H format or quotes as illustrated in Fig. 3-7. An exception is that 1X can be used as a blank control character.

In each of the remaining program samples illustrated in this text, the first character of the output format will be designated for use as the control character.

FORMAT Extension Exercises

1 Evaluate samples (a) to (g), and detail the column-by-column output. Assume that the real variables X and Y have the values 62.33 and 28.007 and the alphanumeric variable NAM has the value of COND.

(a)   WRITE(6,101)X
   101 FORMAT(1X,E14.7)
(b)   WRITE(6,102)Y
       WRITE(6,102)X
   102 FORMAT(1H ,E10.3)
(c)   WRITE(6,103)NAM
   103 FORMAT(1H0,A4)
(d)   WRITE(6,104)
   104 FORMAT('1PRODUCTION GOAL')
(e)   WRITE(6,105)X,Y
   105 FORMAT('+',30X,2E12.5)

(f)   WRITE(6,106)X,Y
  106 FORMAT('0X=',E12.5/'0Y=',E12.5)
(g)   WRITE(6,107)NAM
  107 FORMAT(9H1NAME IS ,A3)

2 Supply the WRITE and FORMAT statements needed to fulfill the stated conditions:
  (a) Create a heading for a report that will print, at the top of a new page, PRODUCTION REPORT.
  (b) After double spacing, generate on one print line the single-precision variables Z, ZEB, and ZEB5. Each has seven significant digits. Separate each of the fields by inserting four blank characters.
  (c) The three variables A, B, and C contain alphanumeric data with four characters each. They are to be printed on three separate lines by using only one FORMAT statement.

3 Furnish the FORMAT statements necessary to process the following records:
  (a) A five-position integer field followed by a seven-digit numeric field.
  (b) A four-character alpha field, a six-digit numeric field, another four-character alpha field, and another six-digit numeric field.
  (c) The same four fields as in (3b); however, separate each field by inserting three blanks.
  (d) The label STANDARD ERROR followed by a seven-digit field. The label should print at the top of a new page.

3-7 Program Sample SALES TAX

Two extensions, the control of line spacing and Hollerith fields within quotes, will be included in the SALES TAX program. Assume that in the problem definition is the requirement that the output begin at the top of a new page. Thus, the first character of the output format must be a 1. Additionally, the H format will be replaced by fields enclosed within quotes.[1] The program logic is still the same as before; hence, Flowchart 3-4 is identical to Flowchart 3-1. The new statements and the output from the program are

---

[1] Since the program samples in this text have been run using an IBM Model 026 keypunch, an "at" (@) sign is used in place of the single quote ('), which is not available. Hence, whenever an "at" sign appears in a program listing, read and consider it as a single quote.

COMMENTS, FORMAT, AND CONTINUATION STATEMENTS

```
C PROGRAM SALES-5
C THIS PROGRAM COMPUTES THE SALES TAX FOR 1 ITEM, AT A RATE OF 4 PERCENT
      SALES = 1000.
      TAXRAT = .04
      SALETX = SALES * TAXRAT
      WRITE(6,401)
      WRITE(6,402)SALES,TAXRAT,SALETX
401   FORMAT(@1SALES@,5X,@TAX RATE@,5X,@SALES TAX@/)
402   FORMAT(1X,F6.0,3X,F8.3,5X,F8.0)
      STOP
      END
```

SALES	TAX RATE	SALES TAX
1000.	0.040	40.

Note that the output appears exactly the same as that from program SALES-3. Also in this sample, the slash in FORMAT 401 could be removed and the same effect enacted by modifying FORMAT 402 as

402   FORMAT('0', F6.0, 3X, F8.3, 5X, F8.0)

since the control character 0 causes double spacing to occur.

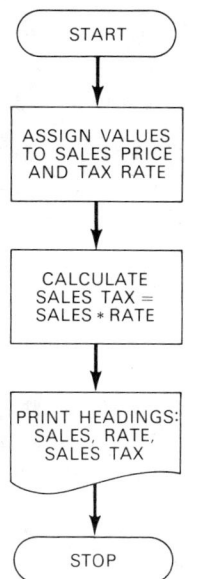

Flowchart 3-4 SALES TAX—FORMAT extensions.

Line spacing and the use of single quotes will also be shown in this sample. Two nondependent, consistent equations can be solved for x and y by using Cramer's rule.[1] Thus, if given two equations in the form

3-8 Miscellaneous Mathematical Samples

$$Ax + By = C$$
$$Dx + Ey = F$$

x and y could be found by substitution or by Cramer's rule. For our purposes the second method is chosen. To solve, the formulas required are

$$x = \frac{CE - BF}{AE - BD} \qquad y = \frac{AF - CD}{AE - BD}$$

Observe that for both x and y the denominator is the same. To be efficient in programming, it should only be calculated once, as shown in Flowchart 3-5. If solving the two equations

$$10x + 4y = -21$$
$$3x - 2y = 15$$

where A is 10, B is 4, C is -21, D is 3, E is -2, and F is 15, the program statements necessary are

```
C THIS PROGRAM SOLVES TWO SIMULTANEOUS EQUATIONS BY USING CRAMERS RULE
      DENOM = 10.*(-2.)-4.*3.
      X = (-21.*(-2.)-4.*15.)/DENOM
      Y = (10.*15.-(-21.)*3.)/DENOM
      WRITE(6,1)X,Y
1     FORMAT(@0THE VALUE OF X IS@,F10.3/@ THE VALUE OF Y IS@,F10.3/
     1@0USING CRAMERS RULE TO SOLVE 2 EQUATIONS@)
      STOP
      END
```

In the assignment statements extra parentheses have been bracketed about the negative values. Are they necessary? Yes, because otherwise two mathematical operators would appear in succession, thus causing an error. Also, because of the FORMAT statement the output would appear on three separate lines.

```
THE VALUE OF X IS     0.563
THE VALUE OF Y IS    -6.656

USING CRAMERS RULE TO SOLVE 2 EQUATIONS
```

[1] It is not necessary for the programmer to understand the mathematical basis of Cramer's rule to solve problems, provided the formulas and calculations are given.

COMMENTS, FORMAT, AND CONTINUATION STATEMENTS

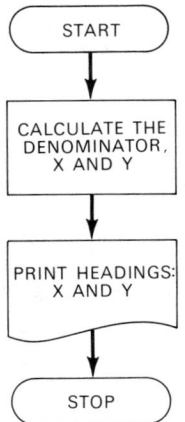

Flowchart 3-5 Cramer's rule—FORMAT extensions.

If the individual values of A, B, C, D, E, and F are to be printed as part of the output, they must be assigned values in separate statements. For this sample, though, it is not necessary. In the next program, the values used in the calculations will be printed.

Given two sides of a right triangle, the third side can be computed by using the formula

$$A^2 + B^2 = C^2 \quad \text{or} \quad (A^2 + B^2)^{1/2} = C$$

Thus, if A and B are 4.5 and 6, respectively, the value of C is 7.5. Flowchart 3-6 identifies the steps required to define values for A and B and then calculate the value of C. The program statements needed and the computer output are

```
C THIS PROGRAM COMPUTES THE THIRD SIDE OF A RIGHT TRIANGLE GIVEN A AND B
      A = 4.5
      B = 6.
      C = (A**2 + B**2)**.5
      WRITE(6,1)A,B,C
1     FORMAT(@1GIVEN TWO SIDES OF A RIGHT TRIANGLE,@F10.2,@ AND@,
     1F10.2/@ THE THIRD SIDE IS@,F10.2)
      STOP
      END
```

```
GIVEN TWO SIDES OF A RIGHT TRIANGLE,      4.50 AND       6.00
THE THIRD SIDE IS       7.50
```

Note that to solve for C, the expression representing $(A^2 + B^2)$ was raised to the .5 power, which is the same as taking the

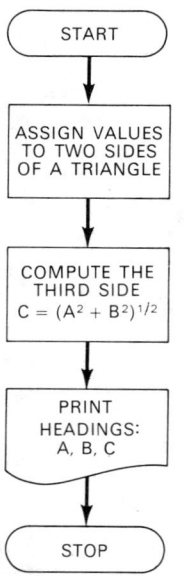

Flowchart 3-6 Right triangle—FORMAT extensions.

square root of the expression. But what would happen if the expression were written as

C = (A**2 + B**2)**1/2

or as

C = (A**2 + B**2)**(1/2)

If the answer is not clear, replace the original statement, and test these by running the programs on the computer.

3-9 Summary

Various format codes are used in FORTRAN to generate particular output data. Codes are available for manipulating integer, real, scientific notation, Hollerith, blank, and alphanumeric fields. Additionally, it is possible to control spacing of the line printer by use of the first character in the format list. In the next chapter, these same codes will be used to process input data.

Questions

1 Revise the program written to solve Question 2 of Chap. 2 so that the output is labeled properly.

COMMENTS, FORMAT, AND CONTINUATION STATEMENTS

2 Revise the program written to solve Question 3 of Chap. 2 to begin the output at the top of a new page. Also provide column headings.

3 Revise the solution for Question 5 of Chap. 2 to provide labels and double-spacing for each answer printed. Print each term on a separate line, but use only one FORMAT statement.

4 Revise the solution for Question 6 of Chap. 2 by changing the F codes designated in the problem to 5E14.7 codes. Label the output appropriately.

5 Write the solution to a problem requiring the computation of a weighted average. Three data values are available, designated by a, b, and c. The weighted average is equal to

$$\frac{[1.5 \times a + (b + c)]/3}{4.5}$$

Print the values of a, b, and c plus the weighted average, beginning at the top of a new page. Label each answer appropriately, and supply your own values for a, b, and c.

6 Grandfather Yarborough states that 10 years from today he will give you $500 if you provide him certain services. How much is the $500 worth today? By using the formula

$$P = \frac{F}{(1 + r)^n}$$

where P = present value
F = future value
r = discount rate
n = number of years

it is a simple question to answer. Write a FORTRAN program, where F is $500, n is 10, and r is 6 percent, to justify your answer that it is not worth the effort. Label the output appropriately.

7 Write a FORTRAN program to calculate X and Y, where

X = 6.21456 × 8.11111
Y = 586932. × 100000.1

and print the results. Check your answers manually. Are the results the same?

8 Write a program to compute the value of x in the equation $ax + b = cx + d$, given values for a, b, c, and d (supply your own). You must first solve for x algebraically. Print the output in the form

THE ROOT X OF THE LINEAR EQUATION IS XXX.XXX

9 The area of a trapezoid can be found by using the formula $A = \frac{1}{2}h(b + b_1)$, where A is the area, h the height, and b and b_1 are the length of the sides. Supply values for the variables; compute; and print this area in the form

A TRAPEZOID WITH SIDES XX.XX AND XX.XX AND A HEIGHT OF XX.XX HAS AN AREA OF XXX.XX.

ADDITIONAL I/O COMMANDS 4

The program samples in Chaps. 2 and 3 were limited as far as flexibility is concerned. In this chapter, a method for introducing the capability of writing flexible programs via the READ statement will be discussed. Several different options will be presented. Additional methods for generating input and output will also be covered.

4-1 The READ Statement

The READ statement, which serves as the primary input instruction in FORTRAN programs, transmits data from a particular input device, such as the card reader, to the memory unit of the computer. There are two general forms of the statement:

sl   READ(ia,b)

and

sl   READ(ia,b) [list of variables, separated by commas]

The sl, as before, represents an optional statement label, the ia is an unsigned integer value specifying a particular input device, and the b refers to a specific FORMAT.

In this text and in most computer installations, the card reader is the standard input device. The device assignment is normally

5; hence, in the program samples shown, the ia in the instruction will be replaced by a 5 or an integer variable.

In use, the first form of the READ simply processes one record (reads one card, for example) but does not normally retain any values. Usually, the required FORMAT statement contains a slash when employing this method (see Fig. 4-1). An exception occurs when the following example is processed:

```
          READ(5,1000)
1000      FORMAT('REPLACED BY INPUT DATA')
or
1000      FORMAT(22HREPLACED BY INPUT DATA)
```

Figure 4-1 Examples of the READ† statement.

	Program Statements		Description
1	READ(5,11)KNT	Data:	Input device number 5 and FORMAT statement 11 are referenced by the READ. The integer value of 82 is assigned to the integer variable KNT when the READ statement is executed during the program run. A three-digit integer field is designated by the specification in the format statement.
11	FORMAT(I3)	82	
12	READ(5,12)REX FORMAT(5X,F5.2)	Data: −2.35	Input device number 5 and FORMAT label 12 are designated by the READ. The real value −2.35 is assigned to the variable REX. The FORMAT statement dictates that the first five columns of the data field are to be skipped and the next five assigned to the variable.
6	READ(5,13)STU,GRADE	Data:	A three-character alpha field is specified by the FORMAT statement for the variable STU. Thus, STU is assigned a value of TSJ at run time. The next two columns of data are skipped by the 2X specification, and the numeric value of 85.5 is assigned to the variable GRADE at run time. Even though the decimal point is not placed in the data field, it is assumed to be between the 5s because of the F4.1 format.
13	FORMAT(A3,2X,F4.1)	TSJ 855	

ADDITIONAL I/O COMMANDS

	Program Statements		Description
14	READ(5,14)G1,G2,G3 FORMAT(3F5.1)	Data: 81.0 79.5 −80.5	During the program run, the three variables G1, G2, and G3 are assigned values of 81.0, 79.5, and −80.5, respectively, as directed by the READ statement.
8 15	READ(5,15)T1 READ(5,15)T2 FORMAT(F8.2)	Data: 8267.33 6167.25 1005.06 1815.76	The variables T1 and T2 are assigned the values of 8267.33 and 1005.06, respectively, because the format indicates only one field per data record. Thus, the values of 6167.25 and 1815.76 are not read as input in this example.
16	READ(5,16)T1,T2 FORMAT(F8.2)	Data: 8267.33 6167.25 1005.06 1815.76	Although only one field is specified in the FORMAT statement, two variables must be assigned values in the READ statement. Thus, the FORMAT statement is repeated for two input records so that T1 and T2 are assigned the values 8267.33 and 1005.06, respectively. The second data value found in each card is not processed by the computer in these examples, as was the case above.
17	READ(5,17) FORMAT(/)	Data: 123.45	The use of the slash (/) in the FORMAT statement causes one entire data record to be processed without using its contents for the program.
18	READ(5,18)II,FAT FORMAT(I3,F8.2)	Data: 1 10.35	This example illustrates how the integer and real format specifications differ. The value 100 is assigned to the variable II because the field is defined as three digits long. Although the data would appear to be simply 1, the value is processed as if it were 100 because the decimal point is fixed. The variable FAT is assigned a value of 10.35, indicating that the computer recognizes the floating decimal point within the field for real values.

†In these samples, the READ statement is shown along with the FORMAT statement and data that would satisfy the condition. It is assumed that column 1 of the data card corresponds to the D listed in the title Data.

FORTRAN IV PROGRAMMING AND APPLICATIONS

In this case, the information processed by the READ instruction replaces the Hollerith data in the FORMAT statement. Subsequently, writing the contents of label 1000 will produce the information read into the program, not the original Hollerith string.

These two options, however, are not used as often as the second form. In the second general form, the variables listed after the READ are assigned values. The values are obtained from data processed by the READ instruction at program execution time. By supplying different data records, the same variables can be assigned different values during the various runs of a program.

The number and mode of the values in the data list must agree with the number and mode of the variables in the READ statement. Figures 4-1 and 4-2 contain examples of various READ statements and many of the rules regarding its use.

Figure 4-2 Common errors that occur with READ statements.

	Program Statements		Description
73	READ(5,10)INT,FNP	Data:	The variable INT is integer mode, and
10	FORMAT(F5.2,I3)	8.45 10	FNP is real mode. Contrarily, the format and data list first a real field and second an integer field. The variable names and their modes must be aligned properly with the format and data. A correct entry would be
			73 READ(5,10)FNP,INT
	READ AVERAG	Data:	The statement as listed does not conform to the standard layout. An input device and a format label must be specified. Corrections necessary include
		689.753	
			READ(5,11)AVERAG
			11 FORMAT(F8.3)
86	READ(5,12)MIN MAX AVER	Data:	The three variables listed in the READ statement must be separated by commas. The other entries are correct as shown. The corrections to the READ statement are
12	FORMAT(2I3,2X,F5.2)	81 95 1.22	
			86 READ(5,12)MIN,MAX,AVER

ADDITIONAL I/O COMMANDS

	Program Statements		Description

13	READ(5,13)A*X+5.6
	FORMAT(2F5.0)
		Data:
		123 284
			Arithmetic operations (*, +) and constants (5.6) are not permitted as part of the READ statement. Only variables may be listed in the READ, and calculations must be made as a separate entry. Corrections necessary to the statement shown are
			      READ(5,13)A,X
			      ANS=A*X+5.6

101 14	READ(5,14)UNITS,PRICE FORMAT(F5.0,F6.1)	Data: 432 47.6	The values assigned to the two variables UNITS and PRICE are 432. and 0.0. The READ and FORMAT statements are constructed properly; however, the second field in the data is assumed to have values of zero since no data exists. The second data record is not processed because there is only one READ statement. To assign the value 47.6 to PRICE, the correct data card would be 432 47.6
15	READ(5,15)CUSTOM,SALES FORMAT(2A4,F10.2)	Data: JONES BR 386.78	Only two variables are listed in the READ statement, but the FORMAT statement identifies three fields: two character fields and one real field. The value assigned to CUSTOM is JONE; S BR is assigned to SALES. The numeric value is not processed by this statement. A third variable must be inserted in the READ to properly assign the data: READ(5,15)CUSTOM,CUSTO2,SALES
72 16	READ(5,16)A FORMAT(1X,F5.1) WRITE(6,16)A	Data: 4239.	This sample does not contain a statement error. However, it does point out a difference between input and output uses of a FORMAT statement. The value assigned to the variable A is 239.0, not 4239.0 as might be assumed. The 1X causes the computer to "skip over" the first column (i.e., the 4) when reading data. But for output purposes, it provides for single spacing, retaining five places for printing A.

Three additional comments are pertinent. First, blanks within a data field are treated as zeros when processed by a READ statement. If the field is entirely blank, it is assumed to be zero. Second, integer fields designated by the I format are often called *fixed-point fields*. This means that the integer constant in the data record must always be right-justified in the field to align properly with the fixed decimal point. Consider as an example an I5 field. If columns 1 to 5 of a data card contain

	Data value	or	the result is interpreted as
Columns	1...5	1...5	
	1	00001	1
	1	00010	10
	1	00100	100
	1	01000	1000
	1	10000	10000

Hence, the decimal point is always assumed "fixed" immediately to the right of the I5 field. But with the F-format code, however, the decimal point can be placed anywhere within the field. The "floating-decimal point" overrides the one indicated by the form Fw.d. For example, consider an F6.1 field; columns 1 to 6 contain

	Data value	or	the result is interpreted as
Columns	1....6	1....6	
	1	0000.1	0.1
	1	0001.0	1.0
	1	0010.0	10.0
	1.	001.00	1.0
	1.	00001.	1.0

Referring again to Figs. 4-1 and 4-2, note the important differences involved with both I- and F-format codes.

Thus, using the READ statement is a second method for assigning values to variables. Recall that the first method was by use of the arithmetic assignment. However, as the samples show, the READ method is much more flexible because only the data cards must be changed to enter different values. Also, large volumes of data are more easily entered by use of the READ statement, as later programs will show.

ADDITIONAL I/O COMMANDS

READ Exercises

1 Supply the necessary data values, in the appropriate form, that will satisfy READ statements (a) to (e). Choose arbitrary values.
   (a) 101 READ(5,100)A,B,C
        100 FORMAT(F5.0,F6.2,F8.1)
   (b) 2   FORMAT(I5,I6,4X,I3)
             READ(5,2)ITER,JTER,KTER
   (c) 3   FORMAT(A4,A2,2E14.7)
        333 READ(5,3)NAME1,NAME2,EXPO,DOUB
   (d)   READ(5,4)F1,F2,I1,I2,I3
        4   FORMAT(2F5.1,3(I3,5X))
   (e) 5   FORMAT(I6,F7.1,A4,E13.6,E12.5)
             READ(5,5)I,F,A,E,D

2 Supply the READ and FORMAT statements that will process each of the following values:

   Columns 1................
   (a)   25   81.233   B0B
   (b)   ALPHA   0.123E−02
   (c)   1 3 5 7 9   6. 7. 8.
   (d)   6.333   5167.3

3 Supply the READ, FORMAT, and data values necessary to enter the following information in the computer:
   (a) Sales are $30,573.35, fixed costs are $12,600.25, and variable costs are $14,820.00
   (b) The month is June, the day is 30, and the year is 1984
   (c) The employee name is John Doer, the rank is SS-3, and the hours worked are 42.75

4 In each of the following statements, what is the last value assigned to the variable A?

	Program Statements	Data Column 1...............	
(a)	READ(5,4)A	SMITH	
	4 FORMAT(A3)		
(b)	READ(5,5)A,B	1234.	3
	5 FORMAT(2F5.1)	2.0	3
	READ(5,5)A,C		
(c)	6 FORMAT(E14.7)	−0.1234567E−02	
	READ(5,6)A		
	A=2.2*A		
(d)	7 FORMAT(E12.5)	0.23E+03	
	READ(5,7)A1,A	0.34E+04	

5 Identify and correct errors, whether they are omitted data values or variables, or an illegal use of the READ and FORMAT statements:

	Program Statements		Data Column 1 . . . .
(a)	151	READ(6,10)BCD	
	10	FORMAT(F6.1)	−674.5
(b)		READ(5,11)B,C,D	
	11	FORMAT(3F5.2)	1.1 3.4 4.6
(c)		READ(5,12)B,CD	
	12	FORMAT(I3,F8.1)	123 6.83
(d)		READ(5,13)BC,D	
	13	FORMAT(E12.4,A4)	BOLT 8.6378903
(e)		READ(5,14)B,C,D	
	14	FORMAT(2E12.5)	1.3864 3.68947
(f)		READ(5,15)BCD	
	15	FORMAT(2(F4.1,2X))	−4.1 62.7
(g)		READ(5,16)B,C	
		READ(5,16)D	16.00
	16	FORMAT(2F5.2)	18.78 8.77

4-2 Program Sample SALES TAX

The previous SALES TAX programs required an arithmetic assignment statement to enter the sales data into the computer. By using the READ statement with an accompanying FORMAT, a flexible program can be created. Flowchart 4-1 indicates the change in logic reflecting the replacement of the assignment statement by the READ statement. Two new cards, a FORMAT (101) and READ, are needed in addition to the others used previously.

```
C PROGRAM SALES-6
C THIS PROGRAM COMPUTES THE SALES TAX FOR 1 ITEM, AT A RATE OF 4 PERCENT
      TAXRAT = .04
      READ(5,101)SALES
      SALETX = SALES * TAXRAT
      WRITE(6,401)
      WRITE(6,402)SALES,TAXRAT,SALETX
101   FORMAT(F6.0)
401   FORMAT(6H1SALES,5X,8HTAX RATE,5X,9HSALES TAX/)
402   FORMAT(1X,F6.0,3X,F8.3,5X,F8.0)
      STOP
      END
```

This version requires a data card containing the sales value $1,000. Because of the F6.0 in label 101, the data must be placed in columns 1 to 6 of the data record. The data card and the output from the program follow:

ADDITIONAL I/O COMMANDS

1000.

SALES   TAX RATE   SALES TAX

1000.   0.040   40.

Note that the output is identical to the earlier versions containing the arithmetic assignment statement. Hence, the READ statement has no effect on the output but concerns only the input.

The astute reader may have noticed in Chap. 3 that the A-format code was discussed but not included in the program samples. How then is the A code used? Suppose that a more explanatory heading containing the date is required. A number of alternatives are available, but because the A code will be illustrated, assume that the date is in the form 09-26-70. The A-format code is required to process these eight characters since two hyphens, which are alphanumeric characters, are included in the field. Also, one variable name can only store

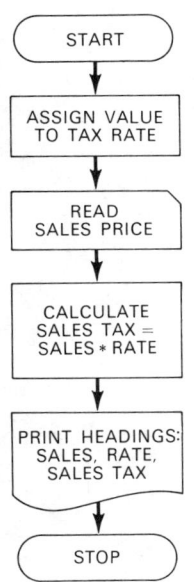

Flowchart 4-1 SALES TAX—READ statement.

four alphanumeric characters, so two distinct variable names are required to process the eight characters listed. The logical flow to incorporate the heading is depicted in Flowchart 4-2. Four new program cards, a READ, a WRITE, and two FORMAT statements, plus a minor change to label 401 to accommodate double-spacing, are needed:

```
C PROGRAM SALES-7
C THIS PROGRAM COMPUTES THE SALES TAX FOR 1 ITEM, AT A RATE OF 4 PERCENT
      READ(5,100)DAY,YEAR
      WRITE(6,400)DAY,YEAR
      TAXRAT = .04
      READ(5,101)SALES
      SALETX = SALES * TAXRAT
      WRITE(6,401)
      WRITE(6,402)SALES,TAXRAT,SALETX
100   FORMAT(2A4)
101   FORMAT(F6.0)
400   FORMAT(21H1SALES REPORT   DATED ,2A4)
401   FORMAT(6H0SALES,5X,8HTAX RATE,5X,9HSALES TAX/)
402   FORMAT(1X,F6.0,3X,F8.3,5X,F8.0)
      STOP
      END
```

Also, one new data card containing the date must be placed in front of the previous card. To show the flexibility of the READ statement, a different sales value has been inserted on the second card. The new data cards and the new output are

```
09-26-70
2000.
```

```
SALES REPORT   DATED 09-26-70

SALES       TAX RATE       SALES TAX

2000.        0.040           80.
```

By using the READ statement in place of the assignment, one version of the program can be used to solve any number of problems. Only new data is required for each run. Thus, use of the READ is a decided advantage when creating flexible programs. As reflected in the program samples, the H code will be used in the SALES TAX problems for Hollerith strings, and single quotes will be illustrated in the STATISTICS problems.

ADDITIONAL I/O COMMANDS

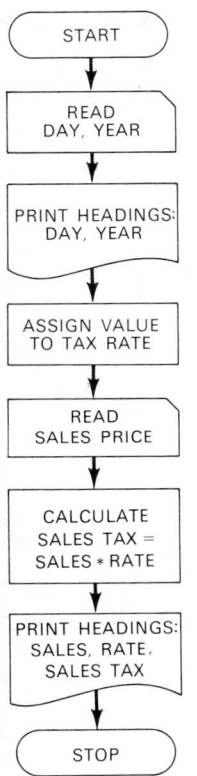

Flowchart 4-2 SALES TAX—READ statement.

In this discussion of the STATISTICS problem the definition remains the same, but the assignment statement will be replaced by the READ statement as the means for entering data into the program. The new data values processed by this program may contain one decimal place. The required logical flow of data is illustrated in Flowchart 4-3. The program statements required are

**4-3
Program
Sample
STATISTICS**

```
C PROGRAM STATISTICS-6
C THIS PROGRAM COMPUTES THE AVERAGE OF THREE VALUES
      READ(5,201)VAL1,VAL2,VAL3
      SUM = VAL1 + VAL2 + VAL3
      AVG = SUM/3.
      WRITE(6,301)VAL1,VAL2,VAL3,SUM,AVG
201   FORMAT(3F5.1)
```

```
301    FORMAT(@11ST VALUE    2ND VALUE    3RD VALUE    SUM    AVERAGE@/1X,F9.1,
       12F11.1,F7.1,F9.1)
       STOP
       END
```

For this program, a data card must be punched according to the form identified in label 201. Because 3F5.1 is the format code, the first value must be located in columns 1 to 5, the second in columns 6 to 10, and the third in columns 11 to 15 of the data card. The card and the output from the program are

75.5 89.5 73.5

1ST VALUE   2ND VALUE   3RD VALUE   SUM   AVERAGE
   75.5   89.5   73.5   238.5   79.5

By now the output should be familiar to the reader. In an expansion of the problem, assume that the definition necessitates the incorporation of a heading containing the date, as was done in the SALES TAX example. However, to show a different method for printing the date, assume that the input data appears in the form 092570 and that the output data is desired as

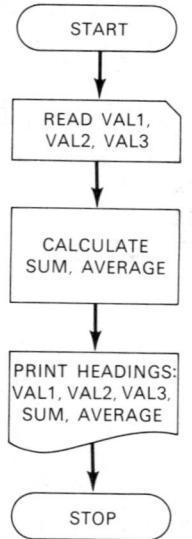

Flowchart 4-3   STATISTICS—READ statement.

ADDITIONAL I/O COMMANDS

09/25/70. Hollerith strings are necessary to print the slashes. But to print the three fields surrounding the slashes requires three integer variables. Flowchart 4-4 details the necessary steps; the program cards needed are

```
C     PROGRAM STATISTICS-7
C     THIS PROGRAM COMPUTES THE AVERAGE OF THREE VALUES
      READ(5,200)MONTH,IDAY,IYEAR
      WRITE(6,300)MONTH,IDAY,IYEAR
      READ(5,201)VAL1,VAL2,VAL3
      SUM = VAL1 + VAL2 + VAL3
      AVG = SUM/3.
      WRITE(6,301)VAL1,VAL2,VAL3,SUM,AVG
200   FORMAT(3I2)
201   FORMAT(3F5.1)
300   FORMAT(@1STATISTICS REPORT   DATED @,I2,@/@,I2,@/@,I2)
301   FORMAT(@01ST VALUE  2ND VALUE  3RD VALUE   SUM    AVERAGE@/1X,F9.1,
     12F11.1,F7.1,F9.1)
      STOP
      END
```

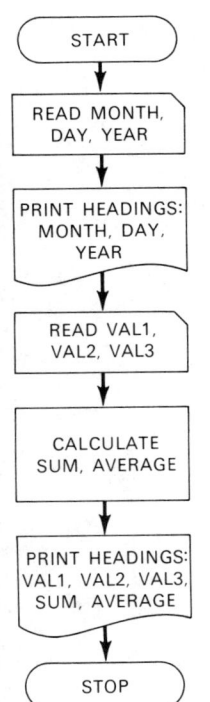

Flowchart 4-4   STATISTICS—READ statement.

To run this program, two data cards are needed: one for the date with information in columns 1 to 6 and the second with values in columns 1 to 15. The data cards, with new values, plus the program output are

```
092570
 855   894   686
```

```
STATISTICS REPORT   DATED   9/25/70

1ST VALUE   2ND VALUE   3RD VALUE   SUM     AVERAGE
   85.5        89.4        68.6    243.5      81.2
```

Note that the data values appearing in columns 1 to 15 of the second card do not contain decimal points. However, since an F code is used in label 201, the point is assumed to be located between the fourth and fifth places in each field. The output reflects the accurate processing of the data so that either form (decimal punched or implied) leads to the correct manipulation of the data.

4-4 Extensions to the Basic I/O Commands

Three additional input/output statements,[1] which are an extension to basic USAS FORTRAN IV, are presented in this section. The first is a simplified form for using the card reader as the standard input device. The general form is

sl   READ b, [list of variables, separated by commas]

where sl is an optional statement label, the device number is omitted (it is assumed to be the card reader), and b refers to a specific FORMAT statement. The only difference between this statement and the previous READ is the omission of a device specification—it functions identically and serves the exact same purpose. Likewise, a simplified form for using the line printer as the standard output device is

sl   PRINT b, [list of variables, separated by commas]

where sl is an optional statement label, the device number is omitted (it is assumed to be the line printer), and b refers to

---

[1] The three statements covered in this section are available for use in most advanced FORTRAN compilers. Refer to the particular systems manual being used for clarification.

ADDITIONAL I/O COMMANDS

Figure 4-3 Examples of the READ and PRINT statements.

	Program Statements		Description
94	READ 100,A	Data:	The standard input device, the card reader, is implied because a specific device has not been listed in the READ statement. The real value 8456.89 is assigned to the variable A.
100	FORMAT(F10.2)	8456.89	
	READ 3,X,Y,K	Data:	FORMAT label 3 specifies that three values, two real and one integer, be assigned to the variables X, Y, and K, respectively. The standard input device is referenced by this form.
3	FORMAT(2F5.1,I3)	23.5 −1.1 7	
872	PRINT 10,A,B		The values of A and B are printed on the standard output device, the line printer. FORMAT label 10 specifies that messages are outputted on the same line with the numeric values.
10	FORMAT(' A=' ,F5.1,5X,'B=' ,F5.1)		
	PRINT 16,XA,XAB		The values of the four variables XA, XAB, XB, and XBB are written on the standard output device according to the A-format code. The first two are printed on one line and the last two on another line.
	PRINT 16,XB,XBB		
16	FORMAT(1X,2A4)		

a specific FORMAT statement. Figures 4-3 and 4-4 show examples of the usage of the READ and PRINT statements along with the common errors that occur in their use.

The third statement discussed in this section involves a more advanced option of the READ statement. Its general form is

sl   READ(ia,b,END=sl) [list of variables, separated by commas]

where sl, ia, and b represent the same items as they did in the earlier READ statements. The END=sl option is a "look-ahead" test for data. If no data is available for the READ, the computer "jumps" or transfers control to the statement label following END=. If there is data, the program continues processing in the normal sequence. This option is used as a method for terminating loops, a concept that will be discussed in great detail in the next chapter. However, it is sufficient now to consider Figs. 4-5 and 4-6 as examples of the READ; in the next chapter it will be shown in program samples.

Figure 4-4 Common errors that occur with READ and PRINT statements.

Program Statements		Description

7	READ, A	A device number and a FORMAT label have been omitted. It is necessary to insert a FORMAT label with this form. Correct entries would be
		     7 READ 5,A
		     5 FORMAT(5X,F10.2)

6	READ (6)TOT FORMAT(5X,F10.2)	To use the READ statement with the standard input device, a comma is necessary, not parentheses as indicated.[1] A correct entry would be READ 6,TOT
9 8	PRINT 8 DEL,ALP FORMAT(2F10.1)	A comma is required to separate the FORMAT designation 8 from the first variable DEL. A correct entry would be 9 PRINT 8,DEL,ALP

6.5	PRINT 6.5,A+B
	 FORMAT(F10.3)
		Two errors are contained in these statements. First, the FORMAT label must be integer mode, not real. Second, the calculation A+B is not permitted. Correct entries would be
		            X=A+B
		            PRINT 6,X
		     6 FORMAT(F10.3)

[1] The use of the READ statement as shown is interpreted as an unformatted read from device number 6 in some systems. For further details, see IBM publication No. C28-6629-2 or the appropriate systems manual for clarification.

ADDITIONAL I/O COMMANDS

Figure 4-5 Examples of the READ statement with END option.

Program Statements		Description
10	FORMAT(F5.3)	The READ statement with the END option, labeled 180, accesses device 5 according to FORMAT 10. Upon execution, a data value is assigned to A and label 190 is performed next. However, if there is no data value for A, control is transferred directly to label 200, bypassing the intervening statements.
180	READ(5,10,END=200)A	
190	.	
	.	
	.	
200	STOP	
11	FORMAT(I7)	If data is available, the READ is processed, a value assigned to the variable I and the next statement in sequence executed. Otherwise, control is passed to the assignment statement labeled 211.
	READ(5,11,END=211)I	
	.	
	.	
	.	
211	KI3=I**3−6	
	READ(5,12,END=212)C	The END= option in the READ statement causes the computer to transfer control to the WRITE statement labeled 212 when there is no data available to satisfy the READ. Otherwise, the next executable statement in the program is processed.
12	FORMAT(1X,A4)	
	.	
	.	
	.	
212	WRITE(6,12)C	

Figure 4-6 Common errors that occur with the READ statement with END option.

	Program Statements	Description
1	READ(5,1,END=10)AL	The END=10 option in the READ statement is not valid because control can be passed only to an executable statement. Label 10, a FORMAT statement, is not executable. A correct entry would be
	FORMAT(5X,F12.3)	
	.	
	.	
	.	
10	FORMAT(F5.1)	
20	STOP	
		READ(5,1,END=20)AL
15	READ(5,2END=15)BL	Two errors occur in this statement. First, a comma must be inserted between 2 and END=15. Second, since the READ is labeled 15 and
	.	
	.	
	.	
25		

Figure 4-6 Common errors that occur with the READ statement with END option *(cont'd)*.

Program Statements	Description
	END=15, when there is no data available control is passed to the same statement repeatedly. Thus, a logic error results. A correct entry would be
	15 READ(5,2,END=25)BL
1 READ(5,3,END=20)IC	No error occurs in the form of
3 FORMAT(6I5)	the READ statement. However,
.	as in the first example, control
.	must be passed to an executable
.	statement. The END statement
20 END	is not executable and can not have a label. Thus, correct entries would be
	20 STOP
	END

Extended I/O Exercises

1 Supply the program statements necessary to read, calculate, and print requirements (*a*) to (*c*). Use the READ and PRINT options contained in this section.
   (*a*) Read values for the maximum and minimum gravitational pull (four decimal places each). Calculate and print the range (maximum minus minimum).
   (*b*) Read two values representing the highest and lowest grades from a test (no decimal places). Calculate and print the range.
   (*c*) Read a two-decimal-place value for gross pay. The net pay is equal to the gross minus 10 percent of the gross. Print the gross and net pay.

2 Supply the READ statements required to process the following verbal descriptions:
   (*a*) Read values for BETA, GAMMA, and DELTA according to FORMAT label 101.
   (*b*) Read values for two integer, three single-precision, and two alphanumeric variables according to FORMAT label 102.
   (*c*) Read two single-precision and four scientific notation variables according to FORMAT label 103.

3 Supply the PRINT statements required to output to the line printer the values processed in Exercise 2(*a*) to (*c*).

ADDITIONAL I/O COMMANDS

4 Using the END=sl option, supply the READ statements equating to the following descriptions:
   (a) Process three integer variables, but if there is no data, transfer control to statement label 9999.
   (b) Process one floating-point and one alphanumeric variable. Transfer control to statement 2 if there is insufficient data to meet the READ requirements.
   (c) Process five alphanumeric variables, but transfer to label 73 if no data is available for the READ.

4-5 Program Sample SALES TAX

In the earlier SALES TAX problem the data was conveniently supplied so that the SALES TAX answer "fitted" the F8.0 format code supplied. However, it is unreasonable to assume that this will always be the case. In the following sample version, a format code of F8.2, indicating two decimal places, will replace the former code along with the use of the READ and PRINT options covered in Sec. 4-4. Another change in this program will show how it is possible to combine two FORMAT statements into one. The minor changes are shown in Flowchart 4-5; the program statements are

```
C     PROGRAM SALES-8
C     THIS PROGRAM COMPUTES THE SALES TAX FOR 1 ITEM, AT A RATE OF 4 PERCENT
      READ 100,DAY,YEAR
      PRINT 400,DAY,YEAR
      TAXRAT = .04
      READ 101,SALES
      SALETX = SALES * TAXRAT
      PRINT 401,SALES,TAXRAT,SALETX
100   FORMAT(2A4)
101   FORMAT(F8.2)
400   FORMAT(21H1SALES REPORT   DATED ,2A4/8H0   SALES,5X,8HTAX RATE,5X,9H
     1SALES TAX/)
401   FORMAT(1X,F8.2,3X,F8.3,5X,F8.2)
      STOP
      END
```

The first revision involves the READ and PRINT statements, replacing the READ and WRITE options employed previously. Note that the only difference concerns the device and format designations. The second revision concerns label 400. The first character in the format is a 1, dictating a page change. Also, the two headings have been combined in this one format, where the first / is used to start another line of print in the output. Finally, the F8.0 code has been replaced by an F8.2

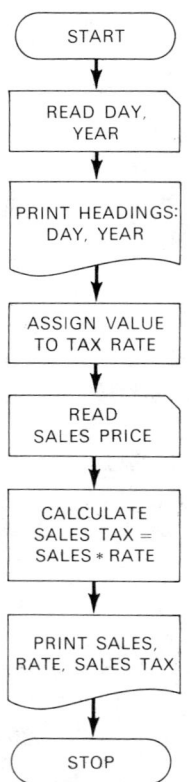

Flowchart 4-5 SALES TAX—READ statement, extension.

code in label 401. New data and the output from the program are

```
10-06-70
 857.67
```

```
SALES REPORT    DATED 10-06-70

   SALES       TAX RATE      SALES TAX

   857.67        0.040         34.31
```

Because of the similarity of the two READs and the WRITE and PRINT statements, the second sample concerning the STATISTICS problem will be omitted here.

4-6 The DATA Statement

In addition to the assignment process and the READ instruction, a third method for entering input into the computer is the DATA statement. Whereas the READ statement should be used for processing most input, the DATA command is preferable when initializing[1] the values of particular variables. The DATA statement is a nonexecutable FORTRAN command that assigns values to variables but only at compile time. Its general forms are

DATA variable/constant/

or

DATA variable-1,variable-2/constant-1,constant-2/

or

DATA variable-1/constant-1/,variable-2/constant-2/

where this is the second statement covered thus far that does not permit an optional statement label. (The END statement was the first.) Within the DATA statement, all the permitted variable types, including Hollerith strings, can be inserted as constants in the DATA statement.

An exception to the general form just listed is a shorthand method for assigning one value to all the variables listed in the DATA statement. For example, the statement

DATA A, B, C/0.0,0.0,0.0/

can be written in shorthand form by

DATA A, B, C/3*0.0/

where the 3* designates the number of variables to be assigned a value of zero.

Figures 4-7 and 4-8 list further examples of its valid use and the common errors that occur. In Sec. 6-4, additional samples in a more powerful application will be shown. However, note that its use is suggested for only two requirements: assigning constant values and initializing variables.

---

[1] The term *initializing* implies setting a variable equal to a constant only at the beginning of a program run.

Figure 4-7 Examples of the DATA statement.

Program Statements	Description
DATA KOT/123/	The integer value 123 is assigned at compilation time to the variable KOT.
DATA A,B/6.21,7.25/	The two real values 6.21 and 7.25 are assigned to the variables A and B, respectively.
DATA X10/5.05/,MAT01/2/	Values are assigned to the two variables X10 and MAT01. The real value 5.05 and the integer value 2 are assigned, respectively.
DATA ANS/4HEOFR/	The Hollerith constant consisting of the four characters EOFR is assigned to the variable ANS.
DATA ANS,DEB/'EOFR','CONT'/	The two Hollerith constants EOFR and CONT are assigned to the variables ANS and DEB, respectively.
DATA M1/1/,M2/1/,M3/1/ or DATA M1,M2,M3/3*1/	In both these statements the integer value 1 is assigned to the variables M1, M2, and M3.

Figure 4-8 Common errors that occur with DATA statements.

Program Statements	Description
DATA KCTY/6.5/	The variable KCTY is integer mode, and the constant 6.5 is real mode. Thus, a mixed-mode assignment results. A correct entry would be 　　　DATA XKCTY/6.5/ 　　　　　　or 　　　DATA KCTY/6/
DATA X/25.1/Y/16.8/	The variables in the DATA statement must be separated by commas. The assignment of X is correct, but a correction is required to separate Y according to 　　　DATA X/25.1/,Y/16.8/

ADDITIONAL I/O COMMANDS

Program Statements	Description

DATA A,B,I,J/1.3,2*0/	The DATA statement is invalid because a constant is missing for the variable B. The value 1.3 is assigned to A, and because 0 is integer mode it can be asasumed that the values of I and J are intended to be 0. A correct entry would be
	    DATA A,I,J/1.3,2*0/
	    or
	    DATA A,B,I,J/1.3,0.,2*0/

DATA XB/EOFR/	The characters EOFR are understood to represent a Hollerith constant. The Hollerith designation, either the H code or quotes, must be included as part of the DATA statement. A correct entry would be either
	    DATA XB/4HEOFR/
	    or
	    DATA XB/'EOFR'/

100 DATA A/7.5/	The label 100 is not permitted as part of the DATA statement. It must be omitted; hence, a correct entry would be DATA A/7.5/

DATA X,Y/A,B/	Within the slashes, only numeric constants are permitted unless the value is assumed to be a Hollerith string. Thus, a correct entry would be either
	    DATA X,Y/0.0,0.0/
	    or
	    DATA X,Y/1HA,1HB/

DATA Exercises

1 List the exact values assigned to the specific variables contained in DATA statements (a) to (f):
- (a) DATA X,Y,I/3.256,4.0007,0/
- (b) DATA X,Y,I/4HAVER,68.87,2HNO/
- (c) DATA X/1.23E+02/,Y/0.0/,I/0/
- (d) DATA Z,T,A,X,S/2*0.0,1.5,2*0.0/

(e) DATA I,J,K,L,M/5*0/
(f) DATA A/'ABCD'/,B/8.46/,C/22.567/,E/0./

2 Supply the DATA statements that will equate to the following verbal descriptions:
   (a) Assign the real values 1.0 through 5.0 to the variables A, B, C, D, and E, respectively.
   (b) Assign the integer values 1 through 5 to the variables I, J, K, L, and M, respectively.
   (c) Assign the labels NAME and DATE to A and B.
   (d) To each of the variables A, B, C, I, K, N, and P assign the value of zero.
   (e) To the variables E9 and E10 assign the values 100,000,000,000 and 200,000,000,000. (Hint: Use the E notation.)

3 Correct errors, if any, contained in the following DATA statements:
   (a) 762   DATA A/2.3/
   (b)   DATA X/1.2/Y/1.3/
   (c)   DATA NAME/4HSUM/
   (d)   DATA R,S,T,U,V/4*0./
   (e)   DATA SUM/2./,SUMA/3.,4./
   (f)   DATA T/'AB/

4-7 Program Sample STATISTICS

The DATA statement, as illustrated in this section,[1] will be used to enter the initial values of the three numbers that are to be summed and averaged. In this simple example, its use is applicable and is analogous to program STATISTICS-2, where the assignment statement was used to enter the initial values. Excluding the title containing the date, Flowchart 4-6 pictures the instructions needed. The program statements and the output are

```
C PROGRAM STATISTICS-8
C THIS PROGRAM COMPUTES THE AVERAGE OF THREE VALUES
      DATA VAL1, VAL2, VAL3 /75.0, 89.0, 73.0/
      SUM = VAL1 + VAL2 + VAL3
      AVG = SUM/3.
      WRITE(6,301)VAL1,VAL2,VAL3,SUM,AVG
301   FORMAT(@11ST VALUE   2ND VALUE   3RD VALUE   SUM   AVERAGE@/1X,F9.1,
     12F11.1,F7.1,F9.1)
      STOP
      END
```

```
1ST VALUE   2ND VALUE   3RD VALUE   SUM     AVERAGE
     75.0        89.0        73.0   237.0      79.0
```

[1] The SALES TAX problem has been purposely omitted here because of the similarity that would arise in illustrating the DATA instruction in both programs.

ADDITIONAL I/O COMMANDS

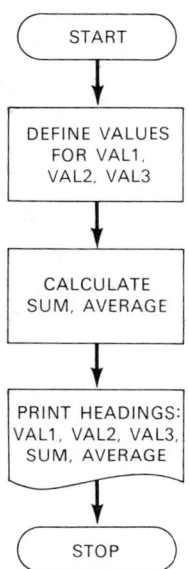

Flowchart 4-6 STATISTICS—DATA statement.

In this program, the DATA statement could have been written alternatively as

DATA VAL1/75.0/, VAL2/89.0/, VAL3/73.0/

without changing the results of the program.

The use of the DATA statement somewhat shortens the length of the program but does not result in the desired flexibility. The READ statement is the recommended procedure for entering problem information into a program; its use will be emphasized in later chapters. However, where applicable, the DATA statement will be employed, as in the next program.

This sample not only illustrates the instructions covered in this chapter but also introduces some ideas that will be useful in later chapters. It is a simple lever problem that concerns two children of different weights. If the first weighs 100 lb and sits on a board 10 ft from a fulcrum, how far from the fulcrum must the second child sit to balance the board if he weighs 75 lb? Graphically, this can be pictured as

**4-8
Miscellaneous
Mathematical
Sample**

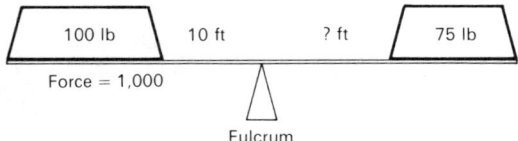

The formula $w_1 d_1 = w_2 d_2$, or $w_1 d_1 / w_2 = d_2$ can be used to solve this problem, where w_1 and w_2 are the weights of the two children and d_1 and d_2 are their respective distances from the fulcrum. To expand the problem slightly, what distance from the fulcrum should the second child sit if his weight is increased by 10 lb? Flowchart 4-7 depicts one solution to the problem with the program statements as

```
C THIS PROGRAM IS BASED ON A SIMPLE LEVER PROBLEM
      DATA WD1/1000./
      PRINT 1
      READ 2, W2
      D2 = WD1/W2
      PRINT 3, WD1,W2,D2
      W2 = W2 + 10.
      D2 = WD1/W2
      PRINT 3, WD1,W2,D2
1     FORMAT(@1FORCE OF CHILD-1    WEIGHT OF CHILD-2    DISTANCE FROM FULC
     1RUM FOR CHILD-2@/)
2     FORMAT(F5.1)
3     FORMAT(8X,F6.1,13X,F6.1,16X,F6.1)
      STOP
      END
```

Several points are pertinent. First, since the first child's force can be readily calculated (100*10) and is constant throughout the program, the resulting calculation (1000) is assigned to the variable WD1 in a DATA statement. Second, the PRINT 1 instruction causes column headings to be listed. Headings are used in this program because there are two sets of answers. In later chapters, extensive use of headings will be made. The next point concerns the statement

W2 = W2 + 10.

Recall that this is a valid instruction because the computer assigns the result of the computation on the right of the equals sign to the variable on the left. The effect is to change the value of W2 from 75.0 to 85.0. This type of statement, too, will be used extensively in later chapters. And, finally, note that two of the statements appear twice within the program. The next

ADDITIONAL I/O COMMANDS

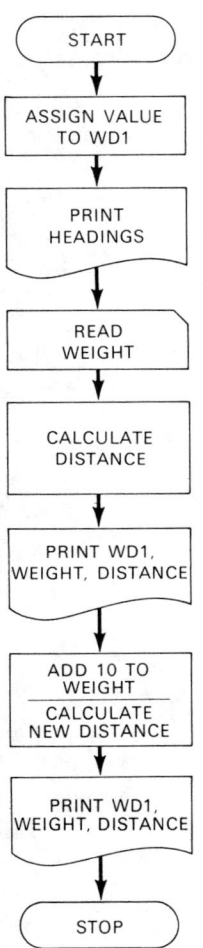

Flowchart 4-7 Simple Lever—DATA and I/O extensions.

chapter covers statements that will permit the elimination of duplicate entries. The data value (weight of the second child) and the output from the present program are

```
75.0
```

FORCE OF CHILD-1	WEIGHT OF CHILD-2	DISTANCE FROM FULCRUM FOR CHILD-2
1000.0	75.0	13.3
1000.0	85.0	11.8

The primary method for entering data into a flexible computer program is by incorporating the READ statement. Three different forms of the statement were designated, with emphasis on the first. Also, a second output method, with the PRINT statement, was presented as an option available for writing output. Finally, the DATA statement, as a means of initializing variables, was discussed.

4-9 Summary

Questions

1. Solve program STATISTICS-7 by using the READ b and PRINT b options discussed in Sec. 4-4.

2. Solve program SALES-3 by using the DATA instruction discussed in Sec. 4-6.

3. Prepare a FORTRAN program that will read the base *b* and height *h* of a triangle. The area can be computed by using the formula Area = $\frac{1}{2}bh$. Calculate and print, with appropriate labels, the area of the given triangle. Supply your own data and be sure to manually compare your answers with the computer's.

4. The circumference of a circle is equal to πd, where π is 3.1416 and *d* is the diameter. Prepare a program that will read the radius ($\frac{1}{2}d$), and calculate and print the radius, diameter, and circumference of the given circle. Supply your own data.

5. Prepare a program to read a value for corporate profit before taxes (assume that the value is greater than $20,000). Compute the tax, which is equal to 12 percent of the first $10,000 and 15 percent of the excess. The net profit is equal to corporate profit minus the tax. Print each of the three values with appropriate labels.

6. Modify Question 5 according to the following parameters:
   (a) The corporate profit is equal to the profit of subsidiary A plus subsidiary B. Hence, two values must be read instead of one.
   (b) The tax is equal to 12 percent of the first $10,000; 15 percent of the amount between $10,000 and $20,000; and 21 percent of the amount over $20,000.

7. Write a program that will read the date, in integer form, for month, day, and year; a growth rate; and an initial value for sales. Assuming that the input is 010172 for the date, .02 for the growth rate, and 10000 for sales, prepare the statements needed to generate the following output:

ADDITIONAL I/O COMMANDS

DATE	SALES
01/01/72	10000
01/01/73	10200
01/01/74	10404
01/01/75	10612
01/01/76	10824

Only the initial values should be read; the rest are calculated by (a) adding 1 to the year for each line of output, and (b) increasing sales each year by the amount (growth X sales at the beginning of the year).

8 Modify Question 7 to include the title heading

SALES   REPORT   GROWTH RATE IS 2 PER CENT

The label SALES should be read into the program by using the A format. If the data is not sales information but is production data, the title headings

PRODUCT. REPORT   GROWTH RATE IS X PER CENT

and

DATE PRODUCT.

should be printed. The X represents the applicable growth rate that is read into the program times 100.

9 Write a program that will use the following name (assume the name has 16 characters or less), pay rate, and hours as input and will print the output in the form:

NAME	PAY	HOURS	PAY
BOB BURNS	1.00	40.0	X
TOM NIEKROS	2.00	30.0	X
STEVE ASQUICK	3.50	25.5	X
JERRY HART	2.75	37.5	X
TOTAL			X

where X is calculated by multiplying pay times hours.

THE TRANSFER COMMANDS 5

The transfer commands listed in this chapter enable the programmer to build program *loops*. A program loop is a sequence of statements that is executed a variable number of times by the computer even though the statements are listed only once. Loops can be constructed by using one of the GO TO, logical IF, arithmetic IF, or computed GO TO instructions. The three latter transfer commands are also used to perform logic tests within the computer.

5-1 The GO TO Statement

In each program sample discussed thus far, the computer has executed the statements in sequence. In other words, the order of the program cards determines the order in which the computer performs the instructions. But in many programs, it is necessary to "jump around." The need arises for altering the sequence of execution by the computer; the GO TO statement solves this need. Its general form is

sl   GO TO sl-1

where the first sl is an optional statement label and the second sl is the label of the next statement recognized and executed by the computer. Upon execution of the GO TO statement, transfer of control within the program is passed from the GO TO instruction to the sl-1 statement label specified. Thus, the normal sequence of processing is changed. For this reason, the GO TO statement is classified technically as an *unconditional transfer of control* or as an *unconditional branch instruction*.

The second label specified in the GO TO statement must be located somewhere within the program—either an earlier or a later instruction must have the valid statement label indicated. Figures 5-1 and 5-2 reflect partial program examples illustrating the GO TO statement.

The main function of the GO TO statement is to build a loop—not a closed loop as discussed in Fig. 5-2, but one that terminates under control of the program. A loop can be defined as a group of statements that are repeated over and over during execution of the program. Perhaps the idea and utilization of loops is the single most important programming tool available. Looping makes it unnecessary to rewrite the same statements within one program; it is possible to reduce significantly the number of instructions required to solve a particular problem.

Figure 5-1 Examples of the GO TO statement.

	Program Statements		*Description*
10	X1 = 10.*6.3**2		The first two lines shown would be processed
	GO TO 20		by the computer and then control would be
	.		passed directly to the statement labeled 20,
	.		bypassing completely any intervening lines.
	.		
20	WRITE(6,10)X1		
	GO TO 1		The first entry directs the computer to pass
2	X = PRICE − COST		control immediately to the WRITE statement
1	WRITE(6,18)		labeled 1. The middle line is not processed in this small sample.
151	READ(5,181)PR,CST	Data:	In this sample, the first two data values 23.5
	X = PR − CST	23.5 47.6	and 47.6 are assigned to the variables PR
	WRITE(6,181)X	61.6 83.9	and CST. The variable X is calculated and
	GO TO 151		written by the next two statements. Control
181	FORMAT(2F5.1)		of the program is then transferred back to the labeled statement number 151, where processing continues and the next two data values are read.

THE TRANSFER COMMANDS

Figure 5-2 Common errors that occur with GO TO statements.

	Program Statements	Description
10	GO TO 10	Erroneously, transfer of control is always passed to the exact same line labeled 10. The computer would endlessly process
11	. . .	the one statement (a closed loop) until terminated by the operator of the system. A correct entry would be
		10 GO TO 11
	GO TO 2	The GO TO statement is not required in this short sample
2	KNT=KNT+1	because processing continues to the next line sequentially without the statement.
5	GO TO 100	The GO TO statement can not be used to pass control to a
	. . .	FORMAT statement. The FORMAT statement is used only as
100	FORMAT(F5.0)	reference for a READ or WRITE
1	READ(5,100)VAR	statement. A correct entry would be
		5 GO TO 1
6	GO TO 5	This is the second example of a closed loop where the computer
	. . .	would process the statements endlessly. Control is alternately
5	GO TO 6	passed back and forth continuously between the two statements. One of the two statements must be deleted or revised.
	GO TO STOP	The actual statement label must be specified in the GO TO state-
	. . .	ment. Use of alphabetic labels or identifiers, such as STOP, is not
8	STOP	permitted. A correct entry would
	END	be
		GO TO 8

Because loops are so important, additional methods for constructing them will be shown later. However, the exercises and program samples pertaining to the GO TO statement will be examined first.

GO TO Exercises

1 Supply the GO TO statements that will transfer control to locations (a) to (c):
   - (a) To the WRITE statement labeled 1, from the current instruction labeled 2
   - (b) To the READ instruction labeled 5000, from the current instruction labeled 50000
   - (c) From the current statement labeled 772 to the STOP instruction labeled 999

2 In each of the three following samples, a required GO TO instruction has been purposely omitted. The GO TO statement should send control back to the READ statement in order to process another set of data. Supply the needed statement and a label for the READ.

   (a) 12   FORMAT (2F10.5)
                  READ(5,12)A,B
                  X=(A+B)**2
                  WRITE(6,12)A,X
                  ─────────────
                  STOP
                  END
   (b)   READ(5,12)A,B,C
        12   FORMAT(3F10.6)
                  X=(A+B)**2+C**2
                  WRITE(6,12)A,X,B
                  ─────────────
                  STOP
                  END
   (c)   READ 12,A,B,C
                  X=(A+B+C)**3−62.5
                  PRINT 12,A,X,C
                  ─────────────
        12   FORMAT(3F12.3)
                  STOP
                  END

3 In the following examples, the GO TO statements pass control to either the READ, WRITE, or STOP statements. Which ones?
   (a) 1   READ 6,X
        2   GO TO 5

THE TRANSFER COMMANDS

	3	READ 6,Y
	4	X=Y
	5	WRITE(6,6)X
	6	FORMAT(F10.5)
	7	STOP
		END
(b)	15	WRITE(6,18)
	16	READ(5,17)A,B
	17	FORMAT(2F10.4)
	18	FORMAT('1TITLE PAGE')
	19	WRITE(6,17)B,A
	20	GO TO 16
	21	STOP
		END
(c)	21	READ(5,22)X,Y
	22	FORMAT(2F9.3)
	23	WRITE(6,22)Y,X
	24	GO TO 26
	25	WRITE(6,22)X,Y
	26	STOP
		END

4 Identify and correct the errors in the GO TO statements found in samples (a) to (c):

(a)	12	FORMAT(6F12.2)
	10	READ(5,12)A,B,C
		PRINT 12,A,B,C
		GO TO 12
		STOP
		END
(b)		READ 14,X,C,XOB
		T=X*C+XOB
	14	FORMAT(3F11.4)
		PRINT 14,X,T
		GO TO READ 14
		STOP
		END
(c)	10	GO TO 30
	11	READ 6,B,C,D
	6	FORMAT(3E12.5)
		E=B/C**2+D/2.2
		PRINT 6,E
		GO TO 11
	30	STOP
		END

The SALES TAX programs written in the earlier chapters had one unique characteristic: each would solve one and only one problem. But what if there is a need to solve two problems, or three or four? One possible solution for handling two sets of data is by simply repeating the statements required to solve one set. The program SALES-9 and the output illustrate the idea:

**5-2
Program
Sample
SALES TAX**

```
C PROGRAM SALES-9
C THIS PROGRAM COMPUTES THE SALES TAX FOR 2 ITEMS, AT A RATE OF 4 PERCENT
      READ 100,DAY,YEAR
      PRINT 400,DAY,YEAR
      TAXRAT = .04
      READ 101,SALES
      SALETX = SALES * TAXRAT
      PRINT 401,SALES,TAXRAT,SALETX
      READ 101,SALES
      SALETX = SALES * TAXRAT
      PRINT 401,SALES,TAXRAT,SALETX
100   FORMAT(2A4)
101   FORMAT(F8.2)
400   FORMAT(21H1SALES REPORT   DATED ,2A4/8H0  SALES,5X,8HTAX RATE,5X,9H
     1SALES TAX/)
401   FORMAT(1X,F8.2,3X,F8.3,5X,F8.2)
      STOP
      END
```

```
11-14-74
 857.67
 628.43
```

```
SALES REPORT   DATED 11-14-74

  SALES     TAX RATE     SALES TAX

 857.67       0.040        34.31
 628.43       0.040        25.14
```

Note that three statements, READ, assignment, and PRINT, have been duplicated within the program to calculate and print the second set of answers. To handle three sets of data, the same entries could be repeated again. But if the program were to process 100 sets of data, it would soon become unnecessarily long. Obviously this method is time-consuming and redundant. A better approach would be to use the same statements over and over, instead of repeating them. This idea

THE TRANSFER COMMANDS

is fundamental to the concept of looping. As already explained, the GO TO statement is one method for building loops. Flowchart 5-1 indicates the minor changes required to include the GO TO statement in the sales problem and to reduce the number of statements needed to solve a large set of data values.

In the flowchart, the dotted line connecting the PRINT and STOP functions is used to specify that the STOP is not directly in line with the other operations. A closed loop has been designed, but the program will not run indefinitely; it will terminate when there is no more data to fulfill the READ statement. When there is no more data, program execution is

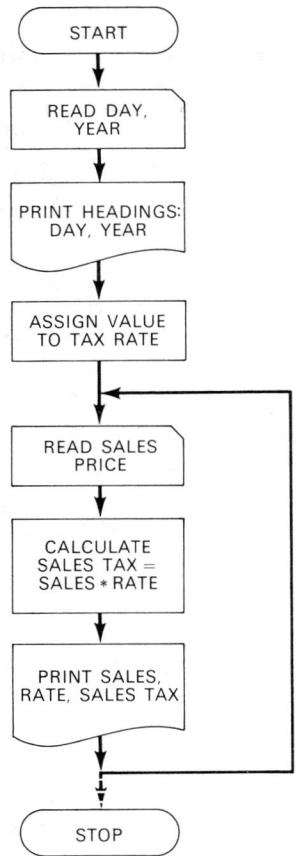

Flowchart 5-1   SALES TAX—GO TO statement.

terminated and an appropriate error message printed. This solution to the problem will handle as many sets of data as the user supplies. The value of loops, especially if 100 sets of data were supplied, should be evident now. The program statements conforming to the flowchart follow:

```
C PROGRAM SALES-10
C THIS PROGRAM COMPUTES THE SALES TAX FOR A NUMBER OF ITEMS BASED ON
C A RATE OF 4 PERCENT.
      READ(5,100)DAY,YEAR
      WRITE(6,400)DAY,YEAR
      TAXRAT = .04
10    READ(5,101)SALES
      SALETX = SALES * TAXRAT
      WRITE(6,401)SALES,TAXRAT,SALETX
      GO TO 10
100   FORMAT(2A4)
101   FORMAT(F8.2)
400   FORMAT(21H1SALES REPORT   DATED ,2A4/8H0   SALES,5X,8HTAX RATE,5X,9H
     1SALES TAX/)
401   FORMAT(1X,F8.2,3X,F8.3,5X,F8.2)
11    STOP
      END
```

Four sales figures as data and the output from the program are

```
11-15-74
 1000.00
  857.67
  628.43
 1575.50
```

```
SALES REPORT   DATED 11-15-74

   SALES      TAX RATE      SALES TAX

  1000.00      0.040          40.00
   857.67      0.040          34.31
   628.43      0.040          25.14
  1575.50      0.040          63.02
```

ERROR CONTROL CARD ENCOUNTERED ON UNIT   5 AT EXECUTION.
   PROBABLE CAUSE-MISSING DATA OR INCORRECT FORMAT

   PROGRAM WAS EXECUTING LINE
   4 IN ROUTINE M/PROG WHEN TERMINATION OCCURRED.

THE TRANSFER COMMANDS

In the sample output, the last lines printed after the valid answers represent the error message generated on the IBM 360 using the WATFIV compiler[1] because of an "out of data" condition. This error results from the closed GO TO loop; however, the message can be ignored since all the valid data has been processed by the READ at this point.

But to remove the error message, the READ with END=sl option can be incorporated in the program, replacing the READ statement labeled 10. By labeling the STOP statement as number 11 and replacing label 10 by the statement

10   READ(5,101,END=11)SALES

the program will print all the answers and terminate under control of the programmer, excluding the error message.

5-3 Program Sample STATISTICS

The STATISTICS program can be revised easily to handle multiple sets of data, as was done with the SALES problem. Flowchart 5-2 reflects the incorporation of the GO TO statement for looping purposes. Also note that the flowchart specifies (1) the use of the READ with END=sl option, (2) that column headings are supplied at the beginning and only for the sum and average, and (3) that the individual values are not printed as part of the answers. The program statements needed to solve the redefined problem are

```
C PROGRAM STATISTICS-9
C THIS PROGRAM COMPUTES THE AVERAGE OF THREE VALUES FOR A NUMBER OF
C GROUPS OF DATA.
      WRITE(6,300)
1     READ(5,201,END=2)VAL1,VAL2,VAL3
      SUM = VAL1 + VAL2 + VAL3
      AVG = SUM/3.
      WRITE(6,301)SUM,AVG
      GO TO 1
201   FORMAT(3F5.1)
300   FORMAT(@1    SUM     AVERAGE@/)
301   FORMAT(1X,F8.2,1X,F8.2)
2     STOP
      END
```

---

[1]Appendix A contains a description of the WATFOR and WATFIV compilers and the significant differences between them and standard FORTRAN IV.

Data for three sets of values and the output from the program are

```
85.5  89.4  68.6
61.4  72.8  68.5
98.3  97.4  96.2
```

```
  SUM      AVERAGE

243.50      81.17
202.70      67.57
291.90      97.30
```

In examining the output it is sometimes necessary to identify each of the problems, especially if a larger number of values were processed. This can be done by labeling the first set of answers with a 1, the second set with a 2, and so on. The numbers 1, 2, 3, . . . , n could be entered as data along with the sales value, or they could be calculated within the program.

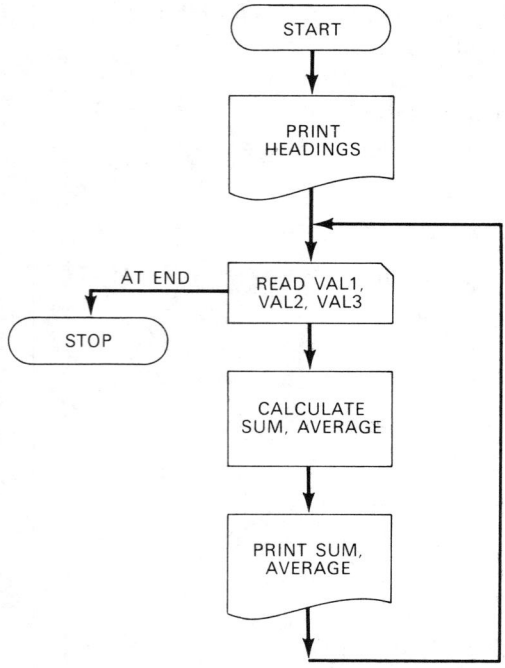

Flowchart 5-2 STATISTICS—GO TO statement.

THE TRANSFER COMMANDS

By inserting a *counter* within the loop, the labels can be computed. A counter is simply a variable that serves to keep track of a running total. Statements such as

KNT = KNT + 1

or

CNTR = CNTR + A

are examples. Assuming that the variable KNT was initialized to zero, the first statement, when inserted within a loop, meets the labeling requirements of the STATISTICS problem. The second statement serves a different purpose; it is used to store the sum of successive values of A in the variable location CNTR, provided that CNTR is initialized first and then placed within a loop. Its use will be illustrated later.

Returning to the STATISTICS problem, to label the output successively by using a counter, two new statements plus three revisions are required.

```
C   PROGRAM STATISTICS-10
C   THIS PROGRAM COMPUTES THE AVERAGE OF THREE VALUES FOR A NUMBER OF
C   GROUPS OF DATA.
      WRITE(6,300)
      KNT = 0
1     READ(5,201,END=2)VAL1,VAL2,VAL3
      SUM = VAL1 + VAL2 + VAL3
      AVG = SUM/3.
      KNT = KNT + 1
      WRITE(6,301)KNT,SUM,AVG
      GO TO 1
201   FORMAT(3F5.1)
300   FORMAT(@1GROUP NUMBER    SUM     AVERAGE@/)
301   FORMAT(5X,I3,4X,F8.1,1X,F8.1/)
2     STOP
      END
```

The location of the two statements containing the variable KNT is important. The first is required to initialize its value to zero. Consequently, it must be placed *ahead* of the loop. If placed inside the loop, the value of KNT would be reinitialized each time the loop were performed. Likewise, the second statement must be placed inside the loop and preceding the WRITE statement. If placed outside the loop, it does not perform the operation of a counter. If placed after the WRITE, the labeling begins 0, 1, 2, ..., $n-1$ instead of 1, 2, 3, ..., n.

An integer variable name is used as the counter variable because an integer constant (1) is to be summed. Note that two of the FORMAT statements plus WRITE 301 have been revised to process the new solution.

New data for four groups and the output from the STATISTICS-10 program are

```
82.2  69.5  74.0
65.5  76.4  83.2
98.8  92.0  90.7
75.5  85.4  68.3
```

GROUP NUMBER	SUM	AVERAGE
1	225.7	75.2
2	225.1	75.0
3	281.5	93.8
4	229.2	76.4

Another use for the variable KNT will be shown in later samples; the second type of counter will be illustrated in the next SALES problem.

5-4 The IF Statements

There are two different types of IF statements to be discussed in this section: the logical[1] IF and the arithmetic IF. The IF statements provide a second method, in addition to the GO TO, of bypassing the normal sequence of statements within a program. They differ from the GO TO statement, however, by permitting a *conditional* branch or transfer of control. The next statement to be processed after an IF statement is dependent upon a test or logical relation involving the values of variables or the results of a computation. The general form of the logical IF is

sl   IF (expression-1 logical operator expression-2) executable statement

---

[1]Not all FORTRAN IV compilers permit the use of logical IF statements. Refer to the particular systems manual being used for clarification.

THE TRANSFER COMMANDS

where sl is an optional label, the expressions are any valid FORTRAN formulas or expressions including variable names and constants, and the logical operator must be one of the following:

Logical Operator	Meaning
.LT.	Is less than
.LE.	Is less than or equal to
.EQ.	Is equal to
.NE.	Is not equal to
.GE.	Is greater than or equal to
.GT.	Is greater than

All six of the logical operators are four characters in length; i.e., the decimal points are an integral part of the symbol and can not be omitted.

The IF statement is a conditional instruction. Transfer of control is passed to the executable[1] statement listed in the IF instruction *only* when the indicated test or relation is met or is true. Consider, for example, the statement

157   IF(A.EQ.B)GO TO 159

In this instruction, only when the value of A is *exactly* equal to the value of B does the computer transfer control to label 159. When the indicated test is not met or is false, the program passes control to the very next statement in line. Referring again to the statement above, if A is not equal to B, the computer bypasses the executable GO TO statement listed in the IF instruction and jumps directly to the next entry.

Contrast this statement with the GO TO, which unconditionally branches control to another line in the program. Figures 5-3 and 5-4 elaborate on the logical IF and detail the conditional branches.

---

[1]The statement following the second expression must be a valid FORTRAN instruction that is executable. Examples of executable statements are the READ, WRITE, and GO TO commands; examples of nonexecutable statements are the COMMENTS, DATA, END, and FORMAT instructions. The two major exceptions of executable statements *not* permitted as part of a logical IF are a second logical IF and a DO statement, discussed in Chap. 6.

Figure 5-3 Examples of the logical IF statement.

	Program Statements	Description
1728	IF(A.EQ.5.1)X=11.3	If the value of A is exactly equal to 5.1, the variable X is assigned the value 11.3. If the value of A is not exactly 5.1, the next statement in the program is executed, bypassing the assignment of X.
	IF(N.LT.M)GO TO 60 . . .	The values of N and M determine the next statement processed by the computer. If the value of N is less than the value of M, statement label 60 is performed after the IF statement. When M is equal to or greater than N, the statement immediately following the IF test is processed.
60		
	IF(N.LE.M+5)GO TO 60 . . .	The value of N and the value of the expression M+5 determines the next statement processed by the computer. If the value of N is less than or equal to the value of M+5, statement label 60 is performed after the IF statement. Only when the value of M+5 is greater than N is the statement immediately following the IF test processed.
60		
	IF(KNT.GT.NOB)WRITE(6,100) . . .	If the value of KNT is greater than the value of NOB, the WRITE statement is executed. The statement following the IF test is executed when the value of KNT is less than or equal to NOB.
	IF(KNT−7.GE.NOB*2)PRINT 100 . . .	The two expressions KNT−7 and NOB*2 determine the next statement processed. When KNT−7 is less than NOB*2, the statement following the IF test is performed. Otherwise, output is generated by the PRINT statement.
	IF(X.NE.Y)X=Y	When the value of X is not equal to Y, the statement X=Y is executed. Hence, the two values are always equal after the execution of the IF test.

THE TRANSFER COMMANDS   111

Figure 5-4 Common errors that occur with logical IF statements.

Program Statements	Description
12345 IF(3.2EQB)STOP	The decimal points are a required part of the logical operator and can not be omitted. A correct entry would be 12345 IF(3.2.EQ.B)STOP

625 IF(N.LT.M)IF(KNT.GE.6)GO TO 10	Only one logical IF can be contained in a statement. This sample attempts to incorporate two erroneously. A correct entry would be
	625 IF(N.LT.M)GO TO 15
	      .
	      .
	      .
	15 IF(KNT.GE.6)GO TO 10

IF(SUM.NE.TOTAL)SUM=TOTAL GO TO 10	Only one executable statement is permitted as the second part of the logical IF statement. The sample here shows two executable statements, one assignment and one GO TO. Correct entries would be
	        IF(SUM.NE.TOTAL)GO TO 5
	        .
	        .
	        .
	5 SUM=TOTAL
	       GO TO 10

IF(I3−6**K.EQ.0)DATA I3,K/2*0/	The DATA statement following the test is a nonexecutable instruction. As such, it is not permitted within the statement. Correct entries to effect the same result would be
	        IF(I3−6**K.EQ.0)GO TO 87
	        .
	        .
	        .
	87 I3=0
	      K=0

IF(3.LT.MON+MNP)END	This is the same type of error that occurred in the case above. The END statement is not executable, whereas the STOP instruction is. Thus, a correct entry would be IF(3.LT.MON+MNP)STOP

The second type of IF statement, the arithmetic IF, provides a three-way branching instruction as compared with just two for the logical IF. The branching is dependent upon the value of an expression or formula in the general form

sl   IF(expression)sl-1,sl-2,sl-3

where sl is an optional statement label, the expression is any valid FORTRAN formula or expression, and sl-1, sl-2, and sl-3 are the labels of valid, executable statements found within the program. When the value of the expression within the parentheses is negative (i.e., less than zero), control of the program is transferred to label sl-1. When the value of the expression is exactly zero, sl-2 is executed next. Finally, if the expression has a positive value (i.e., greater than zero), control is transferred to the statement labeled sl-3.

When using this form, the first executable statement following the arithmetic IF should have a label. Otherwise, it can never be executed or referred to because the next entry in line is never directly processed, as happens with the logical IF. Figures 5-5 and 5-6 contain examples of the use of arithmetic IF statements.

How does the programmer decide which of the two IFs to use? In most cases, the logical IF should be employed unless a three-way branch is necessary. The program samples will illustrate their use in applications.

Figure 5-5 Examples of the arithmetic IF statement.

	Program Statements	Description
4	IF(X)1,2,3	The value of the variable X
1	X=6.5	determines the next statement
	.	processed by the computer. If X
2	X=7.5	is negative, the statement labeled
	.	1 is processed next. If X is
3	X=1.25	exactly zero, control is passed to
		label 2. If X has a value greater
		than zero, label 3 is processed
		next.
7	IF(A−6.)4,8,5	If the value of the expression
4	.	A−6. is positive, control is

THE TRANSFER COMMANDS

	Program Statements	Description
5	.	passed to label 5. When it is
8	.	exactly zero, control is passed to statement 8. Only when the value is negative is control passed to label 4.
11	IF(I**2−J/6)16,8,10	The two expressions I**2 and
10	.	J/6 are evaluated first. The
16	.	second is subtracted from the
8	.	first, and the result is used to determine which statement is executed next. When the result is negative, label 16 is performed. When the result is exactly zero, label 8 is performed next by the computer. When the result is positive, label 10 is executed.
7	IF(TOTAL+ARR)3,5,5	When the value of the expression
3	STOP	TOTAL+ARR is negative,
5	WRITE(6,100)TOTAL	control is passed to label 3. If the value is zero or positive, control is passed to statement labeled 5. (The logical IF would be more effective in this set of statements since only a two-way branch is required.)

Figure 5-6 Common errors that occur with arithmetic IF statements.

	Program Statements	Description
12	IF(VAR)5,8	Three labels must be identified
5	.	in the arithmetic IF statement.[1]
8	.	Omission of one or more causes
10	.	an error. A correct entry would be
		12 IF(VAR)5,8,10
	IF(SUM−2.*A)2,4,4	The first executable statement
	STOP	(STOP) following the IF test
2	SUM=0.	should have a statement label.
4	WRITE(6,101)SUM	Otherwise, the statement can never be referenced or executed.

Figure 5-6 Common errors that occur with arithmetic IF statements *(cont'd)*.

Program Statements		Description
		A correct entry would be
		1 STOP
		where it is intended that control be passed to label 1 to terminate execution of the program.
281	IF(2I)8,26,18	The expression 2I could be
18	.	interpreted as an illegal variable
26	.	name or as the expression 2∗I.
8	.	In either case, it is not permitted as shown but must be revised accordingly. Two corrections are possible:
		281 IF(I2)8,26,18
		or
		281 IF(2∗I)8,26,18

[1] Some FORTRAN compilers permit less than three labels; however, in USAS FORTRAN all three are required.

IF Exercises

1 Write the logical IF statements that will make the following tests:
   (*a*) If sigma is less than 21.1, transfer control to statement label 600
   (*b*) If chi is not equal to alpha plus 6, transfer control to label 1
   (*c*) If fixed costs plus variable costs are equal to sales minus returns, transfer control to label 7
   (*d*) If inventory is equal to or greater than the sales order quantity, transfer to label 7005

2 Supply the arithmetic IF statements that will make the following tests:
   (*a*) If profits are negative, transfer to label 600; if equal to zero, transfer to 700; if positive, transfer to 800
   (*b*) If normal earnings plus overtime pay minus $200 are less than, equal to, or greater than zero, transfer control to lines 6, 5, and 12, respectively
   (*c*) If the average grade is not equal to 72, transfer control to label 16; otherwise, pass control to label 17

3 In the following samples, supply either logical or arithmetic IFs to satisfy the indicated tests (it may be necessary to write two IF statements for certain exercises):
   (*a*) If the product code is not equal to 7, pass control from label 174 to 176

THE TRANSFER COMMANDS

(b) If inventory is less than 10,000 or greater than 13,500 units, pass control to label 652

(c) If the engineering code is 1 or 2, pass control to label 221; otherwise transfer control to label 223

(d) If chi-square is between 2.25 and 2.65, transfer control to label 1450; otherwise pass control to 2450

(e) If sales minus returns are less than $25,000 or greater than $70,000, transfer control to label 621

(f) If rho is less than 4, pass control to label 60; if rho is equal to 4, pass control to label 45; if rho is neither of these, pass control to label 55

4 Identify and correct errors, if any, that occur in IF statements (a) to (f):

(a) IF(A)GO TO 20
(b)   IF(X+5.25)1,2,3,4
(c) 1014 IF(A AND B EQ C)WRITE(6,101)A,B,C
(d) 60   IF(I-J**2+6)60,20,45
(e)   IF(A+B GT C+D)X=1.267
(f)   IF((M+N+N7)-17)2,12

5-5 Program Sample SALES TAX

In the SALES-10 program, the valid output was followed by an error message. By inserting a *dummy* data value at the end of the data cards, the program can be terminated without an error[1] by testing for the specific dummy value. A dummy value is a data value placed at the end of the data list and used by the programmer to terminate a loop. When selecting a dummy value, it can be any number but should not resemble valid program data. For example, a large negative value such as -9999. does not resemble the actual data in the SALES problem. Flowchart 5-3 incorporates a logical IF and a dummy value to terminate the loop in the SALES problem. The diamond symbol is used to represent logical or arithmetic IF tests on a flowchart; the connector symbol represents the GO TO instruction passing control back to the READ. Program SALES-11, reflecting the one added IF statement and a revised STOP statement with a label, is

```
C PROGRAM SALES-11
C THIS PROGRAM COMPUTES THE SALES TAX FOR A NUMBER OF ITEMS BASED ON
C A RATE OF 4 PERCENT.
      READ(5,100)DAY,YEAR
      WRITE(6,400)DAY,YEAR
      TAXRAT = .04
```

---

[1] The method outlined here is used when the READ with END=sl option is either not available or can't be used (for example, it can't be used when operating under WATFOR or WATFIV).

```
10      READ(5,101)SALES
        IF(SALES.EQ.-9999.)GO TO 11
        SALETX = SALES * TAXRAT
        WRITE(6,401)SALES,TAXRAT,SALETX
        GO TO 10
100     FORMAT(2A4)
101     FORMAT(F8.2)
400     FORMAT(21H1SALES REPORT   DATED ,2A4/8H0  SALES,5X,8HTAX RATE,5X,9H
       1SALES TAX/)
401     FORMAT(1X,F8.2,3X,F8.3,5X,F8.2)
11      STOP
        END
```

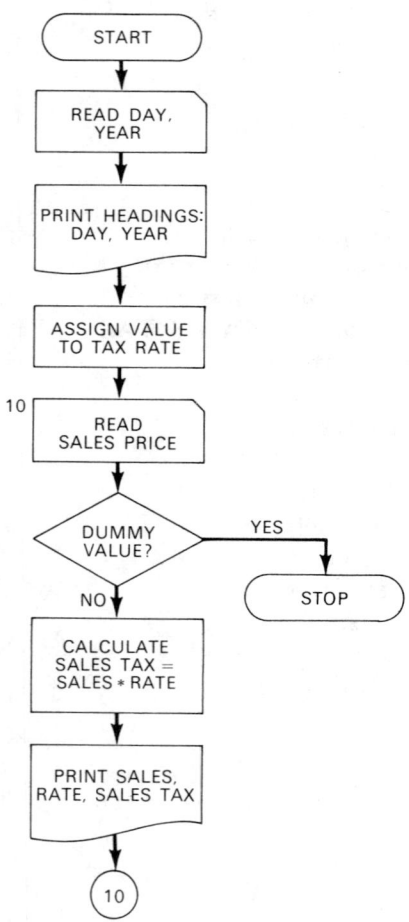

Flowchart 5-3   SALES TAX—Logical IF statement.

THE TRANSFER COMMANDS
117

Notice that the logical IF statement is placed immediately after the second READ. It must be placed here since the program loop should be terminated as soon as the dummy value is read. Otherwise, if placed, for example, after the second WRITE, the program would generate the last line as bad data because the $-9999.$ is used as one of the values in the calculation.[1]

The new data list, including the dummy value, and the output are

```
12-30-75
 1000.00
  857.67
  628.43
 1575.50
-9999.00
```

```
SALES REPORT   DATED 12-30-75

    SALES      TAX RATE      SALES TAX

    1000.00     0.040          40.00
     857.67     0.040          34.31
     628.43     0.040          25.14
    1575.50     0.040          63.02
```

By inserting the IF statement, the only difference from previous versions is that the program terminates without an error. The output is exactly the same. Also, an arithmetic IF (plus a revised sales tax calculation to add a label)

```
        IF(SALES)11,12,12
12      SALETX = SALES * TAXRAT
```

could replace the logical IF without affecting the results. However, in this case the logical IF is more effective since only a two-way branch is required.

There are more important reasons for terminating a loop under program control rather than just to avoid an error message. For example, what if the total sales processed by the program are required? The user could certainly add the sales values manually

---

[1]The reader might prefer to confirm this statement by punching the program statements, inserting the IF card at various places in the program, and running the resultant programs.

in the examples shown. But what if there are 200 values? It would be much easier to permit the computer to do the adding. To do so requires the second type of counter discussed in Sec. 5-3. Each of the individual values of the sales quantity must be added together. Flowchart 5-4 reflects the inclusion of a counter, a revised IF test, and a new WRITE statement. The new program statements are

```
C     PROGRAM SALES-12
C     THIS PROGRAM COMPUTES THE SALES TAX FOR A NUMBER OF ITEMS BASED ON
C     A RATE OF 4 PERCENT. A TOTAL FOR SALES IS ALSO COMPUTED.
      READ(5,100)DAY,YEAR
      WRITE(6,400)DAY,YEAR
      TOTSAL = 0.0
      TAXRAT = .04
10    READ(5,101)SALES
      IF(SALES.EQ.-9999.)GO TO 11
      SALETX = SALES * TAXRAT
      TOTSAL = TOTSAL + SALES
      WRITE(6,401)SALES,TAXRAT,SALETX
      GO TO 10
11    WRITE(6,402)TOTSAL
100   FORMAT(2A4)
101   FORMAT(F8.2)
400   FORMAT(21H1SALES REPORT   DATED ,2A4/8H0  SALES,5X,8HTAX RATE,5X,9H
     1SALES TAX/)
401   FORMAT(1X,F8.2,3X,F8.3,5X,F8.2)
402   FORMAT(1H0,F8.2)
      STOP
      END
```

Observe that the counter TOTSAL, for total sales, must be initialized to zero at the beginning and that the label 11 has been removed from the STOP statement. The statement label 11 now identifies a new WRITE, which eventually prints the total sales. Output from SALES-12, using the same data as before, appears as

```
01-11-76
 1000.00
  857.67
  628.43
 1575.50
-9999.00
```

THE TRANSFER COMMANDS

```
SALES REPORT   DATED 01-11-76

  SALES      TAX RATE    SALES TAX

1000.00       0.040        40.00
 857.67       0.040        34.31
 628.43       0.040        25.14
1575.50       0.040        63.02

4061.60
```

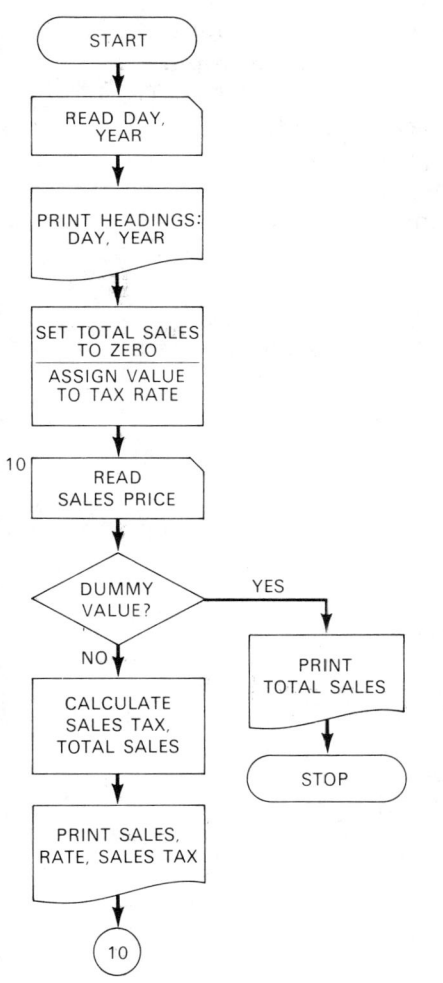

Flowchart 5-4   SALES TAX—Logical IF with counter.

The same arithmetic IF (plus a revised sales tax calculation)

```
      IF(SALES)11,12,12
12    SALETX = SALES * TAXRAT
```

could be substituted in the program as was possible with SALES-11. As stated before, the output would be exactly the same.

5-6 Program Sample STATISTICS

A method for terminating a loop with a counter instead of a dummy value will be included in the second program sample. Problem definition remains the same—compute the average of three values for four different groups. When the value of the counter is four, processing is complete. Thus, a logical IF can be substituted for the GO TO statement appearing in STATISTICS-10 to terminate processing. Flowchart 5-5 reflects the one change to the program. The statements needed are

```
C PROGRAM STATISTICS-11
C THIS PROGRAM COMPUTES THE AVERAGE OF THREE VALUES FOR A NUMBER OF
C GROUPS OF DATA.
      WRITE(6,300)
      KNT = 0
1     READ(5,201)VAL1,VAL2,VAL3
      SUM = VAL1 + VAL2 + VAL3
      AVG = SUM/3.
      KNT = KNT + 1
      WRITE(6,301)KNT,SUM,AVG
      IF(KNT.LT.4)GO TO 1
201   FORMAT(3F5.1)
300   FORMAT(@1GROUP NUMBER    SUM    AVERAGE@/)
301   FORMAT(5X,I3,4X,F8.1,1X,F8.1/)
      STOP
      END
```

When the value of KNT, the counter, is less than four, control is passed back to the READ for more processing. Otherwise, the program is terminated. The output, using the data from STATISTICS-10, appears as

```
82.2  69.5  74.0
65.5  76.4  83.2
98.8  92.0  90.7
75.5  85.4  68.3
```

THE TRANSFER COMMANDS

GROUP NUMBER	SUM	AVERAGE
1	225.7	75.2
2	225.1	75.0
3	281.5	93.8
4	229.2	76.4

An arithmetic IF (plus a revised STOP to add a label)

```
        IF(KNT-4)1,2,2
2       STOP
```

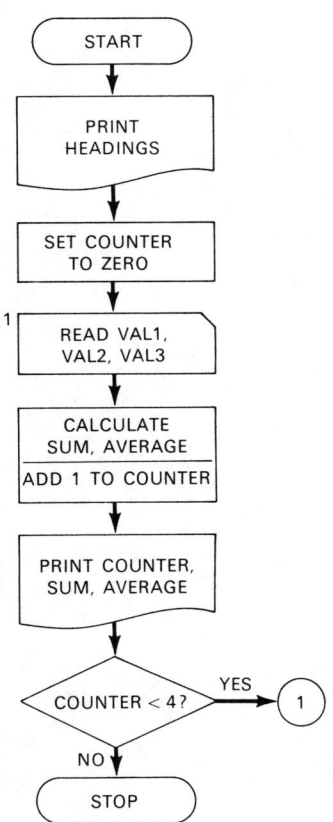

Flowchart 5-5 STATISTICS—Logical IF statement.

could be inserted in the program without affecting the processing.

To add a degree of flexibility to the program, a variable number of groups should be processed. The number of groups can be identified by inserting a READ statement and a data card with the actual number. To incorporate this idea, a new READ and a revised IF are required:

```
C PROGRAM STATISTICS-11 REVISED
C THIS PROGRAM COMPUTES THE AVERAGE OF THREE VALUES FOR A NUMBER OF
C GROUPS OF DATA.
      WRITE(6,300)
      KNT = 0
      READ(5,201)NOG
1     READ(5,200)VAL1,VAL2,VAL3
      SUM = VAL1 + VAL2 + VAL3
      AVG = SUM/3.
      KNT = KNT + 1
      WRITE(6,301)KNT,SUM,AVG
      IF(KNT.LT.NOG)GO TO 1
200   FORMAT(3F5.1)
201   FORMAT(I3)
300   FORMAT(@1GROUP NUMBER    SUM    AVERAGE@/)
301   FORMAT(5X,I3,4X,F8.1,1X,F8.1/)
      STOP
      END
```

In the new IF statement, the variable NOG replaces the constant 4 contained in the previous sample. Thus, the number of times the loop is performed is dependent upon the value of NOG, not upon a constant. To process the same four groups, the data and the output from the revised program are

```
   4
82.2 69.5 74.0
65.5 76.4 83.2
98.8 92.0 90.7
75.5 85.4 68.3
```

GROUP NUMBER	SUM	AVERAGE
1	225.7	75.2
2	225.1	75.0
3	2811 5	93.8
4	229.2	76.4

THE TRANSFER COMMANDS

The first data card containing the 4 is required to assign a value to the variable NOG. This card controls the number of times the loop is performed. (As with the other samples, an arithmetic IF statement could be used in place of the logical IF.)

These few samples certainly do not show all the uses of the IF statements. In later sections, additional applications will illustrate more ideas concerning their deployment.

5-7 The Computed GO TO Statement

The simple GO TO statement was classified as an unconditional transfer of control instruction. When the computer processes a GO TO statement, control is passed directly to the label specified. With the IF statements, a condition is tested and control is passed to, at most, one of three statements. The third type of transfer statement is the computed GO TO instruction. The computed GO TO statement provides a multibranched conditional transfer. Control of the execution of a program is passed to one of a *group* of statements, rather than to one, two, or three, as is possible with the other branch instructions. The general form of the statement is

sl   GO TO(sl-1,sl-2,...,sl-n),i

where sl is an optional statement label, sl-1, sl-2, . . . , sl-n are the labels of executable statements located within the program, and i is an unsigned integer variable whose value is in the range $1 \leq i \leq n$. The next statement processed after the computed GO TO is dependent upon the value of i.

Control of the program is passed to sl-1 when i is equal to 1. Control is passed to sl-2 when i is 2, sl-3 when i is 3, and so forth. In the statement

1087   GO TO (11, 5, 72, 84), KEY

statement 11 is executed next if the value of KEY is 1, statement 5 if KEY is 2, statement 72 if KEY is 3, and statement 84 if KEY is 4. If the value of KEY is *out of range*, i.e., less than 1 or greater than 4, the next executable statement in the program is then processed.[1] "Out of range" means, in general, that the

---

[1] In certain compilers, an out-of-range condition causes a termination error. Refer to the particular systems manual being used for clarification.

value of the variable is less than 1 or greater than the number of statement labels specified within the parentheses.

Any number of labels can be placed in the computed GO TO statement—thus the term *multibranch*. Generally, its use should be restricted to cases where four or more branches are needed. Figures 5-7 and 5-8 reflect samples.

Figure 5-7 Examples of the computed GO TO† statement.

	Program Statements	Description
68	I=1	The value of I is evaluated by the computed GO
	GO TO(10,11,12),I	TO statement. Control is passed to label 10
10	.	because a value of 1 is assigned to I. If I were
11	.	equal to 2, control would be passed to label 11.
12	.	If I were 3, control would transfer to label 12.
	READ(5,100)ITEM	The value assigned to ITEM via the READ
	GO TO(5,24,14,24),ITEM	statement is used to determine which labeled
24	.	statement is processed after the computed GO TO.
5	.	If ITEM has a value of 1, label 5 is performed next.
14	.	If ITEM is 2 or 4, label 24 is performed next. If ITEM has a value of 3, label 14 is performed after the computed GO TO statement.
	GO TO(6,5,13,14,6,8,3,3),NUM	Control of the program would be passed to

Statement Labeled	If the value of NUM is
6	1 or 5
5	2
13	3
14	4
8	6
3	7 or 8

If the value of NUM is not between 1 and 8 inclusively, the next executable statement in the program is processed then.

	Program Statements	Description
	MONTH=5	The program will execute the next statement in
	GO TO(6,5,4,3),MONTH	sequence because the value of MONTH is out of range, i.e., it is greater than 4, the number of labels specified in the GO TO statement.

†In actual use, the computed GO TO statement should only be used when there are four or more labels within the parentheses.

Figure 5-8 Common errors that occur with computed GO TO statements.

	Program Statements	Description
5	GO TO 10,20,30,40 NO	The statement has not been constructed according to the specified form. Parentheses must encompass the labels, and a comma is required in front of the variable NO. A correct entry would be 5 GO TO(10,20,30,40),NO
	GO TO (1,5,13,8),ADM	The variable in the computed GO TO statement must be integer mode.[1] ADM implies real mode, so a correction is required: GO TO(1,5,13,8),IADM
	GO TO(16,17,15,14),I*J+5	The expression I*J+5 is not permitted as part of the computed GO TO statement. Correct entries would be II=I*J+5 GO TO(16,17,15,14),II
	GO TO(10,15,15,10),IN	As discussed with the unconditional GO TO statement, the computed GO TO can not pass control to a FORMAT statement or any other nonexecutable statement. A correct entry would be GO TO(10,20,20,10),IN
10	.	
15	FORMAT(8I3)	
20	WRITE(6,15)IN	

[1] It must also be a nonsubscripted variable. Subscripted variables are discussed in Chap. 6.

Computed GO TO Exercises

1. Supply the computed GO TO statement that satisfies details (a) to (c):
    (a) If the engineering code is 1 to 5, transfer control to labels 100, 150, 200, 250, and 300, respectively, from label 57.
    (b) If the class code is 1 to 8, transfer control to label 600; if it is 9 to 12, transfer to label 601; if it is 12 to 16, transfer control to label 602 from label 81.
    (c) Assuming that Monday is represented by 1, Tuesday by 2, and so forth, transfer control to lines 100, 101, 102, 103, 104, 105, and 106, respectively, based on the day code.
2. In the following samples, determine which statement is processed after the computed GO TO:
    (a)   K = 1+2*2
          GO TO (3,6,4,6,4,6), K
          .
          .
          .

(b) 100   IBETA = 8/4+2
           GO TO (1,1,2,2,3,3), IBETA
           .
           .
           .

(c) 40804 MONTH = 12*2/4−3*2
    40805 GO TO (7,3,7,6,5), MONTH
           .
           .
           .

(d)   MORES = 4+5−6*2+5**1+2
    667   GO TO (80,70,60,50,45), MORES
           .
           .
           .

3. Correct errors appearing in the following statements. Also revise those that could be written more efficiently by using a different type of statement.
   (a)   GO TO (7,8,6,5)X
   (b) 1   GO TO (10,15,9,12,1),I
   (c) 256   GO TO (4,5),2+J**2
   (d)   256 GO TO 170,180,190,200,210,NBAT
   (e)   GO TO (READ,PRINT,END),KLTY
   (f)   GO TO (7,8,9,10),IXT
        7   FORMAT(F10.2)
                 .
                 .
                 .

5-8 Program Sample SALES TAX

For purposes of continuity, the use of the computed GO TO instruction will be illustrated in the SALES program. However, without expanding the problem definition significantly, it should be noted that the arithmetic IF could be used equally well.

In the problems discussed thus far, a tax rate of 4 percent has been applied to each item processed. In this version, assume that two rates, either 4 or 4.5 percent, are applicable. Also, note that the actual rate is not supplied, but a code is placed in the input record to identify the tax rate. Thus, the input data consists not only of the sales quantity but also of a tax-rate code. In setting up the program, a code 1 represents the 4 percent rate and a code 2 the 4.5 percent rate. In program SALES-

THE TRANSFER COMMANDS

12, a dummy value was inserted to terminate the loop. In this version, a third code (3) represents the dummy value keying the termination of the loop. Flowchart 5-6 depicts the steps necessary to incorporate these ideas. Note that the total sales counter has been omitted from this sample. The program instructions follow:

```
C PROGRAM SALES-13
C THIS PROGRAM COMPUTES THE SALES TAX FOR A NUMBER OF ITEMS BASED ON
C A RATE OF 4 PERCENT.
      READ(5,100)DAY,YEAR
      WRITE(6,400)DAY,YEAR
10    READ(5,101)SALES,IRATE
      GO TO (12,13,11),IRATE
12    SALETX = SALES * .04
      GO TO 14
13    SALETX = SALES * .045
14    WRITE(6,401)SALES,IRATE,SALETX
      GO TO 10
100   FORMAT(2A4)
101   FORMAT(F8.2,I2)
400   FORMAT(21H1SALES REPORT   DATED ,2A4/8H0   SALES,5X,8HTAX CODE,5X,9H
     1SALES TAX/)
401   FORMAT(1X,F8.2,5X,I5,6X,F8.2)
11    STOP
      END
```

Here the computed GO TO replaced the IF statement found in the earlier versions. A three-way branch is set up in this program by the instruction. An additional comment relates to the GO TO 14 instruction. It is essential to the program in order to obtain the correct answers. Why?

The new data is listed with one sales quantity (in floating-point form) and one tax-rate code (in integer mode) on each card. The dummy values—two are required because the READ processes two variables—are placed behind the valid data. Output from the program is similar to that shown before.

```
02-12-76
 1000.00 1
  857.67 1
  628.43 2
 1575.50 1
-9999.00 3
```

```
SALES REPORT   DATED 02-12-76

   SALES      TAX CODE     SALES TAX

   1000.00        1          40.00
    857.67        1          34.31
    628.43        2          28.28
   1575.50        1          63.02
```

In this program, the computed GO TO statement could be replaced by an arithmetic IF of the form

IF(NRATE−2)12,13,11

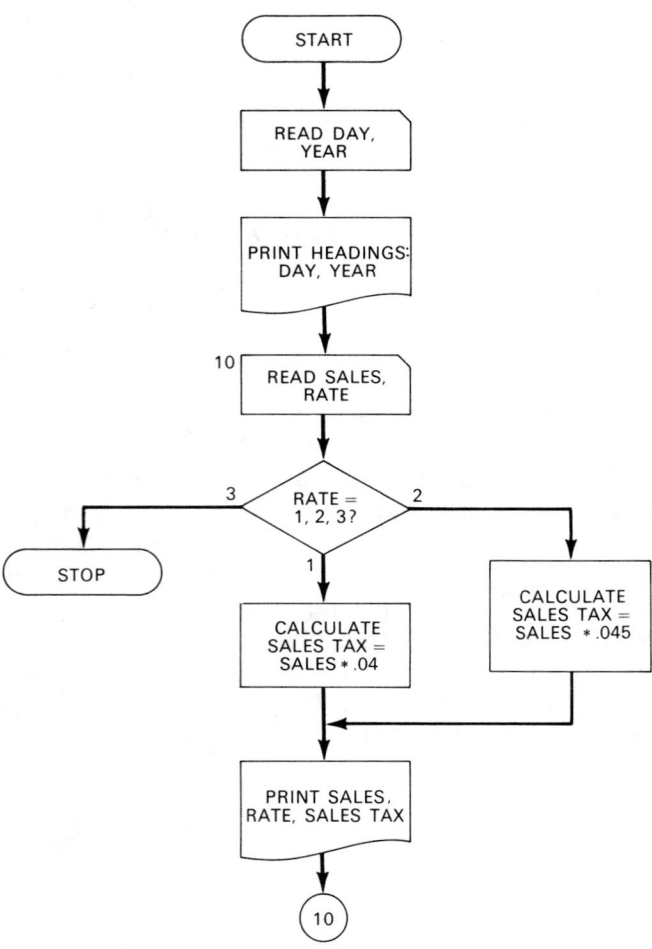

Flowchart 5-6 SALES TAX—Computed GO TO statement.

THE TRANSFER COMMANDS

without changing the results of the program. Normally the computed GO TO should only be used when a four-way (or more) branch instruction is required. For this reason, the STATISTICS problem will be omitted, since, in the present statement of the problem, its use is not recommended.

5-9 Miscellaneous Business Sample

Assume that the FORPRO CO. produces four different products, each with a different cost function. At the end of each day, a printout of the number of units of each type produced, along with its cost, is required. The cost functions for the products are

Product	Cost Function
1	Units · $2.25 + $150
2	Units · $3.86 + $300
3	Units · $4.20 + $500
4	Units · $5.00 + $600

Besides cost by product, the total cost is required. Flowchart 5-7 identifies the steps needed to read the product type and units produced, to compute the cost for the product, to accumulate the total cost, and, finally, to print the answers. The program statements conforming to the flowchart are

```
C   COST REPORTING PROGRAM FOR FORPRO CO. VALID PRODUCT TYPES
C   ARE CODES 1,2,3, AND 4. A 5 IS USED AS THE DUMMY VALUE.
C   ANY OTHER CODE WILL CAUSE THE PROGRAM TO STOP WITH AN
C   ERROR MESSAGE PRINTED AS OUTPUT.
        DATA TOTAL/0.0/
        WRITE(6,100)
500     READ(5,1)IPT,UNITS
        GO TO (10,20,30,40,50),IPT
        WRITE(6,101)IPT,UNITS
        STOP
10      COST = UNITS*2.25 + 150
        GO TO 6
20      COST = UNITS*3.86 + 300
        GO TO 6
30      COST = UNITS*4.20 + 500
        GO TO 6
40      COST = UNITS*5.00 + 600
6       TOTAL = TOTAL + COST
        WRITE(6,102)IPT,UNITS,COST
        GO TO 500
50      WRITE(6,103)TOTAL
1       FORMAT(I2,F6.0)
```

```
100     FORMAT(@1PRODUCT NO    UNITS     COST@/)
101     FORMAT(@0BAD PRODUCT CODE@,I4,@ UNITS@,F6.0)
102     FORMAT(4X,I3,3X,F8.0,F10.2)
103     FORMAT(@0TOTAL COST@,8X,F9.2)
        STOP
        END
```

In the solution, the variable IPT represents the product type. An integer variable is required here for its use in the computed GO TO instruction that follows the READ. A new programming

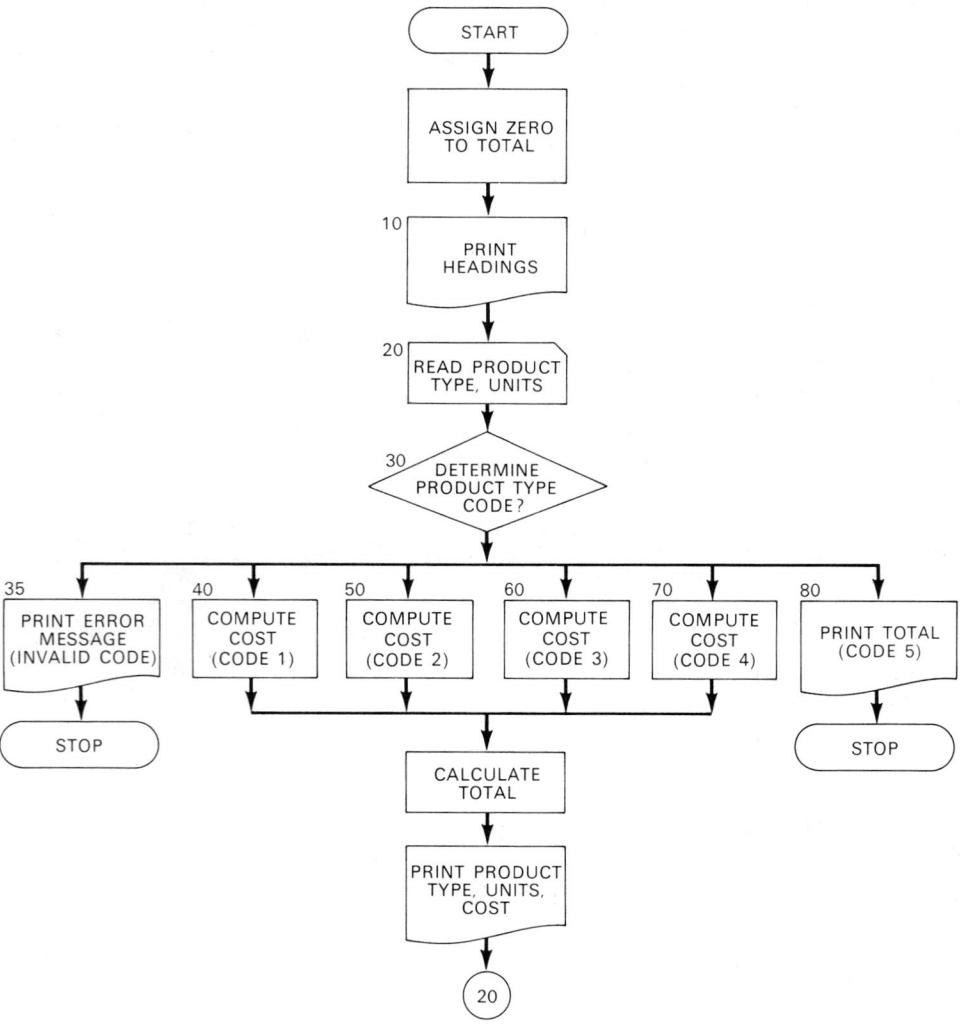

Flowchart 5-7 Cost Reporting—Computed GO TO statement.

THE TRANSFER COMMANDS

idea is incorporated after the computed GO TO. The valid product types are 1, 2, 3, and 4, with a code 5 acting as the dummy value that terminates the loop. But what will happen if a keypunch error occurs and a code 10 is entered as data? The output from a run with bad data in the second record is

```
 1   160.
10   280.
 2  1260.
 3  4140.
 5
```

```
PRODUCT NO     UNITS      COST

     1          160.      510.00
BAD PRODUCT CODE   10 UNITS   280.
```

Because the code 10 is out of range of the computed GO TO, execution falls through to the immediately following WRITE and STOP statements. A printed error message indicates bad data and processing is stopped. The user must correct the invalid code and rerun the program. The use of these two statements here is an example of what is called a "built-in error routine," which ensures that only correct data is processed by the program. Correct data and output from the computer run follow:

```
1   160.
4   280.
2  1260.
3  4140.
5
```

```
PRODUCT NO     UNITS       COST

     1          160.       510.00
     4          280.      2000.00
     2         1260.      5163.60
     3         4140.     17888.00

TOTAL COST                25561.60
```

Note that the sequence of input data is not important in this sample. In Chap. 6, sequencing will be discussed along with additional new material.

Prior to this chapter, all the FORTRAN program samples discussed were assumed to be executed sequentially by the computer; in other words, the statements were processed one after another. The transfer commands in this chapter allow the programmer to alter and control the normal sequence of execution. GO TO statements permit an unconditional transfer of control; the IF statements and the computed GO TO allow for conditional transfers. These control statements form the nucleus of most programs. By properly applying them, many useful programs can be constructed.

5-10 Summary

Questions

1. The AJACKS Company pays its sales employees $100.00 plus 6 percent of net sales weekly. Net sales are equal to sales minus returns. Write a FORTRAN program (using dummy values to terminate the loop) that will calculate the net sales and the pay and will also print a report according to the following format:

NAME	SALES	RETURNS	NET SALES	PAY
SUTFIELD	12000.00	1000.00	11000.00	760.00
HOLMES	15000.00	2500.00	12500.00	850.00
PACEK	10500.00	500.00	10000.00	700.00
TOTALS	37500.00	4000.00	33500.00	2310.00

   The data to be read into the program should include *only* the employee name (2A4 format), sales (F9.2), and returns (F8.2). In addition to calculating the net sales and pay, the totals for each of the four columns should be computed. Use the above data plus one or two sets of additional data values of your own choice.

2. Write a FORTRAN program that will solve Question 1, but substitute the counter method (for the dummy values) to terminate the loop.

3. Revise the program for Question 1 to include the two parameters: If sales are more than $15,000, pay the salesman an additional $50; if returns are less than $500, pay the salesman an additional $50. Supply your own data that pertains to both categories to test the program.

4. The polynomial
$$y = \frac{3x^3 - 5x^2 + 7x - 14}{(x^2 - 4)}$$
can be evaluated for values of x other than ± 2. When x is equal to ± 2, the denominator is zero, and division by zero is not permitted either by mathematical operations or by the computer.

Using the counter method for terminating a loop, evaluate y for successive values of x in the range $-5 \leq x \leq 4$ (that is, $-5, -4, -3, \ldots, 4$). Be sure to exclude the values ± 2. Print all the values for x and y with appropriate labels. The successive values of x may be calculated within the program or supplied via the READ instruction.

5 Solve Question 4 by using a dummy value to terminate the loop. Note that the problem statement implies that the values of x will be read into the program.

6 What will be the relative frequencies of the three genotypes in the next generation of a large population of flies that shows no mating preference and in which the relative frequency of A genes is 0.1 and of a genes is 0.9? By using the formula $(0.1A + 0.9a)^2$, the answers are calculated to be $0.01AA$, $0.18Aa$, and $0.81aa$. Write a FORTRAN program using the generalized formula $(pA + qa)^2$ to calculate a table of values for AA, Aa, and aa when the pairs of data 0.19 and 0.81, 0.3 and 0.7, 0.31 and 0.61, 0.4 and 0.6, 0.45 and 0.55, and 0.5 and 0.5 are read into the program. Supply column headings for A, a, AA, Aa, and aa. Use dummy values to terminate the loop.

7 On a 10-point test, the grades ranged from 3 to 9. The actual test scores for 30 students were

8, 6, 3, 4, 6, 5, 7, 9, 9, 3, 6, 4, 4, 5, 8, 7, 5, 8, 6, 6, 8, 9, 7, 5, 7, 8, 7, 4, 6, 4

Using the grades as the *only* input data, write a FORTRAN program that will calculate the
(a) Sum and the average (sum/30)
(b) Number of students who answered three correctly (that is, 2), and the number who answered four correctly (that is, 5), and so forth
(c) Percent who answered three correctly [the number computed in (b) divided by 30, that is, $2/30 = 0.0666$], the percent who answered four, and so forth

Print the sum and average and a table for the answers computed in (b) and (c). The following column headings should be used for identifying the table numbers:

TEST SCORE   NUMBER OF STUDENTS   PERCENT OF TOTAL

Use any method to terminate the loop. (Hint: The computed GO TO and counters of the type KNT=KNT+1 are very useful in this problem.)

8 Revise Question 7 so that any number of student grades can be processed by your program. Replace the constant 30 by a variable whose value is READ at the beginning of the program and identifies the number of students. As the last line of output,

print the number and the percent of the students who received a grade of 8 or 9. Supply additional grades to test your program. (Note: Do not use mixed-mode expressions within the program.)

9. Let $y = \begin{cases} x^2 + 4x - 7 & \text{when } x = 1, 3 \\ (x^2 - 2x + 1)^2 & \text{when } x = 2, 5, 6 \\ 2x & \text{when } x = 4, 8, 10 \\ 7 - x - \dfrac{x^2}{2} - \dfrac{x^3}{3} & \text{when } x = 7, 9 \end{cases}$

Write a FORTRAN program that will calculate each value of y when x is assigned successively 1, 2, 3, ..., 10. Select the proper formula from the list defined, and print the values of y and x with appropriate labels. (A programming hint: The computed GO TO statement simplifies the problem.)

10. Let $y = \begin{cases} x^3 - 3x + 8 & \text{when } x < 0 \\ 2 & \text{when } x = 0 \\ x^4 + 7x^2 + 17 & \text{when } x > 0 \end{cases}$

Write a FORTRAN program that will read several different values for x and will calculate the proper value for y. Print the value of x and the calculated value of y as output. Label appropriately. Terminate by using the counter method.

THE DO CONTINUE AND DIMENSION STATEMENTS 6

In Chap. 5 simple loops were developed by using the various transfer commands. However, the construction forms employing dummy values and counters were somewhat cumbersome. This chapter introduces a more convenient, straightforward approach for establishing loops.

6-1 The DO and CONTINUE Statements

The powerful technique of performing repetitive calculations by employing the same instructions over and over is made simpler by the DO statement. A DO loop can be constructed by placing the DO statement as the first instruction in the loop and identifying, with a specific label, the last line of the loop. The general form of the DO statement is

sl   DO sl-1 i = n_1, n_2, n_3

where sl is an optional statement label, sl-1 is the label of an executable statement designating the last instruction in the DO loop, i is a nonsubscripted integer variable, and n_1, n_2, and n_3 (called parameters of the DO loop) are either unsigned integer constants greater than zero or integer variables greater than zero. Although n_1 and n_2 are always required, parameter n_3 is optional; if omitted, its value is assumed to be 1. The DO statement is an instruction to the computer to execute, at least once, all the statements following the DO, up to and including the statement labeled sl-1. The first time the loop is performed the value of the variable i is initialized to the value n_1. Thus, n_1 is called the *initial value* of the index i. After the loop has been performed once, the incremental value n_3 (or +1, if n_3 has been omitted) is added to the value of i. Thus, n_3 is called the *increment*. The loop statements are repeated and i incremented as long as the value of i is less than or equal to n_2, the *terminal value* of the loop. For example,

125   DO 11 KK = 1,3,2

.

.

.

11   WRITE(6,100)X,Y

125 is the optional label of the DO statement, 11 identifies the last line or the *object* of the loop, KK the variable or index of the loop, 1 the initial value assigned to KK, 3 the terminal value, and 2 the increment. The *range* of the loop, represented by the three dots and the statement labeled 11, is performed twice in this case, for KK = 1 and KK = 3. When the cycle is completed, control of the program is passed to the next executable statement following the object of the DO loop. Generally, the number of times the statements in the range of the DO are performed is given by the formula

$$\left[\frac{n_2 - n_1}{n_3}\right] + 1$$

where the square brackets indicate an integer function (i.e., "the greatest integer value less than or equal to"), unless n_1 is greater than n_2. If n_1 is greater than n_2, the loop is executed once.

In building a DO loop, the programmer must make sure that the last statement in the range is executable. However, it can't be a GO TO of any form, an arithmetic IF, a STOP, RETURN (discussed later), or another DO statement. Another type of statement, CONTINUE, is used when it appears that one of the statements above signifies the logical end of the loop. Its general form is

sl   CONTINUE

where sl is an optional statement label. CONTINUE is a dummy or nonoperating command that may be placed anywhere in the source program without affecting the execution.

THE DO, CONTINUE, AND DIMENSION STATEMENTS

Its primary purpose is in conjunction with the DO. It is placed as the last statement in the range in order to avoid ending the loop with one of the invalid instructions mentioned earlier. Figure 6-1 illustrates some examples with the statements com-

Figure 6-1 Examples of the DO statement.

	Program Statements	Description
72	DO 10 I=1,3,1 . . .	The computer assigns the initial value of 1 to the variable I. The range of the loop, consisting of the statements below the DO statement down to and including statement labeled 10, is then performed.
10	IK=IK+1 X=SUM	The variable I is increased by the increment 1, and the loop is repeated as long as I is less than or equal to 3. As soon as I is greater than 3, control of the program is passed to the line immediately following statement 10. Thus, this DO loop is performed three times.
75	DO 11 J=1,5 . . .	The initial value of the variable J is 1. Subsequently, J takes on the values of 2, 3, 4, and 5 as the loop is processed a total of five times, once for each value of J. The increment can be omitted because a 1 is
11	CONTINUE	assumed by the computer.
	DO 12 K=2,8,3 . . .	The loop is performed a total of three times because the initial value of K is 2 and the increment is 3, which causes the variable K to take on successive values of 2, 5, and 8. When the value of K becomes
12	CONTINUE	11, the loop is terminated.
	READ(5,100)N DO 13 J1=1,N . . .	The loop is performed N number of times depending upon the value assigned to N in the READ statement. The initial value of J1 is 1 and the last value N.
13	CONTINUE	
79	READ(5,101)M,N DO 14 KJ=M,N . . .	The loop is processed a variable number of times (N−M+1) depending upon the values assigned to M and N in the READ statement. As before, the variable KJ is assigned the value of M initially. Its last value is N.
14	CONTINUE	
	READ(5,102)M,N,N1 DO 15 I=M,N,N1 . . .	The values assigned to M, N, and N1 in the READ statement are evaluated to determine the number of times the DO loop is processed. The initial value of I is the value of M. The terminal value is N; the incremental value is N1.
15	CONTINUE	

prising the loop omitted. Before more advanced examples are shown, a few rules that apply to the DO loop are pertinent:

1. The physical end of a DO loop is signified by the object statement, which contains a label that is also included in the DO.
2. Any number of instructions may be placed inside a DO loop.
3. Loops may be placed within other loops, called *nested loops*,[1] provided they are properly constructed. For example,

```
┌──── Outer loop              ┌──── DO statement-1
│ ┌── Inner loop              │ ┌── DO statement-2
│ └── End of inner loop       │ └── End of DO-2 loop
└──── End of outer loop       └──── End of DO-1 loop
```

An example of nested loops violating the construction rules is

```
┌──── Outer loop              ┌──── DO statement-1
│ ┌── Inner loop              │ ┌── DO statement-2
└─│── End of outer loop       └─│── End of DO-1 loop
  └── End of inner loop         └── End of DO-2 loop
```

4. The index variable identified in the DO may be used inside the loop provided its value is not changed. For example,

```
       DO 10 I = 1, 5
       K3 = K3 + I**3
10     CONTINUE
```

5. It is permissible to transfer out of a loop by means of the GO TO and IF statements. It is, however, bad programming practice to jump into the middle of a loop.
6. When control is passed to the statement following the object of the DO after completion of the loop, the value of the index i is indefinite. Its value is a function of the compiler being used on the particular system.

A second set of examples, Fig. 6-2, shows more advanced uses of the DO while common errors are shown in Fig. 6-3. The DO statement permits the building of loops, especially nested, with a minimum amount of effort. The two program samples will illustrate its use.

---

[1] Nested implies falling within the range of the statements of the outer loop. It does not extend the loop.

THE DO, CONTINUE, AND DIMENSION STATEMENTS

Figure 6-2 More examples of the DO statement.

	Program Statements	Description
6 1	ISUM=0 DO 1 I=1,4 ISUM=ISUM+I WRITE(6,10)ISUM	The DO loop is processed four times, once for each value of I (1,2,3,4). Statement 1 is used to accumulate the total of the four different I values. The WRITE statement would consequently print the value 10.
84 2	MSQ=0 DO 2 M=1,5,2 MSQ=MSQ+M**2 CONTINUE WRITE(6,11)MSQ	The variable M is assigned successive values of 1, 3, and 5; therefore, the loop is processed a total of three times. MSQ is used to store the sum of the squared values for M. The WRITE statement would consequently print the value 35.
95 3	SUM=0. READ(5,100)NOB DO 3 I=1,NOB READ(5,101)OBS SUM=SUM+OBS CONTINUE	The loop is processed a variable number of times depending on the value assigned to NOB in the READ statement. The two statements inside the loop serve to enter observation values and store the sum of the observations in the variable SUM.

4
5
	SUM=0.
	DO 5 I=1,2
	DO 4 J=1,3
	READ(5,101)OBS
	SUM=SUM+OBS
	CONTINUE
	CONTINUE
		The READ and SUM statements constitute the loop and are processed a total of six times. The outer DO loop is performed twice, and the inner loop is processed three times for each of the two values of I. The statements could also be written
		    SUM=0.
		    DO 5 I=1,2
		    DO 5 J=1,3
		    READ(5,101)OBS
		    SUM=SUM+OBS
		5 CONTINUE
		where the one CONTINUE statement serves as the object of both DOs.

346 6	ISUM=0 DO 6 I=1,3,2 DO 6 J=1,4 ISUM=ISUM+I*J WRITE(6,100)ISUM	The ISUM statement inside the nested loops is processed eight times. The inner J loop is performed four times for each of the two values of I. The statements serve to store the sum of the product of each of the values of I and J. The value written would be 40.

Figure 6-2 More examples of the DO statement *(cont'd)*.

	Program Statements	Description
	READ(5,111)NOB	In this sample, the I loop is performed a
	DO 10 I=1,8	maximum of eight times. However, if the
	IF(NOB/10−72.EQ.I) GO TO 12	value of the expression NOB/10−72 were
10	CONTINUE	equal to I during the processing of the loop,
	I=0	control would be transferred outside the
12	KX=NOB+ITER**2	loop and the value of I would be retained and
	WRITE(6,112)I,KX	printed by the WRITE statement. For example, if NOB were equal to 750, the value 3 would be printed for I in the WRITE statement.

Figure 6-3 Common errors that occur with DO statements.

	Program Statements	Description
68	DO 1 K=1,5	The label 1 must be an executable statement appearing after the DO statement. A correct entry would be
	·	
	·	
	·	1 CONTINUE
3	CONTINUE	
	DO 2 L=2,8	As defined above, the DO loop must be terminated with an executable statement appropriately labeled. A correct entry would be
	·	
	·	
	·	
	END	2 CONTINUE END
	DO 3 X=1,A	The variables X and A are real mode, but only valid nonsubscripted integer modes are permitted in the DO statement. A correct entry would be
	·	
	·	
	·	
3	CONTINUE	DO 3 IX=1,IA
48	DO 4 N=0,−5	The integer constants or variables serving as the DO parameters must be unsigned and greater than zero. Thus, both the 0 and the −5 are illegal. A correct entry would be
	·	
	·	
4	CONTINUE	
		48 DO 4 N=1,5
	DO 5 J=3,1	The DO statement is not invalid as written but is misleading. The loop statements would be performed only one time because the initial value 3
	·	
	·	
5	CONTINUE	

Program Statements	Description
	is greater than the terminal value 1. A more logical statement would be
	DO 5 J=1,3
49 DO 61 MN=1, 5	The object of the DO loop can not be a transfer command. To continue processing the DO, label 61 should be replaced by
.	
.	
.	
61 GO TO 49	61 CONTINUE
76 DO 6 KK=1,4	The value of the variable KK in the DO statement should not be changed within the loop. In this example, as a result of statement 6, the loop is performed only once instead of four times as intended by the DO statement. Two corrections are possible:
.	
.	
6 KK=KK+5	
	76 DO 6 KKK=1,4
	or
	6 KKK=KKK+5
DO 7 L=1,5	The object statement of a DO loop must be an executable statement, excluding those listed in the description. The STOP is not permitted; hence, a correct entry would be
.	
.	
7 STOP	
	7 CONTINUE
	STOP
77 IX=0	The two DO loops are nested incorrectly. The inner loop (J) must be terminated before the second loop (I) is terminated. The loops must be constructed in the proper sequence as
IY=0	
DO 8 I=1,3	
DO 9 J=1,2	
IX=IX+I*J	
8 IY=IY+I*J+IX	
9 CONTINUE	77 IX=0
	IY=0
	DO 8 I=1,3
	DO 9 J=1,2
	IX=IX+I*J
	9 IY=IY+I*J+IX
	8 CONTINUE

DO–CONTINUE Exercises

1   Identify the successive values of each index in the following DO statements. How many times is each loop performed?

(a) 2576   DO 1576 KB = 1, 5
              .
              .
              .
      1576   CONTINUE
(b)   786   DO 62 I = 2,7
              .
              .
              .
      62   CONTINUE
(c)   87   DO 1 K = 2,9,3
              .
              .
              .
      1   CONTINUE
(d)   IX = 2**3+1
             DO 6 IY = 1,IX,2
              .
              .
              .
      6   CONTINUE
(e)   DO 2 M = 1,4
             DO 2 N = 2,3
              .
              .
              .
      2   CONTINUE

2 In the following group of statements, what is the last value assigned to the variable IBD after all the statements have been executed?

(a)   IBD = 7
             DO 66 I = 1,6
      66   IBD = IBD + 1
(b)   IBD = 1
             DO 67 J = 1,6
      67   IBD = IBD * J
(c)   IBD = 0
             DO 71 KL = 2,6
             DO 71 KLL = 3,7,2
      71   IBD = IBD + 1
(d)   IBD = −3
             DO 72 KL = 2,6,2
             DO 72 KLL = 3,8,3
      72   IBD = IBD + KLL

(e)   I9 = 6
         DO 74 M = 1,I9
   74   IBD = I9 * M

3 Write the DO loop statements that are needed to satisfy descriptions (a) to (d):
   (a) Use a DO loop to sum the integer numbers from 73 to 123, inclusive.
   (b) Use a DO loop to calculate 14!, where the ! represents factorial. For example, 3! is equal to 1 × 2 × 3 and 4! is equal to 1 × 2 × 3 × 4.
   (c) Use a DO loop to sum all the odd and all the even numbers in the range from 10 to 100, inclusive.
   (d) Construct a DO loop that will read 14 values into a program.

4 Identify and correct all the errors listed:
   (a) 22   DO 22 I = 1,8
                .
                .
                .
        23   CONTINUE
   (b) DO 83 KJ = 3,L,−1
                .
                .
                .
        83   CONTINUE
   (c)   DO 77 JB = M,N
                .
                .
                .
        77   READ(5,10)J,JA,JB
   (d)   DO 1 JBK = 10
   (e)   DO 2 A = 1,6,5
                .
                .
                .
        2   CONTINUE

6-2 Program Sample SALES TAX

Assuming a slightly different definition for the SALES problem, two methods of utilizing DO loops are possible in the solution. The first version is sufficient only when the same number of items are to be processed each time the program is run. The second solution is much more flexible in that it handles a variable number of items for each run.

In examining program SALES-13, the reader might well ask the question, "Why place a tax code in the input data when the actual rate could be inserted?" In this sample, the code will be replaced by the actual rate. Thus, the computed GO TO test is no longer required. Flowchart 6-1 reflects the inclusion of a DO loop to control processing and the exclusion of the computed GO TO test. The two symbols ⟨⎯⎯⟩ and ◯ illustrate in the flowchart the beginning and end of the DO loop. The dotted line following the connector (◯) indicates that the connection is not direct but is made upon completion of the loop. Program SALES-14 lists the necessary statements conforming to the pictorial diagram:

```
C PROGRAM SALES-14
C THIS PROGRAM COMPUTES THE SALES TAX FOR A NUMBER OF ITEMS
C
      READ(5,100)DAY,YEAR
      WRITE(6,400)DAY,YEAR
      DO 14 I = 1, 4
      READ(5,101)SALES, RATE
      SALETX = SALES * RATE
      WRITE(6,401)SALES, RATE,SALETX
14    CONTINUE
100   FORMAT(2A4)
101   FORMAT(F8.2,F5.3)
400   FORMAT(21H1SALES REPORT  DATED ,2A4/8H0  SALES,5X,8HTAX RATE,5X,9H
     1SALES TAX/)
401   FORMAT(1X,F8.2,3X,F8.3,5X,F8.2)
      STOP
      END
```

In this program, the DO contains constant parameters (I = 1, 4). Therefore, it can be used only when there are four items to be processed. However, by using the DO, dummy values for terminating the loop can be omitted from the data list. Note also that the loop is ended with a CONTINUE statement but that the preceding WRITE could be the object of the DO by labeling it statement 14 and removing the CONTINUE. Four sets of data and output from SALES-14 are

```
03-13-76
 1000.00  .04
  857.67  .04
  628.43  .045
 1575.50  .04
```

THE DO, CONTINUE, AND DIMENSION STATEMENTS   **145**

```
SALES REPORT   DATED 03-13-76

   SALES       TAX RATE      SALES TAX

  1000.00       0.040         40.00
   857.67       0.040         34.31
   628.43       0.045         28.28
  1575.50       0.040         63.02
```

The output is very similar to that from SALES-13, except the actual tax rate, instead of the code, is printed. But how must this program be revised to make it flexible enough to handle any number of items?

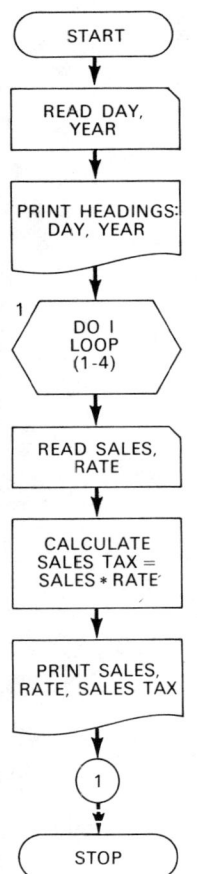

Flowchart 6-1   SALES TAX—DO statement.

By replacing the terminal constant (4) in the DO loop with an integer variable and assigning a value to the variable, the loop can be executed a variable number of times; hence, it is flexible. Therefore, the DO can be written as

DO 14 I = 1,N

where N identifies the number of items to process. But what is the value of N? It must be defined and a logical place to define it is in the first READ:

READ(5,100)DAY,YEAR,N

where the FORMAT statement 100 is revised accordingly

100   FORMAT(2A4,I3)

With these three changes, the program becomes an efficient solution to the stated problem. New data, with the number of items (5) to be processed found in the rightmost field of the date card, and the output are

```
04-12-76   5
 1000.00  .04
  857.67  .04
  628.43  .045
 1575.50  .04
  175.64  .045
```

```
SALES REPORT   DATED 04-12-76

   SALES      TAX RATE     SALES TAX

  1000.00      0.040        40.00
   857.67      0.040        34.31
   628.43      0.045        28.28
  1575.50      0.040        63.02
   175.64      0.045         7.90
```

In both of these examples the value of I, the index of the DO, is not used within the loop. In the next problem, the value of the index will be used.

6-3 Program Sample STATISTICS

In the revised version of program STATISTICS-11, the variable NOG was used to terminate the loop by the counter method. Without redefining the problem, a DO loop containing the variable NOG will be illustrated here. Its use will permit

THE DO, CONTINUE, AND DIMENSION STATEMENTS

elimination of one IF and two assignment statements by using the value of the index within the loop. Flowchart 6-2 shows the logic with the DO. The statements necessary are

```
C   PROGRAM STATISTICS-12
C   THIS PROGRAM COMPUTES THE AVERAGE OF THREE VALUES FOR A NUMBER OF
C   GROUPS OF DATA.
        WRITE(6,300)
        READ(5,201)NOG
        DO 2 I = 1, NOG
        READ(5,200)VAL1,VAL2,VAL3
        SUM = VAL1 + VAL2 + VAL3
        AVG = SUM/3.
        WRITE(6,301) I, SUM,AVG
2       CONTINUE
200     FORMAT(3F5.1)
201     FORMAT(I3)
300     FORMAT(@1GROUP NUMBER    SUM    AVERAGE@/)
301     FORMAT(5X,I3,4X,F8.1,1X,F8.1/)
        STOP
        END
```

Note that the variable KNT has been eliminated from this version. Its elimination is possible since the value of the index I takes on successive values of 1, 2, 3, . . . , NOG, which serves the same purpose. Using the same data from STATISTICS-11, the output is identical although fewer program statements are used in this solution.

```
 4
82.2 69.5 74.0
65.5 76.4 83.2
98.8 92.0 90.7
75.5 85.4 68.3
```

GROUP NUMBER	SUM	AVERAGE
1	229.7	75.2
2	225.1	75.0
3	281.5	93.8
4	229.2	76.4

A critique of this program and all the preceding STATISTICS problems yields one far too stringent assumption. It is recognizable? How many values are averaged in each group? The answer

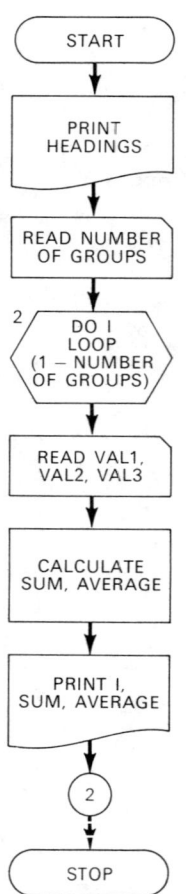

Flowchart 6-2 STATISTICS—DO statement.

is always three, and this certainly is not very flexible. To remove this limitation, nested loops will be incorporated in the solution.

The outer loop will serve as before to indicate the number of groups to process. But within each group an inner loop will be constructed to sum a variable number of values. To program this change, a number of statements must be revised and others added. A discussion of Flowchart 6-3 and program STATISTICS-13 will outline these ideas.

```
C PROGRAM STATISTICS-13
C THIS PROGRAM COMPUTES THE AVERAGE FOR A VARIABLE NUMBER OF VALUES
C IN MULTIPLE GROUPS OF DATA.
```

THE DO, CONTINUE, AND DIMENSION STATEMENTS

```
           WRITE(6,300)
           READ(5,201)NOG
           DO 2 I = 1, NOG
           SUM = 0.
           READ(5,201)NOV
           DO 1 J = 1, NOV
           READ(5,200)VALUE
           SUM = SUM + VALUE
1          CONTINUE
           XNOV = NOV
           AVG = SUM/XNOV
           WRITE(6,301)I,NOV,SUM,AVG
2          CONTINUE
200        FORMAT(F5.1)
201        FORMAT(I3)
300        FORMAT(@1GROUP NUMBER   NUMBER IN GROUP     SUM      AVERAGE@/)
301        FORMAT(5X,I3,13X,I3,5X,F8.1,1X,F8.1/)
           STOP
           END
```

In the program statements, the variable NOG defines the number of groups to process. The variable SUM, used as a counter, must be initialized to zero for each new group processed, or otherwise the calculation of the average would only be correct for the first group of data. Another new variable NOV defines the number of values to be read one at a time and summed for each group. Although NOV identifies the number of values to average, it should not be used in computing AVG (mixed mode). Thus, its value is converted to real mode and assigned to XNOV; XNOV is then used as the divisor in the calculation of the average.

When the inner loop is completed, the average is calculated and the answers printed. Control is then passed to the outer loop, and provided there is more data, another group is summed and averaged. In this version, the data values must be placed on separate cards because the numbers are read into the program one at at time. Data for two groups, with only three values in the first and five in the second, plus the resulting output, are

```
   2
 003
  82.2
  69.5
  74.0
 005
  79.9
  87.3
```

68.2
69.2
87.8

GROUP NUMBER	NUMBER IN GROUP	SUM	AVERAGE
1	3	225.7	75.2
2	5	392.4	78.5

It is important to understand how the data is supplied to this program. Unless placed in the proper sequence, errors will occur during the program run. Thus, only one value is supplied for NOG since it is read once. But NOV is read a variable number of times based on the value of NOG. Likewise, within each group the number of times VALUE is read is dependent upon NOV. Therefore, when supplying data to a program similar to the one above, these dependencies must be taken into account.

6-4 The DIMENSION Statement

In every example considered thus far, only the current value of a variable has been retained. However, it is possible and sometimes necessary to retain all the values assigned to a specific variable. The DIMENSION statement in FORTRAN supplies the capability of storing a large number of values in a table or an array within a program. Subscripted variables are used to reference and retain values in tables or arrays. An analogy with a warehouse permits a better understanding. For a warehouse with many aisles, it is efficient to number the aisles consecutively 1, 2, ..., n in order to easily find materials or parts.

The DIMENSION statement can be thought of as setting up a table or warehouse with a number of locations or aisles reserved. The general form of the statement is

DIMENSION [variable (constant)]

or

DIMENSION [variable (constant), variable (constant)]

where the constants in the forms refer to the maximum number of locations reserved. Note that a statement label is omitted from the general form. The label is not permitted because the

THE DO, CONTINUE, AND DIMENSION STATEMENTS

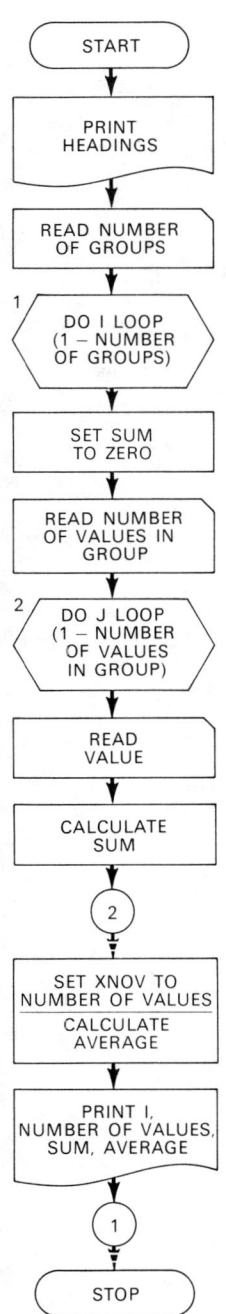

Flowchart 6-3 STATISTICS—Nested DO statements.

DIMENSION is a nonexecutable statement. It is also one example of a declaration type statement used at compilation time, providing the name, mode, and number of elements in a table. The statement must be placed at the beginning of the program before variable names listed in the DIMENSION are referenced. For clarification, assume the statement

DIMENSION A(5)

appears in a program. The statement simply identifies a real table called A, with five locations shown schematically as

```
         A
      ┌─────┐
(1)   │     │
      ├─────┤
(2)   │     │
      ├─────┤
(3)   │     │
      ├─────┤
(4)   │     │
      ├─────┤
(5)   │     │
      └─────┘
```

The variable A is used to refer to the entire table. However, subscripted variables are required to reference individual locations in the table. The first location is referenced by the form A(1), read as "A-sub-1." The second is referenced by A(2), the third by A(3), and the *N*th location by the form A(N). The subscript enclosed in parentheses points to or indexes the specific table location. It should be an integer constant or variable[1] not less than 1 or greater than the number indicated in the DIMENSION statement itself.

The example above is called a table or one-dimensional array. Two-dimensional arrays or matrices are also permitted. The form of the statement for two dimensions is

DIMENSION [variable (constant, constant)]

or

---

[1] Integer-valued expressions such as I−5, 2∗M, and 4∗K−3 are also valid subscripts.

THE DO, CONTINUE, AND DIMENSION STATEMENTS

DIMENSION [variable (constant, constant), variable (constant, constant)]

where the first constant following the variable name identifies the number of rows in the array and the second constant identifies the number of columns. Referring back to the warehouse, if each aisle has a specified number of bins, a specific location such as aisle 2, bin 3 can be referenced directly. Similarly, two-dimensional arrays require two subscripts. Assume an array

DIMENSION I(2,4)

In the integer table I, eight locations are reserved. There are two rows with each row containing four columns, shown schematically as

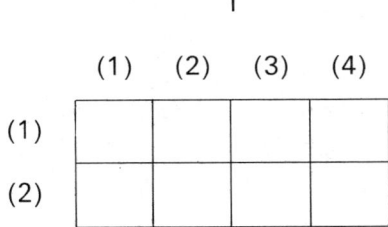

I can be denoted as a 2 × 4 array or as a 2 × 4 matrix. The variable I is used to refer to the entire eight positions. The first location is referenced by the variable I(1,1), read as "I-sub-1-comma-1." The variable I(2,3) refers to the third column in the second row, and I(2,1) refers to the second row, first column. The first subscript *always* refers to the row; the second *always* references the column.

More than two dimensions[1] are permitted in some FORTRAN compilers, but the discussion here will be limited because the same rules and ideas apply to higher dimensions. Like other valid variables, the locations in tables must be assigned values prior to their use. Subscripted variables can be used in assignment, READ, WRITE, PRINT, arithmetic and logical IF statements in place of unsubscripted variables. Figures 6-4 and 6-5 show examples of various DIMENSION statements.

---

[1] The standard number of dimensions is three. Refer to the systems manual in use for clarification.

Figure 6-4 Examples of the DIMENSION statement.

Program Statements	Description
DIMENSION IDN(10)	The statement reserves (in the computer memory unit) a list or table identified as IDN with a maximum number of 10 locations. Because the name of the variable IDN is integer mode, the list can only be used to store integer numbers.
DIMENSION SQD(7)	Seven locations are reserved in the computer memory unit for a table identified as SQD. Only real values can be stored in the table SQD.
DIMENSION X(5),Y(5),ITEM(10)	Three lists have been identified: the first two are used to store real values, and the third is used for integer values. The maximum number of locations for each of the tables X, Y, and ITEM is five, five, and ten, respectively.
DIMENSION IX(60,5),SX(10,8),SSX(18,20)	Three two-dimensional arrays have been reserved: IX, SX, and SSX. Array IX consists of a maximum of 300 integer locations: 60 rows with 5 columns in each row. Array SX consists of 80 real locations: 10 rows with 8 columns each. Array SSX consists of 360 real locations: 18 rows with 20 columns in each.
DIMENSION X(5) READ(5,100)X(1),X(2),X(3),X(4),X(5) WRITE(6,101)X(1),X(2),X(3),X(4),X(5) or DIMENSION X(5) READ(5,100)X WRITE(6,101)X	A table X is reserved with five locations. Values are assigned to each of the five locations by the READ statement and then written on the output device. Note that both sets of statements are equivalent in that the data values are assigned to the same table locations. In the second set, when the specific subscripts are omitted, the number of locations reserved in the DIMENSION dictates the number of values read and written.
DIMENSION X(4) . . . I=1 WRITE(6,200)X(I),X(I+1),X(I+2),X(I+3)	The sample serves to illustrate only that the expressions I+1, I+2, and I+3 are permissible subscripts for referencing table locations.
DIMENSION NOB(100) DO 1 I=1,25 NOB(I)=0 1 CONTINUE	Although a table NOB has been reserved with 100 locations, only the first 25 locations are accessed by the statements in the loop. However, by changing the number of times the loop is performed, all 100 locations can be utilized.

THE DO, CONTINUE, AND DIMENSION STATEMENTS

	Program Statements	Description
	DIMENSION X(2000) DATA X/2000*0./	Table X is established with 2000 locations. All the locations are set equal to zero at compile time by use of the DATA statement.
6	DIMENSION X(3,4),Y(3,4) DO 6 I=1,3 DO 6 J=1,4 READ(5,100)X(I,J) Y(I,J)=X(I,J)**2.56728 CONTINUE	Two tables X and Y are established with 12 locations each. Individual values of X are read into the program and then raised to the 2.56728 power. The results are stored in the corresponding elements of Table Y.
1	DIMENSION SALES(100,12) . . . SUM=0. DO 1 I=1,100 SUM=SUM+SALES(I,5)	Assuming that values have been assigned properly to the table SALES, the short DO loop calculates the sum of the quantities found in the fifth column of each row, that is, SALES(1,5)+SALES(2,5)+⋯+SALES(100,5)

Figure 6-5 Common errors that occur with DIMENSION statements.

	Program Statements	Description
472	DIMENSION X(N),Y(20.)	Labels are not permitted as part of the DIMENSION statement, nor can variable names (N) and real constants be used to reserve the number of locations for a table. Unsigned integer constants must be inserted in place. A correct entry would be DIMENSION X(10),Y(20)
	DIMENSION XSQ(5) YSQ(5) VARIABLE(100)	The table names XSQ, YSQ, and VARIABLE must be separated by commas in the statement. Also, VARIABLE contains too many characters. A correct entry would be DIMENSION XSQ(5),YSQ(5),VAR(100)
	DIMENSION OBS(3) READ(5,100)OBS(1),OBS(2),OBS(3),OBS(4)	Only three locations have been reserved for Table OBS in the DIMENSION statement. The READ statement contains reference to the fourth location OBS(4). Because the DIMENSION statement does not allow for four values, an error results. A correct entry would be DIMENSION OBS(4)

Figure 6-5 Common errors that occur with DIMENSION statements *(cont'd)*.

	Program Statements	Description

100	READ(5,101) VALUE(4)
	DIMENSION VALUE(10)
		The DIMENSION statement appears in the program after the executable READ statement. An error results since the DIMENSION statement must precede all executable statements. A correct entry would be
		    DIMENSION VALUE(10)
		    READ(5,101) VALUE(4)

	DIMENSION X(3,2) . . . Z=X(5)*6.113	A two-dimensional array X, with six locations, is established by the DIMENSION statement. In the calculation of Z, reference is made to the fifth location in Table X. Thus, a specification conflict occurs. A correct entry would be Z=X(2,2)*6.113

	DIMENSION A(2,4)
	.
	.
	A(5,1) = 5*6**(M+2)
		The error in this sample is that the subscript 5 points to a nonexistent row. A correct entry would be
		    DIMENSION A(2,4)
		    .
		    .
		    .
		    A(1,1) = 5*6**(M+2)
		Note also that the integer expression is converted to a real variable in the assignment.

	DIMENSION ZT(6)
	.
	.
	.
	ZT = ZT*2.81281
	DIMENSION ZT(12)
		The assignment statement causes a specification conflict error. The entire Table ZT can be referenced only in a READ or WRITE statement. To multiply each item in Table ZT by the constant 2.81281, a DO loop is required:
		    DIMENSION ZT(6)
		    .
		    .
		    DO 1 I=1,6
		  1 ZT(I) = ZT(I)*2.81281
		Also, a variable can be listed only in one DIMENSION statement. Thus, the second reference to ZT must be omitted.

A more detailed discussion is required for two specific cases:

(A) DIMENSION X(2,3)
      DO 1 I = 1,2
      DO 1 J = 1,3
1   READ(5,10)X(I,J)

(B) DIMENSION X(2,3)
      READ(5,10) X

In Example (A), the values are read into the table in the order: X(1,1), X(1,2), X(1,3), X(2,1), X(2,2), and X(2,3). Thus, the columns in the first row are completed first and then the second row is assigned values. However, when the entire table is read according to Example (B), the order of assignment is X(1,1), X(2,1), X(1,2), X(2,2), X(1,3), and X(2,3); that is, the columns are processed first. Ordinarily, these rules do not cause the programmer problems, but it is necessary to be aware of them. The ideas also apply to the printing of tables. Thus, when the statements

DIMENSION BE(3,2)
.
.
.
WRITE(6,100)BE

appear in a program, the locations are printed in the order BE(1,1), BE(2,1), BE(3,1), BE(1,2), BE(2,2), and BE(3,2).

The DIMENSION statement and subscripted variables are an important part of programming when there is a need to store data that will be used over and over within one program. In addition to the SALES and STATISTICS problems, two other samples will be discussed.

DIMENSION Exercises

1   Identify the table name, mode, total number of locations reserved, and number of rows and columns established by DIMENSION statements (a) to (d):
    (a)   DIMENSION H(6), IHR(165)
    (b)   DIMENSION ZER(3,16), TOTAL(72,2)
    (c)   DIMENSION LOB(5,4), LOC(4,4), ALOC(3,4)
    (d)   DIMENSION K(4), AL(43,13), BL(6,7), K2(17)

2   Supply the DIMENSION statement that will reserve the number of locations and the mode type required:
   (a)   Establish a table that can store a maximum of 25 integer values.
   (b)   Establish a matrix that can store up to 4 years of real data, by month and by year. (Note: A total of 48 locations is necessary.)
   (c)   Establish an array that can store a maximum of 15 real values for each of 6 products.
   (d)   Establish tables that can store 50 real values for inventory balance and 50 integer inventory codes.

3   In the following samples, sketch a table or an array with the specified number of locations (determined from the DIMENSION statement). Enter values in the proper location in each table as indicated by the program.

   (a)   DIMENSION X(5)
               DATA X(1),X(3),X(5)/1.5,2.4,3.3/
   (b)   DIMENSION ALPHA(3)
               DATA ALPHA/2HNO, 3HYES, 4HPOST/
   (c)   DIMENSION I57(6)
               DO 2 K = 1000,1005
         2   I57(K−999) = K
   (d)   DIMENSION IE(3,4)
               DO 7 J = 1,3
               DO 7 K = 1,4,2
         7   IE(I,J) = J*K

4   Indicate and correct errors in DIMENSION statements (a) to (d):
   (a)   READ(5,20)N
               DIMENSION X(N), Y(N), Z(N)
   (b)   DIMENSION X(12)
               READ(5,70)X
               .
               .
               .
               DIMENSION X(5,6)
               READ(5,75)X
   (c)   123   DIMENSION ZEBRA(6,100)
         124   DIMENSION BEBRA(6,100)
   (d)   DIMENSION TAPS(3,15)
               DO 4 I = 1,15
               DO 4 J = 1,3
         4   TAPS(I,J) = 0.

THE DO, CONTINUE, AND DIMENSION STATEMENTS

In the SALES problem, only a minor use for the DIMENSION statement will be shown. More useful techniques will be illustrated in the other sample programs. The problem definition remains the same as that for SALES-14. Hence, Flowchart 6-4 resembles Flowchart 6-1. The program, including the DIMENSION statement, is

**6-5
Program
Sample
SALES TAX**

```
C PROGRAM SALES-15
C THIS PROGRAM COMPUTES THE SALES TAX FOR A NUMBER OF ITEMS
C
        DIMENSION DATE(2)
        READ(5,100)DATE,N
        WRITE(6,400)DATE
        DO 14 I = 1, N
        READ(5,101)SALES, RATE
        SALETX = SALES * RATE
        WRITE(6,401)SALES, RATE,SALETX
14      CONTINUE
100     FORMAT(2A4,I3)
101     FORMAT(F8.2,F5.3)
400     FORMAT(21H1SALES REPORT   DATED ,2A4/8H0   SALES,5X,8HTAX RATE,5X,9H
       1SALES TAX/)
401     FORMAT(1X,F8.2,3X,F8.3,5X,F8.2)
        STOP
        END
```

Note that the only addition is the DIMENSION statement and the only revision involves the reading and writing of the report date. The two variables DAY and YEAR are replaced by one, DATE. Since it is dimensioned with two locations, the same effect results. However, note that the computer executes this new version faster because only one variable is referenced in the READ and WRITE. Supplying the data from program SALES-14, the output appears identical.

```
05-12-76  5
1000.00 .04
 857.67 .04
 628.43 .045
1575.50 .04
 175.64 .045
```

```
SALES REPORT   DATED 05-12-76

   SALES     TAX RATE     SALES TAX

  1000.00     0.040         40.00
   857.67     0.040         34.31
   628.43     0.045         28.28
  1575.50     0.040         63.02
   175.64     0.045          7.90
```

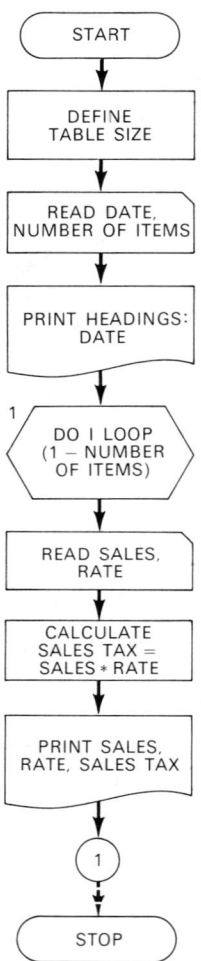

Flowchart 6-4 SALES TAX—DIMENSION statement.

For the STATISTICS problem, assume that only one large group of data is to be summed and averaged. Assume also that once the average is calculated and printed, the input values are to be printed in order from highest to lowest, regardless of their input order. The first part of the problem can be solved easily; however, the second part requires a programming technique called *sorting*.

A sample program showing sorting with switching will be discussed first and then incorporated in the STATISTICS problem.

**6-6
Program
Sample
STATISTICS**

Given data on one card as

14 -23 62 35 -7

and the statements

```
          DIMENSION IX(5)
          READ(5,100) IX
100       FORMAT(5I3)
```

Table IX would appear in storage as

IX

(1)	14
(2)	-23
(3)	62
(4)	35
(5)	-7

The purpose of sorting is to rearrange the data in either ascending or descending order. After the sort has been executed, Table IX should appear in storage as

IX

(1)	62
(2)	35
(3)	14
(4)	-7
(5)	-23

The method begins by searching for the largest value in the table by comparing the value in the first location against all the other locations; that is, $IX(1) \geq IX(2)$, $IX(1) \geq IX(3)$, and so on. If the first location is smaller than the one it is compared with, the two values are switched around in the table. The following statements make the comparisons and the switches, when necessary:

```
        DO 1 J = 2, 5
        IF(IX(1).GE.IX(J))GO TO 1
        ITEMP = IX(1)
        IX(1) = IX(J)
        IX(J) = ITEMP
1       CONTINUE
```

where ITEMP is a variable that temporarily stores the value of the first location during the switch process. When completed, these statements would place the largest value in the first location of IX

	IX
(1)	62
(2)	−23
(3)	14
(4)	35
(5)	−7

The method is repeated by searching for the second largest value and placing it in the second location of the table; that is, $IX(2) \geq IX(3), IX(2) \geq IX(4)$, and so on. The statements

```
        DO 2 J = 3, 5
        IF(IX(2).GE.IX(J))GO TO 2
        ITEMP = IX(2)
        IX(2) = IX(J)
        IX(J) = ITEMP
2       CONTINUE
```

accomplish this task, and IX would be stored as

	IX
(1)	62
(2)	35
(3)	−23
(4)	14
(5)	−7

The logic is repeated until the table is completely sorted. To print the sorted values, the statements

```
        WRITE(6,101)IX
101     FORMAT(1X,6I5)
```

are required.

However, the sorting technique above can be shortened considerably by using nested loops as

```
        DO 10 K = 1, 4
        N = K+1
        DO 10 J = N, 5
        IF(IX(K).GE.IX(J))GO TO 10
        ITEMP = IX(K)
        IX(K) = IX(J)
        IX(J) = ITEMP
10      CONTINUE
```

where K is assigned values of 1 to 4 and J is assigned values up to 5, depending on K. When K is 1, these statements are exactly equivalent to the DO-1 loop shown above; when K is 2, they are equal to the DO-2 loop. The nested loops, therefore, reduce the number of statements in the sort significantly. Flowchart 6-5 summarizes the complete program steps. A final note concerning the sorting technique: all the values must be read into the table *before* the sorting loops can be started. Thus, the DIMENSION statement is required to store the values before the sort can be initiated.

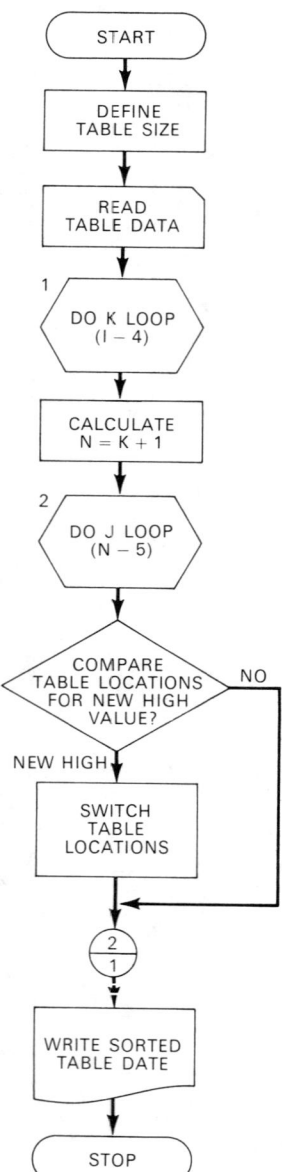

Flowchart 6-5 Sort routine—DIMENSION statement.

The sort routine can now be placed in the STATISTICS problem. Flowchart 6-6 identifies the logic required. The statements for STATISTICS-14 are

THE DO, CONTINUE, AND DIMENSION STATEMENTS

```
C PROGRAM STATISTICS-14
C THIS PROGRAM COMPUTES THE AVERAGE FOR A VARIABLE NUMBER OF VALUES
C AND THEN PRINTS THEM IN ORDER FROM LARGEST TO SMALLEST.
      DIMENSION VALUE(100)
      WRITE(6,300)
      SUM = 0.
      READ(5,201)NOV
      DO 1 J = 1, NOV
      READ(5,200)VALUE(J)
      SUM = SUM + VALUE(J)
1     CONTINUE
      XNOV = NOV
      AVG = SUM/XNOV
      WRITE(6,301)   NOV,SUM,AVG
C START SORT ROUTINE
      NV = NOV - 1
      DO 3 K = 1, NV
      N = K + 1
      DO 3 J = N, NOV
      IF(VALUE(K).GE.VALUE(J))GO TO 3
      TEMP = VALUE(K)
      VALUE(K) = VALUE(J)
      VALUE(J) = TEMP
3     CONTINUE
      WRITE(6,303)
      DO 4 J = 1, NOV
4     WRITE(6,304)VALUE(J)
C
200   FORMAT(F5.1)
201   FORMAT(I3)
300   FORMAT(@1NUMBER IN GROUP    SUM    AVERAGE@/)
301   FORMAT(7X,I3,5X,F8.1,1X,F8.1/)
303   FORMAT(@0SORTED VALUES-LARGEST TO SMALLEST@/)
304   FORMAT(1X,F8.1)
      STOP
      END
```

In this program, the DIMENSION establishes a table with a maximum of 100 locations, although it is not necessary to use all 100. The first part of the program reads the values into the table, accumulates the sum, and computes and prints the average. Since the individual values must still be sorted, a subscripted variable places the numbers in the table so they may be referenced again.

The second part of the program sorts the data in descending order. The constants representing the terminal values in the DO loops have been replaced with variables to make the program flexible. The final part prints the data. Six data values, the first identifying the number of values in the group, and the output follow:

```
005
 79.9
 87.3
 68.2
 69.2
 87.8
```

```
NUMBER IN GROUP    SUM     AVERAGE

       5          392.4     78.5
```

SORTED VALUES-LARGEST TO SMALLEST

```
    87.8
    87.3
    79.9
    69.2
    68.2
```

One final change improves this program. Immediately after the first READ, insert the statements

```
        IF(NOV.LE.100)GO TO 1
        WRITE(6,402)NOV
        STOP
1       SUM = 0.
```

where FORMAT 402 contains a message to reflect the fact that the table is limited to 100 values. In the case where NOV is greater than 100, the program will print the error message and terminate. If a larger table is needed, the DIMENSION and logical IF statements can be revised accordingly. These statements constitute what is known as a "built-in" error routine that allows the programmer to control execution.

6-7 Miscellaneous DIMENSION Samples

Three miscellaneous samples that are solved efficiently by using matrices are added in this chapter. The three samples concern two mathematical operations and one inventory application. Consider two matrices A and B and the sum

	A (1)	(2)	(3)	(4)
(1)	6.1	4.3	9.2	7.5
(2)	8.3	4.8	6.6	7.9

THE DO, CONTINUE, AND DIMENSION STATEMENTS 167

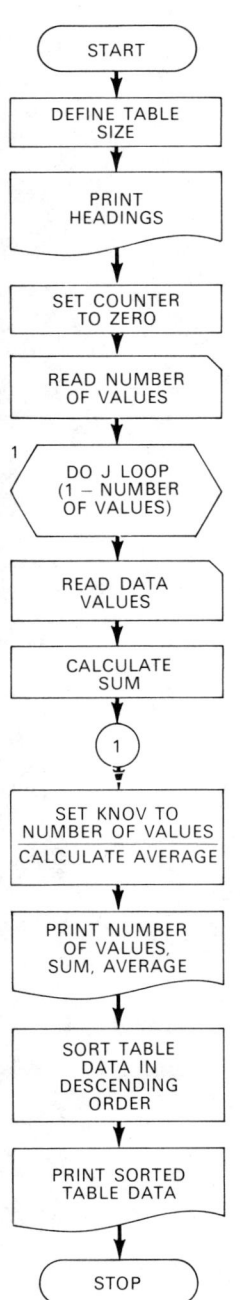

Flowchart 6-6 STATISTICS—Sort routine.

	B			
	(1)	(2)	(3)	(4)
(1)	22.1	21.1	28.7	27.6
(2)	14.3	9.8	12.6	13.4

	A + B			
	(1)	(2)	(3)	(4)
(1)	28.2	25.4	36.9	35.1
(2)	22.6	14.6	19.2	21.3

of their respective elements. A short program including a DIMENSION and nested DO statements facilitates the calculation of the sum. Flowchart 6-7 identifies the logic; the needed statements are

```
C PROGRAM FOR MATRIX ADDITION
      DIMENSION A(2,4), B(2,4), AB(2,4)
      READ(5,100)A,B
      DO 1 I = 1,2
      DO 1 J = 1,4
1     AB(I,J) = A(I,J) + B(I,J)
      WRITE(6,200) AB
100   FORMAT(16F5.1)
200   FORMAT(@1THE SUM OF MATRICES A AND B IS@//( F8.1/))
      STOP
      END
```

The input and output are the same as shown in the matrices above, so they are omitted here. With minor changes, the program can be made flexible. Likewise, matrix subtraction is possible with a sign change.

Matrix multiplication is also easily performed by storing the input data in arrays and including three nested loops. Consider arrays K, L

THE DO, CONTINUE, AND DIMENSION STATEMENTS

	K (1) (2)			L (1) (2) (3)			K × L				K × L		
(1)	2	6	(1)	9	8	5	2·9+6·7	2·8+6·8	2·5+6·6		60	64	46
(2)	3	4	(2)	7	8	6	3·9+4·7	3·8+4·8	3·5+4·6	=	55	56	39
(3)	7	5					7·9+5·7	7·8+8·5	7·5+5·6		98	96	65

and their product. In matrix multiplication, each new element KXL(I,J) is the sum of the products of row I entries times column J entries. For example, matrix element KXL(1,1) is equal to K(1,1)∗L(1,1) + K(1,2)∗L(2,1). The resulting product matrix will have as many rows as K and as many columns as L.

Flowchart 6-8 and the necessary program statements are

```
C PROGRAM FOR MATRIX MULTIPLICATION
      DIMENSION K(3,2), L(2,3), KXL(3,3)
      DATA KXL/9*0/
      READ(5,100)K, L
      DO 1 I1 = 1, 3
      DO 1 I2 = 1, 3
      DO 1 I3 = 1, 2
1     KXL(I1,I2) = KXL(I1,I2)+K(I1,I3)*L(I3,I2)
      WRITE(6,200)KXL
100   FORMAT(12I3)
200   FORMAT(@1THE PRODUCT OF K * L IS@//9I6)
      STOP
      END
```

The program can be made flexible by inserting appropriate variables in place of constants. To attempt to solve this problem without the use of subscripted variables would be a significant task. It is important for the reader to recognize applications similar to these, where the problem is simplified by using tables and the index in a DO loop to reference the data.

Another common problem solved by table manipulation concerns inventory records. The two types of data normally found in an inventory file are (1) an identification number for each particular part, and (2) the number of units in stock. Schematically, the data would reasonably be aligned in tables as

	ID No. (1)	No. of Units (2)
(1)	72	15606
(2)	321	95705
⋮	⋮	⋮

where the first column contains each ID number and the second column the number of units for the respective item in column 1. The question to be solved by this example is, "How many units of item 321 are in stock?" without printing the entire inventory. The problem can be solved by comparing the data value 321 with each ID number in the first column of the table. When

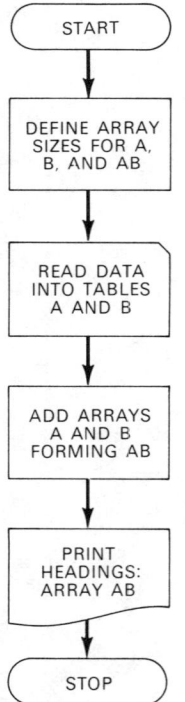

Flowchart 6-7 Matrix addition—DIMENSION statement.

THE DO, CONTINUE, AND DIMENSION STATEMENTS

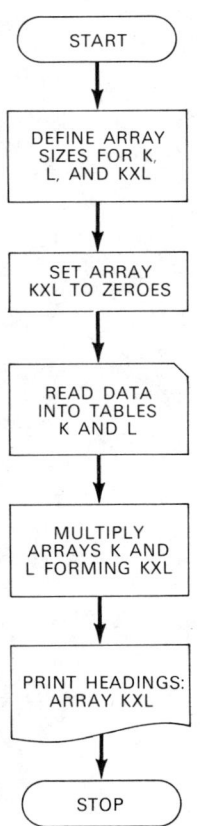

Flowchart 6-8 Matrix multiplication—DIMENSION statement.

the ID number 321 is found in the table, the units in the respective second column are printed. Flowchart 6-9 details the logic required for a *table lookup* solution. The statements capable of processing 500 inventory items are

```
C TABLE SEARCH - INVENTORY
      DIMENSION INV(500,2)
      READ(5,100) INV
1     READ(5,100,END=4) ITEM
      DO 2 I = 1, 500
      IF(ITEM.EQ.INV(I,1))GO TO 3
2     CONTINUE
      WRITE(6,200) ITEM
      GO TO 1
3     WRITE(6,201) ITEM, INV(I,2)
      GO TO 1
```

```
100     FORMAT(2I5)
200     FORMAT(@1ITEM NOT FOUND IN FILE@, I7)
201     FORMAT(@ FOR ID NO@,I6, @ THE BALANCE IS@,I6)
4       STOP
        END
```

In this sample, the first READ loads the table INV, and the second reads the item number to be located in the table. Note that the END-sl option is used to terminate processing. In the DO loop, when an equal condition is found, the WRITE labeled 3 prints the item number and the number of units in stock. Recall that transferring out of a DO loop is permissible. If the item is not found in the table, the DO loop is completed

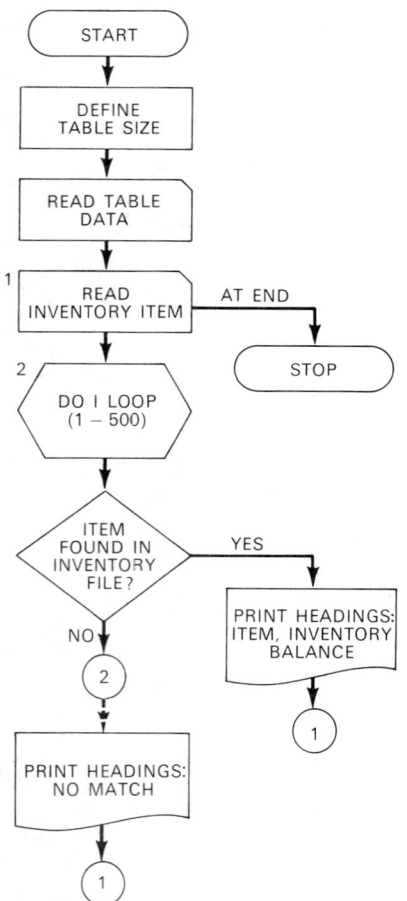

Flowchart 6-9 Inventory table search—DIMENSION statement.

THE DO, CONTINUE, AND DIMENSION STATEMENTS

and the error message ITEM NOT FOUND IN FILE is printed. The message is the second type of error routine built into the sample programs.

6-8 Implied DO Loops in I/O

When reading, writing, or assigning initial values to arrays or tables, it is possible to combine features of the DO statement with a particular input/output instruction. The cominbation of the DO and an input/output statement together form an *implied* DO loop.

The general forms of the implied DO for one-dimensional arrays are

DATA(X(i),i=n_1,n_2,n_3)/n*0./
READ(5,100)(X(i),i=n_1,n_2,n_3)
WRITE(6,200)(X(i),i=n_1,n_2,n_3)

where it is assumed that the variable X has been dimensioned previously. The variable i serves as the subscript index, and n_1, n_2, and n_3 are the parameters of the implied DO, having the same significance as those in an explicit DO statement. Thus, n_1 is the initial value of the index, n_2 the terminal value, and n_3 the increment. In the general forms, the outer parentheses and the comma preceding the DO index are required. Two-dimensional arrays may also be assigned values by incorporating implied DO loops.

DATA((Y(i,j),i=n_1,n_2,n_3),j=m_1,m_2,m_3)/m*0./
READ(5,100)((Y(i,j),i=n_1,n_2,n_3),j=m_1,m_2,m_3)
WRITE(6,200)((Y(i,j),i=n_1,n_2,n_3),j=m_1,m_2,m_3)

where it is concluded that the variable Y has been dimensioned previously. In these forms, i is the row subscript and j the column subscript. The n parameters control the values of i (the rows), and the m parameters control the values of j (the columns). The inner implied DO with subscript i is processed first; the j loop is the outer implied DO. Thus, values are assigned by columns in this form. Alternately, if the statements were constructed as

DATA((Y(i,j),j=n_1,n_2,n_3),i=m_1,m_2,m_3)
READ(5,100)((Y(i,j),j=n_1,n_2,n_3),i=m_1,m_2,m_3)
WRITE(6,200)((Y(i,j),j=n_1,n_2,n_3),i=m_1,m_2,m_3)

i is still the row and j the column subscripts. However, since the j loop is now the innder loop, the rows would be assigned values first. Figures 6-6 and 6-7 illustrate various examples.

Figure 6-6 Examples of implied DO loops.[1]

	Program Statements	Description
	DATA(X(K),K=1,3)/3*0./	The effect of the statement is to assign a value of zero to each of the first three locations in Table X.
	DATA(Y(K),K=1,7,3)/3*0./	The value zero is assigned to three locations in Table Y, Y(1), Y(4), and Y(7) because the index K takes on values of 1, 4, and 7.
72	READ(5,100)(CNT(I),I=1,3)	Three values are processed by the READ statement: CNT(1), CNT(2), and CNT(3). The implied DO causes the variable I to take on the successive values of 1, 2, and 3. Observe that the incremental value may be omitted because a 1 is assumed.
	READ(5,101)(ACT(J),J=1,5,2)	Three values are processed by the READ statement: ACT(1), ACT(3), and ACT(5). The implied DO causes the variable J to take on the successive values of 1, 3, and 5.
83	READ(5,102)(X(I),I=1,N),(Y(I),I=1,M)	N plus M data values are processed by the READ statement. The first group is assigned to the first N locations in Table X; the next group is assigned to the first M locations in Table Y. The two implied DOs in the statement dictate the order in which the values are assigned.
	WRITE(5,103)(X(1,J),J=1,4)	Four data values are outputted by the implied DO statement. The values referenced are located in a two-dimensional array identified as X. The locations referenced are X(1,1), X(1,2), X(1,3), and X(1,4).
	READ(5,104)(A(I),B(I),I=5,7)	A total of six values are processed by the one READ statement. Alternate data values are assigned to A and B because the parentheses surround both variables. Thus, the first two values are assigned to A(5) and B(5), the second two to A(6) and B(6), and the final two to A(7) and B(7).
	WRITE(6,10)((ARRAY(I,J),J=1,3),I=1,2)	A total of six values are processed by the one WRITE statement containing two implied DOs. A two-dimensional array is referenced first by the inner DO and second by the outer DO.

THE DO, CONTINUE, AND DIMENSION STATEMENTS

Program Statements	Description
	The output would reflect sequentially the contents of ARRAY(1,1), ARRAY(1,2), ARRAY(1,3), ARRAY(2,1), ARRAY(2,2), and, last, ARRAY(2,3). Note the contrast in the following example:
WRITE(6,11)((ARRAY(I,J),I=1,2),J=1,3)	Six values contained in a two-dimensional array are referenced by the implied DOs. The output would reflect sequentially the contents of ARRAY(1,1), ARRAY(2,1), ARRAY(1,2), ARRAY(2,2), ARRAY(1,3), and ARRAY(2,3).

[1] In each of these examples, appropriate DIMENSION statements must precede the statements shown.

Figure 6-7 Common errors that occur with implied DO loops.[1]

	Program Statements	Description
757	READ(5,100)CNT(I),I=1,3	The implied DO specification must be enclosed within a set of parentheses. Omission of the parentheses results in an error. A correct entry would be 757 READ(5,100) (CNT(I),I=1,3)
	WRITE(6,10)(TOT(J)J=1,4)	Commas must separate the implied DO parameters from the variable name of the table or array. A correct entry would be WRITE(6,10)(TOT(J),J=1,4)
	READ(5,101)(XSUM(A),A=1,5)	The implied DO variable index name must be integer mode. The variable A is real and hence in error. A correct entry would be READ(5,101)(XSUM(I),I=1,5)
	WRITE(6,11)(A(I,J),I=1,2,J=1,3)	As in the first two samples shown, commas and parentheses must be inserted in the proper locations. A correct entry would be WRITE(6,11)((A(I,J),I=1,2),J=1,3)

[1] In each of these examples, it is assumed that a properly constructed DIMENSION statement precedes the information shown.

Implied DO Exercises

1 Supply the DATA statement, containing implied DO loops, that will satisfy the following. Assume the statement

DIMENSION AB(5,12), IKT(32)
- (a) Assign zeros to the first three rows of Table AB.
- (b) Assign zeros to the odd-numbered locations in Table IKT and ones to the even-numbered locations.
- (c) Assign ones to the first column in Table AB.
- (d) Assign twos to the second column in Table AB.
- (e) Assign twelves to the twelfth column in Table AB.
- (f) Assign zeros to the first, fourth, seventh, and so forth locations in Table IKT.

2 Supply the READ and WRITE statements, containing implied DO loops, that will satisfy the following. Assume the statement
DIMENSION AX(10), BX(10), IKX(10,10)
- (a) Read seven values into the first seven locations of Table AX. Print only the first, third, fifth, and seventh locations.
- (b) With one READ, process 10 values so that the first, third, fifth, seventh, and ninth data values are assigned to the first five locations in Table BX while the remaining five are assigned to the first five locations in Table AX. Print the data in the order BX(1), BX(2), ..., BX(5), AX(1), AX(2), ..., AX(5).
- (c) Read 50 values into the odd-numbered rows of Table IKX. Assign the values to all the columns in the first row, then to all the columns in the third row, and so on. Print the data in the same order as it is read.
- (d) Read 50 values into the even-numbered rows of Table IKX. Assign the values to all the even rows in the first column, then to all the even rows in the second column, and so on. Print the data in the same order as it is read.
- (e) Read and print 30 data values in the order AX(1), BX(1), IKX(1,1), AX(2), BX(2), IKX(2,2),...,AX(10), BX(10), IKX(10,10).

3 Identify and correct errors contained in samples (a) to (g):
- (a) DIMENSION X(10)
  READ(5,10)(X(I),I=1,20,2)
- (b) DIMENSION A(100), B(100)
  READ(5,11)((A(I),B(I)),I=1,100)
- (c) DIMENSION Z(50)
  DATA((Z(I,J),I=1,5),J=1,10)/10*1.5,40*2.5/
- (d) DIMENSION T(3,4)
  DATA(T(K),K=1,12)/12*0.0/
- (e) DIMENSION SUM(M,N)
  .
  .
  .
  WRITE(6,200)((SUM(I,J),I=1,M),J=1,N)

(f) DIMENSION TAB(2,3)
.
.
.
WRITE(6,200)((TAB(I,J),I=1,3),J=1,2)
(g) DIMENSION AR(3,3)
.
.
.
WRITE(6,200)((AR(I,J),I=1,3,J=1,3))

6-9 Program Sample STATISTICS

In this section[1] the definition of the STATISTICS problem remains the same: Read a set of data values, calculate and print the sum and average, and print the input data in descending order. An implied DO loop will be used to read the data into the table before summing and sorting the values. An implied DO will also be used to print the sorted values. Flowchart 6-10 identifies the required logic. For brevity, the error routine detailed in Sec. 6-6 has been omitted here. The required statements are

```
C PROGRAM STATISTICS-15
C THIS PROGRAM COMPUTES THE AVERAGE FOR A VARIABLE NUMBER OF VALUES
C AND THEN PRINTS THEM IN ORDER FROM LARGEST TO SMALLEST.
      DIMENSION VALUE(100)
      WRITE(6,300)
      SUM = 0.
      READ(5,201)NOV,(VALUE(I),I=1,NOV)
      DO 1 J = 1, NOV
      SUM = SUM + VALUE(J)
1     CONTINUE
      XNOV = NOV
      AVG = SUM/XNOV
      WRITE(6,301)   NOV,SUM,AVG
C START SORT ROUTINE
      NV = NOV - 1
      DO 3 K = 1, NV
      N = K + 1
      DO 3 J = N, NOV
      IF(VALUE(K).GE.VALUE(J))GO TO 3
      TEMP = VALUE(K)
      VALUE(K) = VALUE(J)
      VALUE(J) = TEMP
3     CONTINUE
      WRITE(6,303) (VALUE(J),J=1, NOV)
```

[1] The SALES program is omitted here since the present definition of the problem does not facilitate the use of implied DO loops.

```
C
201    FORMAT(I3,(15F5.1))
300    FORMAT(@1NUMBER IN GROUP   SUM    AVERAGE@/)
301    FORMAT(7X,I3,5X,F8.1,1X,F8.1/)
303    FORMAT(@0SORTED VALUES-LARGEST TC SMALLEST@//(1X,10F5.1/))
       STOP
       END
```

Since the logic is very similar to that used in STATISTICS-14, the statements are essentially the same, with the exception of the READ and WRITE, where implied DO loops have been employed. The input data can be placed across the card by using this form, thereby increasing the speed in which the input data is processed. Likewise, the output can be written across the same line, speeding up the output process. Also, two fewer statements, a READ and a DO, are needed in this solution. New data, where the first value represents the number of items to sum and sort, plus the actual data, and the output follow:

```
6  71.8 61.4 98.6 45.8 47.7 78.4
```

```
NUMBER IN GROUP    SUM    AVERAGE
       6          403.7    67.3
```

SORTED VALUES-LARGEST TO SMALLEST

```
98.6 78.4 71.8 61.4 47.7 45.8
```

Particular attention should be focused on the two FORMAT statements that control the manner in which the input is read and the output written. Up to 15 values can be placed on each input card using label 201, and up to 10 items will be printed on each output line by employing label 303.

6-10 Miscellaneous Implied DO Samples

The same three samples illustrated in Sec. 6-7 will also be illustrated here, employing implied DO loops in the solution. In the matrix addition problem, the DIMENSION statement established three 2 × 4 arrays. However, to create a flexible program, sufficiently large matrices should be reserved in the DIMENSION statement. To include this idea, consider the following statements:

THE DO, CONTINUE, AND DIMENSION STATEMENTS

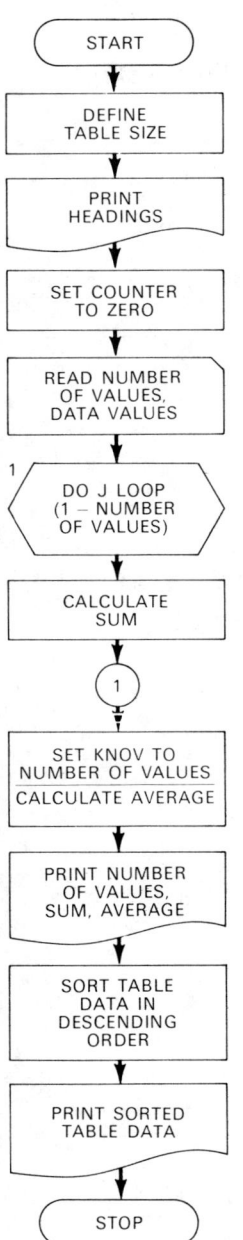

Flowchart 6-10 STATISTICS—Implied DO statements.

```
C PROGRAM FOR MATRIX ADDITION - REVISED
      DIMENSION A(50,50), B(50,50), AB(50,50)
      READ(5,100)M,N,((A(I,J),J=1,N), I=1,M),((B(I,J),J=1,N),I=1,M)
      DO 1 I = 1,M
      DO 1 J = 1,N
1     AB(I,J) = A(I,J) + B(I,J)
      WRITE(6,200)((AB(I,J),J=1,N),I=1,M)
100   FORMAT(2I5,(14F5.1))
200   FORMAT(@1THE SUM OF MATRICES A AND B IS@//(8F8.1/))
      STOP
      END
```

With the revised DIMENSION statement, the program is flexible now because it is possible to add the respective elements of two matrices, each with as many as 50 rows and 50 columns. In these statements, M represents the number of rows and N the number of columns in each array. The data is read into the tables A and B row-wise, that is, A(1,1), A(1,2), ..., A(1,M), A(2,1), ..., A(N,M), and similarly for B. The output is also printed in the same manner because of the construction form of the implied DO loops in the READ and WRITE statements. Both the input and output are omitted here. However, the chapter questions will ask the reader to supply values for the program.

The second matrix sample concerned multiplication of two arrays. As shown in Sec. 6-7, it is also inflexible because of the DIMENSION statement. By increasing the number of locations reserved and also replacing the DO parameter constants with variables, the desired capability can be programmed. The new program fits the description.

```
C PROGRAM FOR MATRIX MULTIPLICATION - REVISED
      DIMENSION K(40,40), L(40,40), KXL(40,40)
      DATA KXL/1600*0/
      READ(5,100)NR1, NC1, NC2
      READ(5,101)((K(I,J),J=1,NC1),I=1,NR1)
      READ(5,101)((L(I,J),J=1,NC2),I=1,NC1)
      DO 1 I1 = 1, NR1
      DO 1 I2 = 1, NC2
      DO 1 I3 = 1, NC1
1     KXL(I1,I2) = KXL(I1,I2)+K(I1,I3)*L(I3,I2)
      WRITE(6,200)((KXL(I,J),J=1,NC2),I=1,NR1)
100   FORMAT(3I5)
101   FORMAT(16I5)
200   FORMAT(@1THE PRODUCT OF K * L IS@//(9I6))
      STOP
      END
```

THE DO, CONTINUE, AND DIMENSION STATEMENTS

Two large matrices, each with as many as 40 rows and columns, can be multiplied by using this version. The DIMENSION reserves the array area, and the DATA statement is very efficient in this program because 1,600 locations are initialized to zero at compilation time. In the first READ, the matrix sizes are defined. The variable NR1 represents the number of rows in the first array; NC1 represents the number of columns in the first array *and also* the number of rows in the second matrix. To conform to the rules of matrix multiplication, the first matrix must have as many columns as the second matrix has rows, defined above as NC1. The final parameter NC2 represents the number of columns in the second matrix. The new product matrix will have NR1 rows and NC2 columns.

The next two READ statements assign values to the arrays row-wise; the three nested loops perform the multiplication. The WRITE statement prints the resulting matrix by row. As before, the input and output are omitted.

The final sample relates to the inventory file containing an identification number and the number of units in stock. To construct a viable program, a sufficiently large table should be reserved and the actual number of items in the file defined. Consider the minor revision to the table search program

```
C TABLE SEARCH - INVENTORY - REVISED
      DIMENSION INV(1000,2)
      READ(5,100) NI,(INV(I,1),INV(I,2),I=1,NI)
1     READ(5,100,END=4) ITEM
      DO 2 I = 1, NI
      IF(ITEM.EQ.INV(I,1))GO TO 3
2     CONTINUE
      WRITE(6,200) ITEM
      GO TO 1
3     WRITE(6,201) ITEM, INV(I,2)
      GO TO 1
100   FORMAT(I5,(2I5))
200   FORMAT(@ITEM NOT FOUND IN FILE@, I7)
201   FORMAT(@ FOR ID NO@,I6, @ THE BALANCE IS@,I6)
4     STOP
      END
```

Only three changes are included in the program: (1) a revised DIMENSION permits up to 1,000 inventory items; (2) the READ is modified to process a variable number (NI) of inventory items; and (3) the terminal DO parameter is changed to the variable NI.

The chapter questions will ask the reader to supply input data to run and analyze the program output.

6-11 Summary

The statements listed in this chapter are very powerful commands. The DO statement permits the building of loops in a convenient manner. The value of the index in the DO can also be used inside the loop for various purposes, the most important being its value as a subscript. The DIMENSION statement establishes tables and matrices, where large groups of data values can be retained individually. The use of matrices is particularly efficient in solving many mathematical problems. Finally, DO loops can be combined with input/output commands to form implied DO statements.

Questions

1. Supply arbitrary data values for program STATISTICS-13 that will process three groups of data with 11 numbers in the first group, 12 in the second, and 10 in the third.

2. Modify program STATISTICS-14 to print the data in ascending order, from smallest to largest.

3. Revise the statements in the matrix addition program found in Sec. 6-7 to add two 4 × 5 arrays. Supply your own data values and run the program.

4. Revise the statements in the matrix multiplication program found in Sec. 6-7 to multiply a 3 × 4 array by a 4 × 5 array. Supply your own data values and run the program.

5. Supply data for the matrix addition program found in Sec. 6-10 that will add two 3 × 7 arrays. Run the program with your data.

6. Supply data for the matrix multiplication program found in Sec. 6-10 that will multiply a 2 × 7 array by a 7 × 3 array. Run the program with your data.

7. Supply $m \times 2$ data values to load the Table INV in the inventory program found in Sec. 6-10. Supply additional values to do a table lookup. Run the program with your data.

8. Write separate solutions to the following mathematical problems:
    (a) Read data into an $m \times n$ matrix, multiply each element by 0.025, and print the results.
    (b) Read data into a 4 × 5 matrix named X, store the sum of the elements in the first row in location X(1,6), store the

THE DO, CONTINUE, AND DIMENSION STATEMENTS

sum of the elements in the second row in location X(2,6), and so on.

(c) As a continuation of (b), store the sum of the elements in the first column in location X(5,1), the sum of the second column in X(5,2), and so on. The grand total for all the elements should be placed in X(5,6).
(d) Find the largest element in an $n \times n$ matrix.
(e) Invert a 3×3 matrix.
(f) Create an identity matrix for a 5×5 array.

9 Write a program to process the following data and print the desired output. On each data card, the first 20 columns contain a student's name. Five grades are in the next 20 columns. Read the student's name into a table (see SALES-15) and each of the five grades into another table. Replace the lowest grade with a zero, sum the grades, and calculate the average grade (SUM÷4). Print the name and the average grade.

10 Sales by month and year for ZEBRAY Co. are stored in a 5×12 table. Net profit by month and year are stored in another 5×12 table. Write a program to compute the net profit as a percent of sales for each of the 60 table elements and print the results with the heading:

NET PROFIT AS A PERCENT OF SALES
YEAR JAN FEB MAR APR MAY JUN JUL AUG SEP OCT NOV DEC

For example, if sales are $1,250 and net profit for the same month and year is $100, net profit as a percent of sales is (100/1,250) × 100, or 8 percent. Supply your own data for the two tables.

11 Using the sales data from Question 10, generate another 5×12 array that stores the manufacturing cost of sales per month. Subtract each of the cost figures from the sales data, and print the answers in the same form as above. Supply your own data for the cost of sales.

12 Again using the sales data from Question 10, compute the average sales for each year, the average sales for the five January months, the five February months, and so on.

13 Revise Questions 7 and 8 from Chap. 5, using subscripted variables in the solution. Use the actual grade as an index for accumulating the totals required.

14 An instructor at Werdo College wanted to divide his class arbitrarily into four groups. The four groups are: (a) male working student; (b) male full-time student; (c) female working student; and (d) female full-time student, organized in array form as

	Male	Female
Working student		
Full-time student		

Supply 150 sets of arbitrary data in the form: M for male, F for female; and W for working student, F for full-time student. Write a program that will read for each student the sex and work category; analyze the data (via the program), and count the number of students that fall into each of the four groups; and print the final totals. Include error routines in your program.

15 Modify Question 14 to permit numeric codes (1 for male, 2 for female, and 1 for working, 2 for full-time student) to be substituted in place of the M, F, W, and F used. (Hint: This problem should be much shorter because direct subscripts can be used for the counting.)

SPECIFICATION STATEMENTS 7

The specification or declaration statements provide the compiler program with information concerning the type of data to be processed in a particular program application. An example of a specification statement is the DIMENSION command listed in the previous chapter; five additional specification commands are discussed in this chapter.

7-1 INTEGER-type Specification

Thus far, variable type or mode has been specified by the first character in the variable name. Hence, variables such as A, B, C, and D are by default assumed to be real mode, and the variables I, J, and K are implied integer mode. The purpose of the INTEGER specification command is to declare the fixed-point type or mode for a particular variable by name rather than by its initial letter. Additionally, array information (dimension sizes) may be included in the statement. The general forms of the statement are

INTEGER [list of variables, separated by commas]

or

INTEGER [variable (constant), variable (constant)]

or

INTEGER [variable (constant, constant), variable (constant, constant)] where the first form refers either to unsubscripted variable names or the names of arrays, the second to one-dimensional arrays, and the third to two-dimensional arrays. In general, the statement replaces or follows the DIMENSION command but precedes the rest of the program. For example,

INTEGER A,B,C,D

declares that the four variables listed are integer mode, overriding the implied real designation. But if the two statements

DIMENSION A(50),B(50)
INTEGER A, B, C, D

are contained in a program, A and B in the INTEGER-type statement refer to the tables defined in the DIMENSION, and C and D are unsubscripted variable names, all four being designated as integer mode. The second form is illustrated in the statement

INTEGER TOTAL(100)

defining an integer-type table containing a maximum of 100 locations. When this form is used, it is invalid to precede the statement with a DIMENSION. Thus, the following is invalid:

DIMENSION SUM(50)
INTEGER SUM(50)

The final form defines a two-dimensional array as integer mode

INTEGER XY(3,4),ZY(3,5)

or

DIMENSION XY(3,4),ZY(3,5)
INTEGER XY, ZY

Figures 7-1 and 7-2 contain examples of the INTEGER-type statement plus examples of the REAL specification statement discussed in the next section.[1]

7-2 REAL-type Specification

The REAL specification command declares the floating-point type or mode for a particular variable by name, overriding the mode implied by the initial character. Dimension sizes may be

---

[1] The program samples illustrating the INTEGER and REAL statements are shown in Secs. 7-4 and 7-5.

SPECIFICATION STATEMENTS

Figure 7-1 Examples of INTEGER and REAL specification statements.

Program Statements	Description
INTEGER SUM, SUMS	The INTEGER specification statement declares that the two variables SUM and SUMS are used to store integer numbers, thus negating the implied real mode.
DIMENSION APPLE(100) INTEGER X,Y,APPLE	The DIMENSION statement reserves 100 locations for Table APPLE. The INTEGER specification defines the fixed-point mode for the unsubscripted variables X and Y plus the Table APPLE.
INTEGER ARRAY(2,3) . . . LBT = ARRAY(2,1)*6	The specification statement declares that the Table ARRAY is integer mode, but it also declares the size of the matrix as having two rows and three columns. In the assignment of LBT, it appears that there is a mixed-mode expression. However, because of the declaration command, the statement is a valid integer expression.
INTEGER A/5/, B(6)/6*0/	An option permitted with some FORTRAN compilers allows variables to be assigned values in the specification statement. The variable A is assigned a value of 5, and all six locations in Table B are set equal to zero.
REAL KN,NOB(5,12)	By implied declaration, KN and NOB are integer mode. However, the REAL specification statement overrides the implicit mode and establishes them as real variables. The size of the array NOB is declared as having 5 rows and 12 columns, or a total of 60 locations.
DIMENSION KLN(3,3) REAL KLN,MM,NN	The REAL specification statement identifies the floating-point mode for the matrix KLN and the unsubscripted variables MM and NN.
REAL LMN . . . READ(5,100)LMN 100 FORMAT(F10.2)	The declaration statement defines the mode of LMN as real. Thus, the READ statement with FORMAT 100 is valid. If the declaration command were omitted, an error would occur when attempting to read an integer variable LMN with a F10.2 format code. The same rules apply when writing output.

Figure 7-2 Common errors that occur with INTEGER and REAL specification statements.

Program Statements	Description
15 INTEGER S,T,U	Statement labels are not permitted as part of the specification commands. A correct entry would be INTEGER S,T,U

INTEGER SUM
.
.
.
.
SUM=A*B+IC
	The implied mode of SUM has been overridden and denoted as INTEGER. Its use in the assignment statement involves real variables A and B plus IC. A mixed-mode expression results. Correct entries would be either
	    INTEGER SUM,A,B
	    or
	    SUM=IA*IB+IC

INTEGER I,J,A
REAL X,Y,M
	The two statements listed do not contain errors. However, it is unnecessary to declare I and J as integer mode and X and Y as real because their mode is implied as such. A more logical set of entries is
	    INTEGER A
	    REAL M

DIMENSION X(3,2),Y(2,2)
INTEGER A,B,X(3,2)
	The array size of variable X can not be defined in both the DIMENSION and INTEGER statements. A correct entry would be
	    DIMENSION X(3,2),Y(2,2)
	    INTEGER A,B,X
	where A and B are unsubscripted variables and X is an array.

REAL NOB NOT NOC
.
.
.
NOB = NOT + 7*NOC
	Two errors are contained in this sample. First, the variables in the REAL declaration must be separated by commas. Second, the assignment statement is a mixed-mode expression as constructed because the variables are real and the constant 7 integer. Correct entries would be
	    REAL NOB, NOT, NOC
	    .
	    .
	    .
	    NOB = NOT + 7.0*NOC

included in the statement also. The general forms of the REAL command are identical to the forms available with the INTEGER specification. Hence, the statement

REAL KOUNT, ITER, MONTY

declares that the three unsubscripted variables are real mode, not integer as implied. If the statement is preceded by a DIMENSION, such as

DIMENSION KOUNT(3), ITER(55), MONTY(7,6)
REAL KOUNT, ITER, MONTY

the REAL specification declares all three as real mode. The same effect is recognized by the computer with the statement

REAL KOUNT(3), ITER(55), MONTY(7,6)

or

REAL KOUNT(3)
REAL ITER(55)
REAL MONTY(7,6)

where the DIMENSION statement must be omitted with this form. Refer again to Figs. 7-1 and 7-2 for examples.

7-3 DOUBLE PRECISION Specification

The DOUBLE PRECISION specification statement is similar in form to the REAL command. It declares the floating-point mode for a particular variable, as does the REAL, but also specifies that the variable occupies more storage area in the computer's memory than either a real or an integer variable. In most advanced FORTRAN compilers, double-precision variables are accurate numerically to approximately 16 digits, but real variables are accurate to only 7. The DOUBLE PRECISION statement, therefore, is employed in programs requiring greater accuracy than that available by using real variables. The statement

DOUBLE PRECISION A, B, M, N

declares that the four variables are double-precision mode. Notice that without the statement, A and B are implied real mode and M and N are implied integer mode. Once identified in the DOUBLE PRECISION specification, the variable names may begin with any letter because the explicit declaration nulls the predefined convention. The DOUBLE PRECISION statement can also be used with tables and arrays as follows:

DOUBLE PRECISION YEAR(12,12),IK(5)

and

DIMENSION YEAR(12,12),IK(5)
DOUBLE PRECISION YEAR,IK

are exactly equivalent, declaring that both the array and the table are double-precision, floating-point variables.

To process extremely large or small values in READ and WRITE statements, a new format code is required in conjunction with the DOUBLE PRECISION statement. The general form for representing real double-precision values is

Dw.d

and

aDw.d

where a, w, and d are the same as in the E-format code discussed in Chap. 3. The D is used to denote a variable that is capable of storing approximately twice as many significant digits as a single-precision variable. Examples of the specification statement and the D-format code are contained in Figs. 7-3 and 7-4.

Specification Exercises

1 Supply the specification statements that meet criteria (a) to (e):
   (a) Define array X, with six rows and five columns, as integer mode.
   (b) Declare X, Y, and Z as integer mode, and matrix ALPHA, with 10 rows and 10 columns, as real.
   (c) Establish H, I, J, and HK as double-precision-type variables. All are 3 × 4 arrays.
   (d) Establish X and Y as integer type, IX and IY as real, and XIX and YIY as double-precision.
   (e) In a DIMENSION statement, define the sizes of F, G, X2, H, HI, and I as 3 × 5 arrays. In specification statements, declare the first two as real mode, the second two as double-precision, and the last two as integer.

2 Supply a FORMAT statement that will process the declared mode of the variables listed in the following READ instructions:

SPECIFICATION STATEMENTS

(a) INTEGER SUX
    READ(5,100)SUX
(b) INTEGER XM, ZM
    REAL LOB
    READ(5,200)XM,LOB,ZM
(c) DOUBLE PRECISION I,A,J,B
    REAL MAX,MIN
    READ(5,300)MAX,I,A
    READ(5,301)J,MIN,B
(d) REAL KK, LL
    INTEGER AVG, RNT
    DOUBLE PRECISION HI,II
    READ(5,400)KK,AVG,HI,LL,RNT,II
(e) REAL K(3,4)
    INTEGER BAT(2,6)
    READ(5,500)K,BAT

3 Identify and correct errors found in the following groups of statements:

(a)   INTEGER GAM FAM
(b)   REAL K(3,4)L(3,4)
(c) 200   DIMENSION X(3,5),I(2,4)
    205   DOUBLE PRECISION X,I
(d)   INTEGER X
          REAL IOTA
          .
          .
          .
          Z=5.28*X
          K=IOTA+8
(e)   DOUBLE PRECISION LK,MK
          .
          .
          .
          READ(5,12)LK,MK
    12   FORMAT(2I12)
(f)   INTEGER T,U,V
          REAL I,K,M
          DIMENSION T(3,4), K(6,17)
(g)   IX=5.**I
          REAL IX
(h)   REAL NAME,NAME
          .
          .
          .
          IBAR = NAME + NAME

Figure 7-3 Examples of DOUBLE PRECISION statements.

	Program Statements	Description
100	FORMAT (D15.8)	Statement number 100 describes a 15-digit, real, double-precision data field, where the output is formatted in modified scientific notation. Eight significant digits are outputted as dictated by the 8 following the decimal point. The modified output expresses the exponent with a D, as D±nn, rather than E±nn, as is the case with the E format discussed in Chap. 3.
	DOUBLE PRECISION A ⋅ ⋅ ⋅ WRITE (6,130) A	The value of the double-precision variable A is printed on output device numbered 6 preceded by a Hollerith label. Eleven significant digits are printed; the field width is 18 positions.
130	FORMAT (' A= ',D18.11)	
	DOUBLE PRECISION CENTER,KMAX	The type of the variables CENTER and KMAX are declared DOUBLE PRECISION. Note that CENTER has an implied real mode and KMAX an implied integer mode, but both are now defined to store double-precision numbers.
	DIMENSION X(3,2) DOUBLE PRECISION X,Y,I ⋅ ⋅ ⋅ READ(5,100)X,Y,I	The Table X, with six locations in total, is defined as DOUBLE PRECISION mode along with the unsubscripted variables Y and I. The D-format code is required to process the variables listed in the READ statement.
100	FORMAT(2D22.15)	
	DOUBLE PRECISION MX/2.13458D−05/	A value is assigned to the double-precision variable MX at compilation time by using this form of the specification statement.
	DOUBLE PRECISION X ⋅ ⋅ X=(1.111D1∗26.237/1D03)/1.8333D−03 ⋅ ⋅ ⋅	An example of a DOUBLE PRECISION assignment statement is illustrated here. The three constants in the calculation of X are double-precision type, denoted by the D indicating exponentiation. The variable X must be explicitly declared; otherwise, it has an implied real mode, and the value assigned to it would be accurate to only seven significant places. However, in this sample X is accurate to approximately 16 digits.
	DOUBLE PRECISION NAME ⋅ ⋅	It was stated in Chap. 3 that one variable location could store only four alphanumeric characters. Here, however, by specifying NAME as DOUBLE PRECISION, eight characters can be stored in the location. Thus, the A8 format code is valid here.
1	FORMAT(A8)	

SPECIFICATION STATEMENTS

Figure 7-4 Common errors that occur with DOUBLE PRECISION statements.

Program Statements	Description
100 FORMAT (D13.10)	The specification D13.10 is not permitted because the length of the field (13) must be seven or more digits greater than the number of decimal places indicated (10). A correct entry would be 100 FORMAT (D17.10)
WRITE (6,103) MON 103 FORMAT (D16.9,' IS X')	The FORMAT statement is correct as shown here; however, the variable MON in the WRITE statement is integer mode. To use the D code, a DOUBLE PRECISION statement is required. A correct entry would be DOUBLE PRECISION MON

DOUBLE PRECISION XBAR
.
.
.
XBAR = SUM/XNOB + 5.12E1
	Although XBAR is defined as a double-precision variable, its use within the program involves three real values. All three values must be double-precision type in order to assign a correct double-precision result to XBAR. Otherwise, a mixed-mode expression is evaluated with only single-precision accuracy. Correct entries would be
	        DOUBLE PRECISION XBAR,SUM,XNOB
	        .
	        .
	        .
	        XBAR = SUM/XNOB + 5.12D1

DOUBLE PRECISION I9(5,5) . . . READ(5,100)I9 100 FORMAT(25I5)	An array I9 is declared as double-precision mode. However, the READ references a format code of I, representing integer type. Thus, during the READ an error occurs. A correct entry requires the D-format code: 100 FORMAT (25(D20.13))

DOUBLE PRECISION Z
DIMENSION X(15,12)
	The DOUBLE PRECISION specification statement must follow the DIMENSION and precede any executable instructions. Correct entries would be
	        DIMENSION X(15,12)
	        DOUBLE PRECISION Z

7-4 Program Sample SALES TAX

When should the specification statements be included in programs? Earlier, it was suggested that the programmer choose variable names having an implied meaning. Thus, when the first SALES program was discussed, real-variable names SALES and TAXRAT were chosen because the data was in floating-point form. In SALES-13, the tax-rate code was defined by the variable IRATE because the variable was used in a computed GO TO statement. However, a more meaningful name suggestive of the data might be TXCODE. The specification statements permit the defining of the variable TXCODE as integer mode. To convert a data name to a mode that corresponds to the type of data which will be stored in a particular location requires the specification statement. Program SALES-13 is repeated here[1] with the inclusion of an INTEGER statement and the substitution of TXCODE for IRATE. Additionally, the two variables DAY and YEAR have been replaced by one, DATE. The REAL specification declares DATE as a table containing two locations.

```
C PROGRAM SALES-13 REVISED
C THIS PROGRAM COMPUTES THE SALES TAX FOR A NUMBER OF ITEMS
C
          INTEGER TXCODE
          REAL DATE(2)
          READ(5,100)DATE
          WRITE(6,400)DATE
10        READ(5,101)SALES,TXCODE
          GO TO (12,13,11),TXCODE
12        SALETX = SALES * .04
          GO TO 14
13        SALETX = SALES * .045
14        WRITE(6,401)SALES,TXCODE,SALETX
          GO TO 10
100       FORMAT(2A4)
101       FORMAT(F8.2,I2)
400       FORMAT(21H1SALES REPORT   DATED ,2A4/8H0   SALES,5X,8HTAX CODE,5X,9H
         1SALES TAX/)
401       FORMAT(1X,F8.2,5X,I5,6X,F8.2)
11        STOP
          END
```

Because of the INTEGER declaration statement at the beginning, TXCODE is integer mode. Its use is valid in the computed GO TO as a result. Also, I-format codes in the READ and WRITE statements are necessary to process TXCODE. The data from SALES-13 is repeated on the next page along with the output from the revised program.

---

[1] The flowcharts are omitted for many of the samples in this chapter because the program logic is the same as that used in previous chapters.

SPECIFICATION STATEMENTS   **195**

```
02-12-76
  1000.00 1
   857.67 1
   628.43 2
  1575.50 1
 -9999.00 3
```

```
SALES REPORT    DATED 02-12-76

    SALES      TAX CODE      SALES TAX

   1000.00        1           40.00
    857.67        1           34.31
    628.43        2           28.28
   1575.50        1           63.02
```

The output from this sample is identical to that shown in Sec. 5-8. As concluded in that section, the computed GO TO in this version could also be replaced by an arithmetic IF of the form

IF(TXCODE-2)12,13,11

because TXCODE is integer mode. Without the specification, a mixed-mode expression would occur within the parentheses. A more practical need for declaration-type statements is in the next sample program.

The largest sales quantity entered as data in any of the SALES programs has been $1,575.50. In the programs, multiplying a six-digit number with two decimal places by 4 or 4.5 percent is accurate to two places with single-precision variables. However, a loss of accuracy occurs if the sales data is large, such as $72,572,646.05, because only the seven most significant digits are used in the calculation. Multiplying the 10-digit number above by 4 percent yields an answer of $2,902,905.84, but by using only the seven most significant digits, the answer is $2,902,905.00, a difference of $0.84. The difference may seem trivial, but it is not if an accountant must balance hundreds of accounts involving such numbers as these. As another example, extreme accuracy is required in the space program; slight errors are magnified immensely when a spacecraft is traveling millions of miles in space.

The DOUBLE PRECISION specification statement permits floating-point variables to be carried more accurately within the memory unit of the computer. To illustrate its use, a modified version of SALES-14 was used to process the following data (FORMAT labels 101, 400, and 401 were revised to accept and print the new form of the data):

```
08-24-84   4
 72572646.05  .04
 14735842.64  .045
 72548654.05  .04
 89600978.74  .045
```

```
SALES REPORT   DATED 08-24-84

   SALES           TAX RATE         SALES TAX

 72572640.00       0.040            2902905.00
 14735840.00       0.045             663112.90
 72548650.00       0.040            2901946.00
 89600970.00       0.045            4032044.00
```

With single-precision variables, although no error message is generated, the answers are only approximately correct. Only the seven most significant digits are retained, and, as the answers illustrate, used in the calculation.

By inserting a DOUBLE PRECISION-type declaration for the variables SALES, RATE, and SALETX, and revised FORMAT statements, the program below computes more accurate answers.

```
C PROGRAM SALES-15
C THIS PROGRAM COMPUTES THE SALES TAX FOR A NUMBER OF ITEMS
C
      DIMENSION DATE(2)
      DOUBLE PRECISION SALES, RATE, SALETX
      READ(5,100)DATE,N
      WRITE(6,400)DATE
      DO 14 I = 1, N
      READ(5,101)SALES, RATE
      SALETX = SALES * RATE
      WRITE(6,401)SALES, RATE,SALETX
14    CONTINUE
100   FORMAT(2A4,I3)
101   FORMAT(2D12.3)
400   FORMAT(21H1SALES REPORT   DATED ,2A4/8H0   SALES,9X,8HTAX RATE,9X,9H
     1SALES TAX/)
401   FORMAT(1X,F12.2,3X,F8.3,7X,F12.2)
      STOP
      END
```

SPECIFICATION STATEMENTS

Observe that it is valid to print the double-precision variables with an F-format code, as contained in label 401. Using the same data, output from the program above yields the expected numerical results.

```
08-21-84   4
 72572646.05  .04
 14735842.64  .045
 72548654.05  .04
 89600978.74  .045
```

```
SALES REPORT    DATED 08-21-84

   SALES           TAX RATE         SALES TAX

 72572646.05        0.040          2902905.84
 14735842.64        0.045           663112.92
 72548654.05        0.040          2901946.16
 89600978.74        0.045          4032044.04
```

A comparison of the printout generated with this program and the previous one indicates the usefulness and accuracy of the DOUBLE PRECISION declaration.

Whenever the input data or a calculation involves more than seven digits, only the seven most significant are used for single-precision variables. If greater accuracy is required, the declaration DOUBLE PRECISION is needed.

7-5 Program Sample STATISTICS

In program STATISTICS-7 the date was printed as part of the heading. Three variable names, MONTH, IDAY, and IYEAR, represented the integer values for the month, day, and year. IDAY and IYEAR were chosen rather than DAY and YEAR because integer data was involved. However, with the specification command, DAY and YEAR can be declared integer mode, as in the following:

```
C PROGRAM STATISTICS-7 REVISED
C THIS PROGRAM COMPUTES THE AVERAGE OF THREE VALUES
      INTEGER DAY, YEAR
      READ(5,200)MONTH,DAY,YEAR
      WRITE(6,300)MONTH,DAY,YEAR
      READ(5,201)VAL1,VAL2,VAL3
      SUM = VAL1 + VAL2 + VAL3
      AVG = SUM/3.
```

```
            WRITE(6,301)VAL1,VAL2,VAL3,SUM,AVG
200         FORMAT(3I2)
201         FORMAT(3F5.1)
300         FORMAT(@1STATISTICS REPORT   DATED @,I2,@/@,I2,@/@,I2)
301         FORMAT(@01ST VALUE   2ND VALUE   3RD VALUE    SUM    AVERAGE@/1X,F9.1,
            12F11.1,F7.1,F9.1)
            STOP
            END
```

However, a more efficient method for writing the program incorporates the dimension capability of the declaration commands. By specifying the variable DATE as an integer table with three locations, the three variables in the first READ and WRITE statements can be replaced by one.

```
C PROGRAM STATISTICS-7 REVISED
C THIS PROGRAM COMPUTES THE AVERAGE OF THREE VALUES
            INTEGER DATE(3)
            READ(5,200)DATE
            WRITE(6,300)DATE
            READ(5,201)VAL1,VAL2,VAL3
            SUM = VAL1 + VAL2 + VAL3
            AVG = SUM/3.
            WRITE(6,301)VAL1,VAL2,VAL3,SUM,AVG
200         FORMAT(3I2)
201         FORMAT(3F5.1)
300         FORMAT(@1STATISTICS REPORT   DATED @,I2,@/@,I2,@/@,I2)
301         FORMAT(@01ST VALUE   2ND VALUE   3RD VALUE    SUM    AVERAGE@/1X,F9.1,
            12F11.1,F7.1,F9.1)
            STOP
            END
```

Reusing the data employed in the original STATISTICS-7, the output from the revised program is identical

```
112570
  855   894   686


STATISTICS REPORT   DATED 11/25/70

1ST VALUE   2ND VALUE   3RD VALUE     SUM    AVERAGE
     85.5        89.4        68.6   243.5       81.2
```

In a later program, STATISTICS-11, the variable KNT was used as a counter representing the number of groups processed. If the problem for STATISTICS-11 is expanded to include an overall average for all groups processed, a different need arises. To calculate the overall average, the sum of all the values must be divided by the number of groups times three.

SPECIFICATION STATEMENTS

For example, if four groups were processed, the overall sum must be divided by 12 (4 × 3). To use the variable KNT in the calculation of an average, it must be real mode. Flowchart 7-1 and program STATISTICS-16 list changes to incorporate these ideas.

```
C  PROGRAM STATISTICS-16
C  THIS PROGRAM COMPUTES THE AVERAGE OF THREE VALUES FOR A NUMBER OF
C  GROUPS OF DATA. IT ALSO COMPUTES THE AVERAGE FOR ALL VALUES COMBINED.
       REAL KNT/0./, TOTSUM/0./
       WRITE(6,300)
1      READ(5,201)VAL1,VAL2,VAL3
       SUM = VAL1 + VAL2 + VAL3
       TOTSUM = TOTSUM + SUM
       AVG = SUM/3.
       KNT = KNT + 1.
       WRITE(6,301)KNT,SUM,AVG
       IF(KNT.LT.4.) GO TO 1
       OAVG = TOTSUM / (KNT*3.)
       WRITE(6,302) TOTSUM,OAVG
201    FORMAT(3F5.1)
300    FORMAT(@1GROUP NUMBER    SUM    AVERAGE@/)
301    FORMAT(5X,F3.0,4X,F8.1,1X,F8.1/)
302    FORMAT(@0SUMMARY@,4X,F8.1,1X,F8.1/)
       STOP
       END
```

The specification statement declares KNT as real mode and sets to zero both KNT and TOTSUM. The variable TOTSUM is a counter, storing the value of the overall sum; the variable OAVG is the overall average. Without the specification command, mixed-mode expressions would occur throughout the program. Output from using the following data is

```
82.2  69.5  74.0
65.5  76.4  83.2
98.8  92.0  90.7
75.5  85.4  68.3
```

GROUP NUMBER	SUM	AVERAGE
1.	225.7	75.2
2.	225.1	75.0
3.	281.5	93.8
4.	229.2	76.4
SUMMARY	961.5	80.1

200 FORTRAN IV PROGRAMMING AND APPLICATIONS

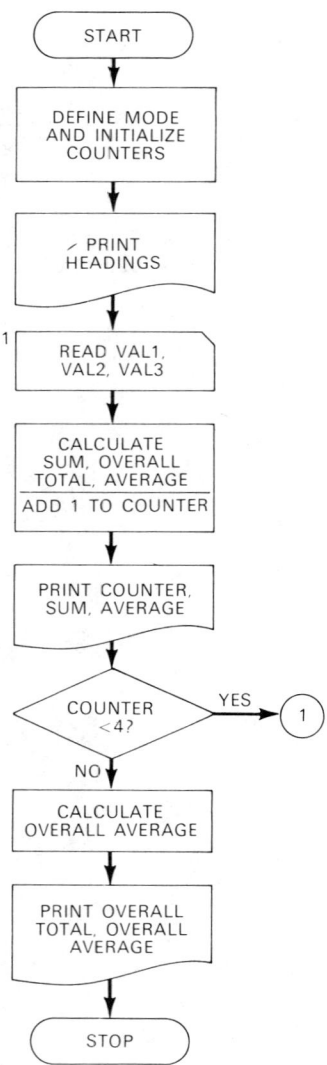

Flowchart 7-1   STATISTICS—REAL statement.

In the printout, note the decimal point listed below the group number. It is printed as part of the output because KNT is declared real mode and is printed using an F code. In this sample the answers are accurate because fewer than seven significant digits are involved. But if each data value consists of eight or nine digits, such as 1,077,899.47, how precise

SPECIFICATION STATEMENTS

is the answer? Using the previous program with revised FORMAT statements to READ and WRITE the data

```
112475.24  236521.78  565017.14
147638.85  245012.87  685247.75
 78874.47   98378.14   25147.68
 32658.87   89562.64   98371.58
```

The output appears as

```
GROUP NUMBER      SUM        AVERAGE

    1.         914014.10    304671.30

    2.        1077899.00    359299.60

    3.         202400.20     67466.75

    4.         220593.00     73531.00


SUMMARY       2414906.00    201242.10
```

with only seven digits retained and used in the computations. To be more precise, double-precision variables should be incorporated in the program. STATISTICS-17 includes specification statements to declare double-precision variables. The statements are

```
C  PROGRAM STATISTICS-17
C  THIS PROGRAM COMPUTES THE AVERAGE OF THREE VALUES FOR A NUMBER OF
C  GROUPS OF DATA. IT ALSO COMPUTES THE AVERAGE FOR ALL VALUES COMBINED.
       DOUBLE PRECISION KNT/0.0000000/, TOTSUM/0.0000000/
       DOUBLE PRECISION VAL1,VAL2,VAL3, SUM,AVG,OAVG
       WRITE(6,300)
1      READ(5,201)VAL1,VAL2,VAL3
       SUM = VAL1 + VAL2 + VAL3
       TOTSUM = TOTSUM + SUM
       AVG = SUM/3.
       KNT = KNT + 1.
       WRITE(6,301)KNT,SUM,AVG
       IF(KNT.LT.4.) GO TO 1
       OAVG = TOTSUM / (KNT*3.)
       WRITE(6,302) TOTSUM,OAVG
201    FORMAT(3D10.2)
300    FORMAT(@1GROUP NUMBER    SUM     AVERAGE@/)
301    FORMAT(5X,F3.0,2X,F10.2,1X,F10.2/)
302    FORMAT(@0SUMMARY@,2X,F10.2,1X,F10.2/)
       STOP
       END
```

Supplying the same data from the previous statement, the output reflecting greater accuracy is

```
GROUP NUMBER     SUM         AVERAGE

    1.       914014.16      304671.39

    2.      1077899.47      359299.82

    3.       202400.29       67466.76

    4.       220593.09       73531.03


SUMMARY      2414907.01     201242.25
```

Note the slight differences in the answers. Although it generally takes slightly more programming and computer time, in certain applications it is imperative that double-precision variables be used to garner the accuracy required.

7-6 The COMMON Statement

As with the DIMENSION statement, the COMMON statement can be used to establish table-sized information for an array, provided the name of the array appears first in the COMMON declaration. If the array has been listed in a declaration-type statement, it can not be dimensioned in a COMMON. For example,

COMMON TXB(10,12)

could be used in place of the statements

DIMENSION TXB(10,12)

or

REAL TXB(10,12)

Likewise, the statement

COMMON I(10), JK(2,7)

could be used in place of the statements

DIMENSION I(10), JK(2,7)

or

INTEGER I(10), JK(2,7)

Figures 7-5 and 7-6 show examples of the COMMON statement as employed in this form plus samples of the EQUIVA-

LENCE statement discussed in Sec. 7-7.† However, a more important attribute of the COMMON statement involves the allocation of storage areas. In Chap. 9 this capability will be discussed in detail.

7-7 The EQUIVALENCE Statement

The EQUIVALENCE statement permits the programmer to reference one storage location within the memory unit of the computer by more than one variable name. The statement

EQUIVALENCE (X,B)

informs the compiler program that the variables X and B refer to the same storage location. The statement

EQUIVALENCE (X,B,GA,BT)

informs the compiler program that all four variables occupy only one storage location. Why is this feature needed?

The statement is useful in two applications, both involving large programs. One case concerns a programmer error that occurs as a result of listing two variable names for the same variable. This occasionally happens by accident when writing a large program over an extended period of time. Assume that the variable GTOTAL (for grand total) was employed during the initial stages of program development but at a later point the variable OTOTAL (for overall total, representing the same grand total) was inadvertently employed. The programmer can rewrite the statements so that only GTOTAL or OTOTAL is used throughout, or if a large number of changes are necessary, the statement

EQUIVALENCE (GTOTAL,OTOTAL)

can be inserted with the effect that both variables reference the same storage location.

In the second case, it is possible that the size of a particular program is larger than that permitted with a certain computer. When a program is too large to "fit" in the computer, means for shortening the length of the program must be examined. One method employs the EQUIVALENCE statement. The form is similar to the one just used. However, assume that in a large program the variables A and B are used in an initial segment

†Program samples illustrating the EQUIVALENCE statement are shown in Secs. 7-8 and 7-9.

Figure 7-5 Examples of the COMMON and EQUIVALENCE specification statements.

Program Statements	Description
COMMON X(10),Y(5,8)	The COMMON statement in this example serves the same purpose as a DIMENSION statement. It establishes a maximum of 10 locations for real Table X and 40 locations (5 rows and 8 columns) for real array Y.
COMMON R(50), S(50), L(3) INTEGER R,S REAL L	Two tables R and S, each with 50 locations, are established by the COMMON declaration. The INTEGER specification overrides the implied real mode of the two tables and declares them as integer tables. Likewise, Table L, with three locations, is declared real mode.
EQUIVALENCE (XSUM,YSUM) or EQUIVALENCE (YSUM,XSUM)	The two variables XSUM and YSUM are assigned the same location within the computer's memory area. This form serves two purposes: (1) It can conserve memory by using one location to store the value of XSUM and then later to store the value of YSUM; and (2) it can be used to reference the same value by either name, XSUM or YSUM.
EQUIVALENCE (A,B) A = 6.2 X = B+1	The value assigned to the variable X is 7.2 because of the EQUIVALENCE statement. A and B share the same location, so when referred to both have the same value of 6.2.
DIMENSION X(100,50),Y(100,50) EQUIVALENCE (X,Y) or DIMENSION X(100,50),Y(100,50) EQUIVALENCE (X(1,1),Y(1,1))	Two large arrays X and Y are established by the DIMENSION statement. To conserve the amount of storage area available, the EQUIVALENCE statement specifies that the two arrays share the same storage area. This implies naturally that only one array can be processed at one time.
DIMENSION X(50),Y(25) EQUIVALENCE (X(26),Y(1)) or DIMENSION X(50), Y(25) EQUIVALENCE (X(26),Y)	Two one-dimensional arrays are established by the DIMENSION statement. The EQUIVALENCE statement declares that the last 25 locations of Table X, beginning with X(26), shares the same storage area as Table Y.
DIMENSION A(30),B(10),C(10),D(10) EQUIVALENCE (A(1),B),(A(11),C),(A(21),D)	In this sample, Table B and the first 10 locations of A share the same area. Likewise, Table C shares the same area as the second 10 locations of Table A. Table D shares the same area as the last 10 locations of Table A.

SPECIFICATION STATEMENTS

Program Statements	Description
DIMENSION A(20,10), B(10,10), C(10,10) EQUIVALENCE (A(1,1),B(1,1)), (A(11,1),C(1,1))	Three arrays are established by the DIMENSION statement. Array A contains 200 locations; B and C each contain 100 locations. The EQUIVALENCE statement causes the array B to share the same storage area as the first 100 locations of Table A, and array C shares the same area as the second 100 locations of Table A. Note that only the first locations of B and C are listed, but it is *implied* that all the array locations are equivalent when this form is used.

Figure 7-6 Common errors that occur with COMMON and EQUIVALENCE specification statements.

	Program Statements	Description

	DIMENSION X(100)
	COMMON X(100)
		The size of Table X has been established in the first statement. It is redundant and wrong to list the size in both statements. A correct entry would be either
		    DIMENSION X(100)
		    or
		    COMMON X(100)

200	COMMON TZ(20)	As with the other specification statements, a label is not valid as part of the COMMON declaration. A correct entry would be COMMON TZ(20)

	COMMON ZEN(5), KEN(3,2)
	INTEGER ZEN(5)
	REAL KEN(3,2)
		The size of tables or arrays must be specified in only one declaration statement. Thus, the dimension sizes must be omitted in the INTEGER and REAL statements as
		    COMMON ZEN(5), KEN(3,2)
		    INTEGER ZEN
		    REAL KEN
		or the COMMON statement omitted:
		    INTEGER ZEN(5)
		    REAL KEN(3,2)

	EQUIVALENCE (A)	The EQUIVALENCE statement must contain more than one variable name if it is to share the same memory location. A correct entry would be of the form EQUIVALENCE (A,B)

Figure 7-6 Common errors that occur with COMMON and EQUIVALENCE specification statements *(cont'd)*.

Program Statements	Description
EQUIVALENCE (A,B) (K,M)	The comma separating the two lists of variables has been omitted. A correct entry would be EQUIVALENCE (A,B),(K,M)
DIMENSION B(50),A(25) EQUIVALENCE (B(26),A(26))	In the EQUIVALENCE statement, A(26) refers to a nonexistent location because Table A is defined as only containing 25 locations. A correct entry would be EQUIVALENCE (B(26),A(1))
DIMENSION X(50),Y(51),Z(52) EQUIVALENCE (X(1),Y(2)),(X(1),Z(3)),(Y(1),Z(1))	Three arrays are established in the DIMENSION statement. The EQUIVALENCE statement specifies that the array Y, beginning with the second location, shares the storage area with X, beginning with the first location. Thus, X(1) and Y(2), X(2) and Y(3), and so on, share the same locations. The statement also specifies that X(1) and Z(3), X(2) and Z(4), and so on, share the same locations. However, the third segment specifies that Y(1) and Z(1), Y(2) and Z(2), and so on, share the same area. This last segment is contradictory because X(1), Y(2), and Z(3) physically share the same location as specified by the first two parameters. A correct entry would simply omit the last segment: EQUIVALENCE (X(1),Y(2)),(X(1),Z(3))

but are not referenced in a later segment of the program. Also assume that the variables X and Y are utilized in the later segment but not in the first. Shown schematically,

Large program

Segment 1	A and B used. X and Y are not referenced.
Segment 2	X and Y used. A and B are not referenced.

SPECIFICATION STATEMENTS

The number of storage locations required and, consequently, the size of the program, can be reduced by causing A and X to "share" the same storage location and likewise for B and Y. The statements

EQUIVALENCE (A,X)
EQUIVALENCE (B,Y)

or

EQUIVALENCE (A,X), (B,Y)

assign one location for A and X and one for B and Y. Care must be exercised when using this method because one location can only store one number at a time. The statements can not be used if it is necessary to store values for A and X or B and Y in the same part of the program at the same time.

Using unsubscripted variables in the EQUIVALENCE declaration does not lead to significant savings. Fortunately, however, the general form of the statement permits the use of subscripted variables or arrays as

EQUIVALENCE (a,b), (c,d,e)

where a, b, c, d, and e may be unsubscripted variables, subscripted variables, or arrays. Thus, the statements

DIMENSION A(10),B(10)
EQUIVALENCE (A,B)

declare that the two Tables A and B share the same 10 storage locations.[1] The statements

DIMENSION BAC(100,100), CAC(100,100)
EQUIVALENCE (BAC,CAC)

declare that the same 10,000 locations are shared by the two Tables BAC and CAC.[†] In this form, substantial reductions in

---

[1] Note that certain compilers, such as on the CDC 6400 and IBM 7094, require for form

DIMENSION A(10),B(10)
EQUIVALENCE (A(1), B(1))

where in the EQUIVALENCE statement the subscript notation must be used. Refer to the particular systems manual being used for clarification.

[†] Here the form required by certain compilers is

DIMENSION BAC(100,100), CAC(100,100)
EQUIVALENCE (BAC(1,1), CAC(1,1))

the size of large programs can be made. Refer again to Figs. 7-5 and 7-6.

More Specification Exercises

1. Define the table sizes by using the COMMON statement in the following samples. Supply additional specification statements as needed.
   (a) Integer array X with six rows and five columns
   (b) Real array AL with 10 rows and 4 columns
   (c) Double-precision Table HI with six locations
   (d) Tables X and Y as integer, Tables M and N as double-precision and Tables T4 and K4 as real, all with five locations

2. Supply the EQUIVALENCE statements required to satisfy descriptions (a) to (e):
   (a) BETA and SAT are to share the same location within the computer's memory.
   (b) X, Y, Z, T, and R are to share the same location within the computer.
   (c) XBAR and ZBAR are to share one location, while TBAR and RBAR are to share a second location.
   (d) Tables A and B, each with 200 locations, are to share the same area.
   (e) Table C contains 20 locations, D and E each 10. The first 10 locations of C and D are to share the same area, while the last 10 locations of C and E are to share the same area.

3. In the following list of problems, supply two sets of statements that cause the same result to occur:
   (a) Tables FG and GF, each with 12 locations, are to share the same storage area.
   (b) Table H contains 10 locations, while H1 and H2 each contain five. The first five locations in H and H1 are to share the same area, and the last five in H are to share the same area as H2.
   (c) Array X is a 10 × 5 matrix, and Y and Z are 5 × 5 matrices. The first five rows and columns of X are to share the same area as Y; the last five rows and columns are to share the same area as Z.

4. Identify and correct errors, if any, in statements (a) to (f):
   (a)   DIMENSION IX(100)
                REAL IX
                COMMON Z(50),IX(100)
   (b)   REAL COMMON IKTM(50)
   (c) 72   COMMON A(5), B(60)
   (d) 73   EQUIVALENCE (A,B)

SPECIFICATION STATEMENTS

(e)   EQUIVALENCE SUM,TOTAL,ALL
(f)   DIMENSION X(100), Y(10)
                  EQUIVALENCE (X(50),Y(50))

As defined at this point, it is unnecessary to incorporate the EQUIVALENCE statement in the SALES problem. However, to illustrate a method that reduces slightly the size of the program, it will be included in a revised version of SALES-11. In this program, the variables DAY and YEAR are read and printed at the beginning of the program but are not used again. The variables SALES and TAXRAT are used in a later segment of the program. It is possible to have the variables DAY and SALES plus YEAR and TAXRAT share one location each, reducing by two locations the size of the program. To incorporate this idea requires the statements

**7-8
Program
Sample
SALES TAX**

```
C PROGRAM SALES-11 REVISED
C THIS PROGRAM COMPUTES THE SALES TAX FOR A NUMBER OF ITEMS BASED ON
C A RATE OF 4 PERCENT.
      EQUIVALENCE (DAY,SALES), (YEAR,TAXRAT)
      READ(5,100)DAY,YEAR
      WRITE(6,400)DAY,YEAR
      TAXRAT = .04
10    READ(5,101)SALES
      IF(SALES.EQ.-9999.)GO TO 11
      SALETX = SALES * TAXRAT
      WRITE(6,401)SALES,TAXRAT,SALETX
      GO TO 10
100   FORMAT(2A4)
101   FORMAT(F8.2)
400   FORMAT(21H1SALES REPORT   DATED ,2A4/8H0   SALES,5X,8HTAX RATE,5X,9H
     1SALES TAX/)
401   FORMAT(1X,F8.2,3X,F8.3,5X,F8.2)
11    STOP
      END
```

Obviously, with this short program, it is not mandatory that the EQUIVALENCE statement be inserted. It does, however, illustrate the concept that may be required when writing large programs. Processing the same data from before results in identical output

```
12-30-75
1000.00
 857.67
 628.43
1575.50
-9999.00
```

```
SALES REPORT   DATED 12-30-75

   SALES       TAX RATE     SALES TAX

   1000.00      0.040         40.00
    857.67      0.040         34.31
    628.43      0.040         25.14
   1575.50      0.040         63.02
```

In program STATISTICS-14, the DIMENSION statement can be replaced by the COMMON command as shown in the following statements:

7-9 Program Sample STATISTICS

```
C PROGRAM STATISTICS-14 REVISED
C THIS PROGRAM COMPUTES THE AVERAGE FOR A VARIABLE NUMBER OF VALUES
C AND THEN PRINTS THEM IN ORDER FROM LARGEST TO SMALLEST.
      COMMON VALUE(100)
      WRITE(6,300)
      SUM = 0.
      READ(5,201)NOV
      DO 1 J = 1, NOV
      READ(5,200)VALUE(J)
      SUM = SUM + VALUE(J)
1     CONTINUE
      XNOV = NOV
      AVG = SUM/XNOV
      WRITE(6,301)   NOV,SUM,AVG
C START SORT ROUTINE
      NV = NOV - 1
      DO 3 K = 1, NV
      N = K + 1
      DO 3 J = N, NOV
      IF(VALUE(K).GE.VALUE(J))GO TO 3
      TEMP = VALUE(K)
      VALUE(K) = VALUE(J)
      VALUE(J) = TEMP
3     CONTINUE
      WRITE(6,303)
      DO 4 J = 1, NOV
4     WRITE(6,304)VALUE(J)
C
200   FORMAT(F5.1)
201   FORMAT(I3)
300   FORMAT(@1NUMBER IN GROUP    SUM    AVERAGE@/)
301   FORMAT(7X,I3,5X,F8.1,1X,F8.1/)
303   FORMAT(@0SORTED VALUES-LARGEST TO SMALLEST@/)
304   FORMAT(1X,F8.1)
      STOP
      END
```

Processing the STATISTICS-14 data by using this version of the program results in the same output. However, to show a

SPECIFICATION STATEMENTS

valid use of the EQUIVALENCE statement, assume the following criteria have been incorporated. Often it is much faster to include in your program segments that have been written by someone else. Provided the segments are not proprietary and are working properly, substantial time savings can be effected. For example, sort routines such as the one included in STATISTICS-14 are essentially alike, with only minor differences. Therefore, if a particular problem requires a sort, it is efficient to use the statements listed in STATISTICS-14 rather than creating your own. Recalling the definition of the problem for STATISTICS-14, assume that the following sort routine is available on cards:

```
C START SORT ROUTINE
      NV = NOV - 1
      DO 3 K = 1, NV
      N = K + 1
      DO 3 J = N, NOV
      IF(X(K).GE.X(J))GO TO 3
      T = X(K)
      X(K) = X(J)
      X(J) = T
3     CONTINUE
```

Rather than repunching these cards, a new DIMENSION statement and an EQUIVALENCE statement[1] can be inserted so that these statements can be used as is with the first and last parts of the STATISTICS-14 program:

```
C PROGRAM STATISTICS-18
C THIS PROGRAM COMPUTES THE AVERAGE FOR A VARIABLE NUMBER OF VALUES
C AND THEN PRINTS THEM IN ORDER FROM LARGEST TO SMALLEST.
      DIMENSION VALUE(100),X(100)
      EQUIVALENCE (VALUE,X)
      WRITE(6,300)
      SUM = 0.
      READ(5,201)NOV,(VALUE(I),I=1,NOV)
      DO 1 J = 1, NOV
      SUM = SUM + VALUE(J)
1     CONTINUE
      XNOV = NOV
      AVG = SUM/XNOV
      WRITE(6,301)NOV,SUM,AVG
C START SORT ROUTINE
```

---

[1] Note once again that the EQUIVALENCE statement must be listed in the form
EQUIVALENCE (VALUE(1), X(1))
on certain computer systems.

```
      NV = NOV - 1
      DO 3 K = 1, NV
      N = K + 1
      DO 3 J = N, NOV
      IF(X(K).GE.X(J))GO TO 3
      T = X(K)
      X(K) = X(J)
      X(J) = T
3     CONTINUE
      WRITE(6,303) (VALUE(J),J=1, NOV)
201   FORMAT(I3,(15F5.1))
300   FORMAT(@1NUMBER IN GROUP    SUM    AVERAGE@/)
301   FORMAT(7X,I3,5X,F8.1,1X,F8.1/)
303   FORMAT(@0SORTED VALUES-LARGEST TO SMALLEST@//(1X,10F5.1/))
      STOP
      END
```

The EQUIVALENCE statement causes the two tables VALUE and X to share the same storage area. Consequently, referral to either VALUE or X results in access to the same computer location. The output from the program, using the new data listed, is

8 71.8 61.4 98.6 45.8 47.7 78.4 58.7 98.9

NUMBER IN GROUP   SUM   AVERAGE

       8   561.3   70.2

SORTED VALUES-LARGEST TO SMALLEST

98.9 98.6 78.4 71.8 61.4 58.7 47.7 45.8

The method outlined here is valuable, especially when limited by the physical size of the computer being used or when large programs are being developed.

7-10 Summary

The INTEGER, REAL, and DOUBLE PRECISION specification statements can be inserted to override the implied mode of variable names. Dimension sizes for tables and arrays can also be specified within the statements. As listed in this chapter, the COMMON declaration can be used at the programmer's option in place of a DIMENSION statement, and the EQUIVA-LENCE statement is useful when it is necessary to reduce the

SPECIFICATION STATEMENTS

size of a program because it causes variables, either unsubscripted or arrays, to share the same storage areas. Consequently, its use can reduce the size of a program. As implied in the last two sections, the use of the EQUIVALENCE statement is limited for the most part to large programming problems. However, the COMMON statement is helpful in processing subroutine subprograms, which are discussed in Chap. 9.

Questions

1. Write a program to add the integer values 6, 7, 8, ... , 26 to the variable SUM. (Avoid a mixed-mode expression by using a specification statement.) Print the value of SUM, with an appropriate label.

2. Write a program to subtract the sum of the real values 3½, 4½, 5½, ... , 12½ from the variable MOMENT. Assign an initial value of 2.3482E+03 to MOMENT. (Avoid mixed-mode expressions.) Print the initial value of MOMENT, the sum of the values, and the difference between MOMENT and the sum. Label each output value appropriately.

3. Write a program that will calculate the sum, average, and standard deviation for the following numbers

14372.6891	18368.2465	1121.2487
222648.8174	69417.4141	37.2478
1178687.6879	28337.6767	3436.2784

    The standard deviation is calculated by the formula

    $$\left[\frac{\Sigma x^2}{n} - \left(\frac{\Sigma x}{n} \right)^2 \right]^{1/2}$$

    where Σ = sum
    Σx = sum of values
    Σx^2 = sum of individual values squared
    n = number of values

    Make sure the answers are numerically correct. Label the output values.

4. Using the data from Question 3 and a COMMON statement in place of a DIMENSION, determine the *median* value. By placing the data in a table and sorting the values from largest to smallest, the median value is determined by examining the fifth, or middle, location of the sorted table of values. Write a program to read the data into a table and print the median value. The correct answer to be printed is 18368.2465.

5. Modify Question 4 so that the program can handle any number of data values. In this version, it is necessary to determine whether

there is an even or odd number of values. If odd, the median value is simply the center value in the sorted array. However, if there is an even number of values, the median is computed by summing the middle two values and dividing by two. For example, the median of the numbers 1, 2, 3, and 4 is $(2+3)/2$ or 2.5.

6. Write a program that will calculate chi-square, given the following information. Tables X and Y contain the data

X	1	2
1	190	320
2	290	200

Y	1	2
1	24.48	26.52
2	23.52	25.48

The formula for chi-square is

$$\frac{\Sigma(X_{ij} - Y_{ij})^2}{Y_{ij}}$$

where the subscripts i and j are used to indicate each of the respective row and column table elements. To check the accuracy of your program, the correct value for chi-square is 4.83. Read the data into the tables, calculate chi-square, and print the value with an appropriate label.

7. Solve STATISTICS-16, from Sec. 7-5, by letting the variables AVG and OAVG share the same storage location.

8. A group of scores for a certain test are

```
92  78  80  65  87  76  58  74  82  66
88  82  58  56  79  74  67  83  87  68
77  84  93  85  94  67  76  72  81  99
```

Write a program that will read the scores, calculate, and print the table information as shown.

SCORE	NO. OF GRADES	PERCENT OF TOTAL
91–100	X	.XXX
81–90	X	.XXX
71–80	X	.XXX
61–70	X	.XXX
51–60	X	.XXX
TOTALS	X	X.XXX

For example, three grades or 10 percent (that is 3/30) of the total were in the range from 51 to 60.

9. Employing the percentages calculated in Question 8, if the same test were given to 1,000 students, how many scores would be expected to be in the range 91 to 100, 81 to 90, and so on? Print a table of values according to the following form:

SPECIFICATION STATEMENTS

Probable Results Based on Question 8 Percentages
(for 1,000 Students)

SCORE	EXPECTED PERCENT	EXPECTED NO. OF GRADES
91–100	.XXX	X
81–90	.XXX	X
71–80	.XXX	X
61–70	.XXX	X
51–60	.XXX	X
TOTALS	X.XXX	X

For example, 100 grades, or 10% × 1,000, is the expected number in the range 51 to 60.

10 The cost functions for five products are given by the general formula

$$\text{Total cost}_i = \text{units} \times \text{unit cost}_i + \text{setup cost}_i$$

The respective and setup costs for the products are

Product	Unit Costs	Setup Costs
1	$52.00	$125.00
2	58.50	150.00
3	63.70	180.00
4	68.75	195.00
5	75.00	255.00

Write a flexible program that stores the five-unit and setup costs in tables and uses a product code to reference them and compute the total cost. The input data consists of the number of units plus the product code. Thus, if the data were 100 units and product code 4, the total cost would be

$$T = 100*68.75 + 195.00$$
$$T = 882.50$$

Accumulate totals for all the items processed. Supply your own data.

11 Write a program that will calculate and print the standard deviation for a group of data. Use the formula

$$SD = \sqrt{\frac{\Sigma(X - \bar{X})^2}{n}}$$

where SD = standard deviation
       X = each input data value
       $\bar{X}$ = average of input data values
       n = number of input data values

[Notes: Supply your own data and avoid mixed-mode expressions. Also, although other formulas can be used for the calculation (see Sec. 8-2), it is suggested that the one above be employed because it requires the use of subscripted variables.]

FUNCTIONS AND SUBPROGRAMS 8

There is a common group of operations performed in many different types of programs. Rather than requiring each programmer to create his own method for each of the functions, a *library* of FORTRAN-supplied functions is available. The library operations are called *subprograms* and may be either mathematical or service routines. The library of subprograms plus user-created functions and FUNCTION subprograms are discussed in this chapter.

8-1 FORTRAN-supplied Subprograms

A category of common operations performed in many scientific programs is that of taking the trigonometric functions, such as the sine or cosine of a number or expression. The FORTRAN-supplied subprograms simplify the task greatly by supplying the operation. To use the FORTRAN-supplied functions, the programmer "calls" the subprogram by inserting, in an assignment statement, one of the entry names listed in Table 8-1 plus an appropriate argument. For example, to calculate the sine of $\pi/2$, the statement

10   X = SIN(3.14/2.)

is used. Likewise, the cosine of $\pi/2$ can be assigned to a variable and used within a program by the statement

15   Y = COS(3.14/2.)

Table 8-1 FORTRAN-supplied Mathematical Subprograms

Subprogram Operation	Function Reference Name[1]	Sample Assignment Statement[2]	Definition
Absolute value	ABS	A = ABS(X)	$\|X\|$
	DABS	DA = DABS(X)	$\|DX\|$
	IABS	IA = IABS(IX)	$\|IX\|$
Arctangent (in radians)	ATAN	A = ATAN(X)	arctan X
	DATAN	DA = DATAN(DX)	arctan DX
Common logarithm	ALOG10	A = ALOG10(X)	$\log_{10} X$
	DLOG10	DA = DLOG10(DX)	$\log_{10} DX$
Cosine	COS	A = COS(X)	cos X
	DCOS	DA = DCOS(DX)	cos DX
Exponential	DEXP	DA = DEXP(DX)	e^{DX}
	EXP	A = EXP(X)	e^X
Fixed point	IFIX	IA = IFIX(X)	Convert X from real to integer.
Floating point	DFLOAT	DA = DFLOAT(IX)	Convert IX from integer to real.
	FLOAT	A = FLOAT(IX)	
Hyperbolic tangent	DTANH	DA = DTANH(DX)	tanh DX
	TANH	A = TANH(X)	tanh X
Natural logarithm	ALOG	A = ALOG(X)	$\log_e X$
	DLOG	DA = DLOG(DX)	$\log_e DX$
Sine	DSIN	DA = DSIN(DX)	sin DX
	SIN	A = SIN(X)	sin X
Square root	DSQRT	DA = DSQRT(DX)	$DX^{1/2}$
	SQRT	A = SQRT(X)	$X^{1/2}$

[1] The functions listed here are available in basic USAS FORTRAN IV. A more complete listing is located in Appendix C.

[2] The variables X and A are real mode, IX and IA are integer mode, and DX and DA are double-precision mode in this group of assignment statements. Also, when using the double-precision operations the function reference name must appear in a DOUBLE PRECISION specification statement.

In addition to the trigonometric functions, other mathematical and service routines are available. Figures 8-1 and 8-2 contain examples of various uses of the subprograms listed in the table.

FUNCTIONS AND SUBPROGRAMS

Figure 8-1 Examples of FORTRAN-supplied subprograms.

	Program Statements	Description
10	AI = ABS(DBMT)	The real variable AI is assigned the absolute value of the variable DBMT.†
20	I = IABS(IA)	The integer variable I is assigned the absolute value of the integer variable IA.
	CNT = FLOAT(KNT)	The value of the variable KNT is converted from integer mode to real mode and assigned to the real variable CNT.
	KNT = IFIX(CNT)	The value of the variable CNT is converted from real mode to integer mode and assigned to the integer variable KNT.
	I3 = IFIX(CNT*3.+X)	The value of the expression CNT*3.+X is converted from real mode to integer mode and assigned to the variable I3.
30	Y = EXP(X)	The variable Y is assigned the value of e raised to the X power or the equivalent of e^X, where e has the value of 2.718282.
	SQA = SQRT(156.25)	The variable SQA is assigned the value of the square root of 156.25 or 12.5.
	DOUBLE PRECISION SQB,DSQRT,A,X . . SQB = DSQRT(6.333*(1.25+A−X**2))	The expression serving as the argument of the square root function is evaluated. The square root of the indicated expression is assigned to the double-precision variable SQB. To use the double-precision subprograms, a specification statement must list the entry name and the argument.
	GAMMA = SIN(PI/4.)	The value of the trigonometric sine for the calculation of PI/4. is assigned to the variable GAMMA. The argument PI/4. must be expressed in radians when using the SIN function.
	X = SQRT(ABS(A))	The variable X is assigned the square root of the variable A. The ABS included as part of the SQRT argument precludes the possibility of taking the square root of a negative number.

†In this and the following statements, using a variable as an argument does *not* cause the variable to lose its value. Thus, DBMT retains its original value after execution of the statement.

Figure 8-2 Common errors that occur with FORTRAN-supplied subprograms.

Program Statements	Description
10 A = ABS(LTG)	The argument LTG is in conflict with the type required. As instructed in Table 8-1, a real argument is required to use the ABS function. LTG can be converted to real mode and the new variable used as shown: GLTG = FLOAT(LTG) 10 A = ABS(GLTG)

AVG = SUM/N	Although the mixed-mode expression here is not an example of a library subprogram error, it highlights one need for the subprograms. The mixed-mode expression can be avoided by the entries
	        XN = FLOAT(N)
	        AVG = SUM/XN
	        or
	        AVG = SUM/FLOAT(N)

I = SIN(PI/6.)	The assignment statement results in a loss of accuracy because the sine function is real and I is an integer variable. A correct entry would be AI = SIN(PI/6.)
X = DSQRT(87689.3345)	To use the double-precision function DSQRT, a specification statement must list the entry name. A correct entry preceding the assignment statement would be DOUBLE PRECISION X,DSQRT

APPLE = TANH(1.2,1.3)	Only one argument can be listed after the entry name TANH: a single constant, variable, or expression. Correct entries would be
	        APPLE1 = TANH(1.2)
	        APPLE2 = TANH(1.3)

Note: The type of the argument for the subprograms must be the same type specified in Table 8-1. For example, to use the subprogram FLOAT, an integer-type argument must be supplied.

FORTRAN-supplied Subprogram Exercises

1   What values are assigned to variables (a) to (h)?
    (a)   4876   X = ABS(−6.25∗1.5)
    (b)   Y = FLOAT(25/5+6)
    (c)   K = IFIX(−6.25∗1.5+7.3∗2.4)
    (d)   A = EXP(0.0)

FUNCTIONS AND SUBPROGRAMS

    (e)   B = ALOG(1.0)
    (f)   C = SIN(3.1416/6.)
    (g)   D = −COS(3.1416/6.)
    (h)   E = SQRT(18.5*18.5+25.)

2 Write the statement that equates to the following verbal descriptions:
   (a) Take the square root of X and assign to Y.
   (b) Take the square root of the variance (VAR) and assign to the standard deviation (STD). VAR and STD are double-precision variables.
   (c) Take the integer value of X and assign to IX.
   (d) Assign to XBX the value of e^Y, where e is assumed to be 2.7148.
   (e) Assign to DBX the value of e^{DY}, where DBX and DY are double-precision variables.
   (f) Assign the values of the sine and cosine of PI to the variables SPI and CPI, respectively.

3 Identify and correct errors in the following statements. Avoid mixed-mode expressions.
   (a) 67842   X = FLOAT(KNT*6.25)
   (b)   I = DABS(7.486*A−B)
   (c)   Y = SIN(3.14/8)
   (d)   E = EXP(5)
   (e)   S = FLOAT(10*B)
   (f)   X = IFIX(9*7*5)
   (g)   A = ABS(−5*I−J*10)
   (h)   H = ATAN(5.5,6.7)

4 Write a program that will calculate (by using the trigonometric functions) and print the answers requested:

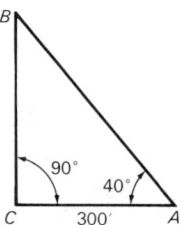

   (a) What is the length of the line BC in the triangle ABC?
   (b) What is the length of the line AB in the triangle ABC?
        (Hint: 1° = π/180 radians.)

5 Each of the equal sides of an isosceles triangle is 40.4 ft. Each of the equal angles is 75°. Write a program that will compute and print the altitude and base of the triangle.

8-2 Program Sample STATISTICS

Three standard functions will be illustrated in the STATISTICS[1] samples: the FLOAT, IFIX, and SQRT operations. These three are probably used more often than any of the others, especially in nonscientific programs. The FLOAT operation is shown first.

In the original version of STATISTICS-13, a variable XNOV was assigned the value of NOV for use in calculating the average. It was observed that the variables NOV and XNOV were assigned the same values, but since NOV is integer mode, it could not be used as the divisor (mixed-mode). By using the FLOAT function, the assignment statement can be removed from the program[2] as shown:

```
C PROGRAM STATISTICS-19
C THIS PROGRAM COMPUTES THE AVERAGE FOR A VARIABLE NUMBER OF VALUES
C IN MULTIPLE GROUPS OF DATA.
      WRITE(6,300)
      READ(5,201)NOG
      DO 2 I = 1, NOG
      SUM = 0.
      READ(5,201)NOV
      DO 1 J = 1, NOV
      READ(5,200)VALUE
      SUM = SUM + VALUE
1     CONTINUE
      AVG = SUM/FLOAT(NOV)
      WRITE(6,301)I,NOV,SUM,AVG
2     CONTINUE
200   FORMAT(F5.1)
201   FORMAT(I3)
300   FORMAT(@1GROUP NUMBER   NUMBER IN GROUP    SUM      AVERAGE@/)
301   FORMAT(5X,I3,13X,I3,5X,F8.1,1X,F8.1/)
      STOP
      END
```

New data for the program and the output from it are

```
   2
 004
  98.9
  82.2
  69.5
```

[1] As presently defined, the SALES problems do not require the use of subprograms. Miscellaneous samples will be inserted in their place.

[2] For programs STATISTICS-19 to 21, the flowcharts are omitted because the program logics are the same as those used for STATISTICS-13, 16, and 13, respectively.

FUNCTIONS AND SUBPROGRAMS

```
 71.9
005
 79.9
 87.3
 82.6
 92.5
 87.8
```

GROUP NUMBER	NUMBER IN GROUP	SUM	AVERAGE
1	4	322.5	80.6
2	5	430.1	86.0

The resultant output is generated with one less statement, using this version. The conversion from integer to real mode shown in this sample arises in many applications. The need for converting a value from real to integer mode also arises occasionally.

In the output from STATISTICS-16, the group number was printed with a decimal point following the numerical value because the variable KNT was designated as real mode. Recall that KNT was designated as real mode to facilitate its usage as part of the divisor in calculating the overall average. To print the group number in integer mode, the subprogram IFIX can be called to make the conversion. The revised statements illustrating the use of IFIX follow:

```
C   PROGRAM STATISTICS-20
C   THIS PROGRAM COMPUTES THE AVERAGE OF THREE VALUES FOR A NUMBER OF
C   GROUPS OF DATA. IT ALSO COMPUTES THE AVERAGE FOR ALL VALUES COMBINED.
        REAL KNT/0./, TOTSUM/0./
        WRITE(6,300)
1       READ(5,201)VAL1,VAL2,VAL3
        SUM = VAL1 + VAL2 + VAL3
        TOTSUM = TOTSUM + SUM
        AVG = SUM/3.
        KNT = KNT + 1.
        K = IFIX(KNT)
        WRITE(6,301)K,SUM,AVG
        IF(KNT.LT.4.) GO TO 1
        OAVG = TOTSUM / (KNT*3.)
        WRITE(6,302) TOTSUM,OAVG
201     FORMAT(3F5.1)
300     FORMAT(@1GROUP NUMBER    SUM    AVERAGE@/)
301     FORMAT(5X,  I3,  4X,F8.1,1X,F8.1/)
302     FORMAT(@0SUMMARY@,4X,F8.1,1X,F8.1/)
        STOP
        END
```

Although the statement containing the IFIX function appears to be in violation of the argument type, it is permitted to because KNT is listed in a REAL specification statement. New data plus the output from STATISTICS-20 are

```
68.4 69.5 47.2
55.6 46.4 58.3
98.8 92.0 90.7
75.5 85.4 68.3
```

GROUP NUMBER	SUM	AVERAGE
1	185.1	61.7
2	160.3	53.4
3	281.5	93.8
4	229.2	76.4
SUMMARY	856.1	71.3

The final function shown in this section, SQRT, requires a modification to the STATISTICS problem. Assume that in the definition of the problem solved by STATISTICS-13 the standard deviation is also required. The standard deviation is a statistic that measures, to a degree, the amount of variation in the data values and is calculated by employing the formula

$$SD = \sqrt{\frac{\Sigma x^2}{n} - \left(\frac{\Sigma x}{n}\right)^2}$$

where n = number of values in group
Σx = sum of values
Σx^2 = sum of each squared value

Flowchart 8-1 details the steps added to calculate and print the standard deviation. The new program statements are

```
C PROGRAM STATISTICS-21
C THIS PROGRAM COMPUTES THE AVERAGE FOR A VARIABLE NUMBER OF VALUES
C IN MULTIPLE GROUPS OF DATA. THE STANDARD DEVIATION IS ALSO COMPUTED.
      WRITE(6,300)
      READ(5,201,NOG
      DO 2 I = 1, NOG
```

FUNCTIONS AND SUBPROGRAMS

```
         SUM = 0.
         SUMSQ = 0.
         READ(5,201)NOV
         DO 1 J = 1, NOV
         READ(5,200)VALUE
         SUM = SUM + VALUE
         SUMSQ = SUMSQ + VALUE**2
1        CONTINUE
         XN = FLOAT(NOV)
         AVG = SUM/XN
         STD = SQRT(SUMSQ/XN - AVG**2)
         WRITE(6,301)I,NOV,SUM,AVG,STD
2        CONTINUE
200      FORMAT(F5.1)
201      FORMAT(I3)
300      FORMAT(@1GROUP NUMBER   NUMBER IN GROUP    SUM     AVERAGE    STANDARD D
        1EVIATION@/)
301      FORMAT(5X,I3,13X,I3,5X,F8.1,1X,F8.1,7X,F10.3/)
         STOP
         END
```

A new counter, SUMSQ, for calculating the sum of the squared values is inserted. It is required to compute the standard deviation. Another change involves the "floating" of the variable NOV from integer mode to the variable XN, real mode. The conversion is made in a separate assignment statement and then employed in two separate calculations. It is more efficient to write the statements as shown rather than using the forms

AVG = SUM/FLOAT(NOV)
STD = SQRT(SUMSQ/FLOAT(NOV) − (SUM/FLOAT(NOV))**2)

which requires three separate conversions. The SQRT function in the assignment statement serves the purpose of obtaining the square root of the expression within the outer parentheses. Also, the WRITE and FORMAT statements for printing the standard deviation are revised. Data for two groups plus the output from STATISTICS-21 follow:

```
    2
  004
   98.9
   82.2
   69.5
   71.9
  005
   79.9
   87.3
```

82.6
92.5
87.8

GROUP NUMBER	NUMBER IN GROUP	SUM	AVERAGE	STANDARD DEVIATION
1	4	322.5	80.6	11.580
2	5	430.1	86.0	4.383

In engineering and other scientific problems it is often necessary to introduce trigonometric functions to arrive at a solution. In this section, two of the functions, the cosine and the sine, will be illustrated in typical applications. In the first sample, consider an airplane that is flying due north at a speed of 356 mph. A strong wind is blowing from the west; in fact, the direction of the plane is N9°0′E. Determine the velocity of the wind and the speed of the plane with respect to the ground. To solve the problem, the first step requires a sketch of the conditions:

8-3 Miscellaneous Samples with Trigonometric Functions

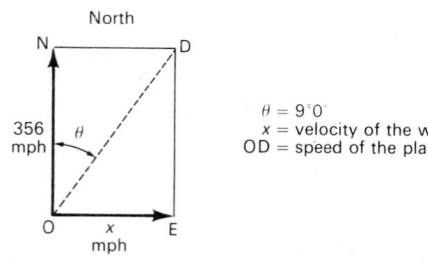

$\theta = 9°0′$
x = velocity of the wind
OD = speed of the plane with respect to the ground

The dotted line OD reflects the speed of the plane with respect to the ground; the angle θ gives the direction. The lighter lines ED and ND complete the rectangle, which permits the formula for x to be written

$$\tan 9° = \frac{x}{356} \quad \text{or} \quad x = 356 \tan 9°$$

Computing x manually yields the answer 56.4 mph, the speed of the wind. To find the speed along the line OD, the formula

$$\cos 9° = \frac{356}{OD} \quad \text{or} \quad OD = \frac{356}{\cos 9°}$$

FUNCTIONS AND SUBPROGRAMS

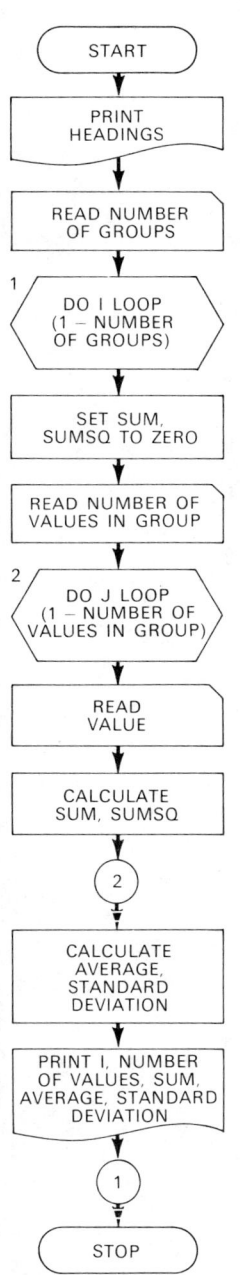

Flowchart 8-1 STATISTICS—FLOAT and SQRT functions.

can be used. The manual solution yields the answer 360.4 mph. Flowchart 8-2 outlines these steps; the program[1] statements required are

```
C AIR SPEED PROGRAM
      REAL MIN
      READ(5,100)AIRSPD,PD,DEG,MIN,WD
C AIRSPD = AIRPLANE SPEED, PD = PLANE DIRECTION, DEG = ANGLE IN DEGREES
C MIN = ANGLE IN MINUTES, WD = WIND DIRECTION
      THETA = .0174528*DEG + .0002909*MIN
      X = AIRSPD*(SIN(THETA)/COS(THETA))
      WRITE(6,200)PD,AIRSPD,PD,DEG,MIN,WD,WD,X
C GRDSPD = ADJUSTED GROUND SPEED
      GRDSPD = AIRSPD/COS(THETA)
      WRITE(6,201)GRDSPD
100   FORMAT(F4.0,A1,2F3.0,A1)
200   FORMAT(@1THE PLANE IS FLYING @,A1,@ AT A SPEED OF @,F5.1,@ MPH@/
     1@ THE DIRECTION CAUSED BY THE WIND IS @A1,2F3.0,A1/
     2@ THE WIND IS BLOWING @,A1,@ AT A SPEED OF @,F5.1,@ MPH@)
201   FORMAT(@0THE AIRPLANE SPEED WITH RESPECT TO THE GROUND IS @,F7.1,
     1@ MPH@)
      STOP
      END
```

The variable THETA, the argument of the functions sine and cosine, must be expressed in radians. Therefore, the input data in degrees and minutes must be converted to radians. The conversions are based on the formulas $1° = \pi/180$ rad and $1' = 1°/60 = 0.0174528/60$ rad.

Using as data the information just given, the output from the program is

```
 356N 9 0E
```

```
THE PLANE IS FLYING N AT A SPEED OF 356.0 MPH
THE DIRECTION CAUSED BY THE WIND IS N 9. 0.E
THE WIND IS BLOWING E AT A SPEED OF   56.4 MPH

THE AIRPLANE SPEED WITH RESPECT TO THE GROUND IS   360.4 MPH
```

For just one air-travel problem, the program is unnecessary, but if many similar problems are to be solved, it is quite useful.

---

[1] In the calculation of X, $\tan \theta$ has been computed by the formula $\sin \theta/\cos \theta$. In basic USAS Fortran IV, the tangent function is not available. However, the function is available in most advanced compilers, and the statement could be written simply as X = AIRSPD*TAN(THETA).

FUNCTIONS AND SUBPROGRAMS

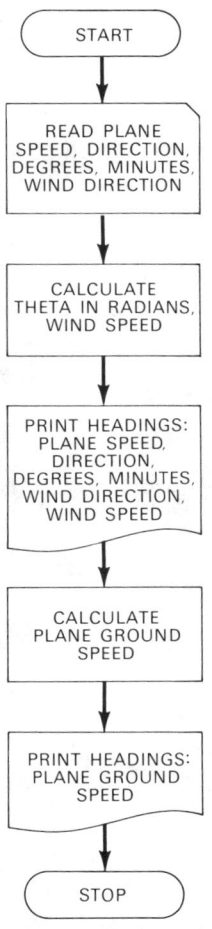

Flowchart 8-2 Air speed—Trigonometric functions.

For our purposes, it illustrates the use of the sine (SIN) and cosine (COS) functions.

A second sample again requires the use of the sine and cosine operations. If a large round stone weighing 734 lb is placed on an incline that makes an angle of 17°30′ with the horizontal plane, what is the minimum force required to prevent the stone from rolling down the incline? What is the force exerted by the stone against the plane? As before, a sketch serves the purpose of clarifying the problem:

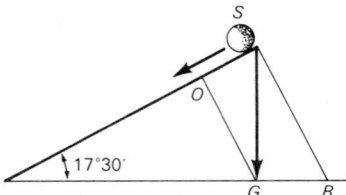

The force of the stone can be resolved into two rectangular components, one parallel to the plane and the other perpendicular. Hence SO, the force required to prevent it rolling, is given by

$SO = SG \sin 17°30'$ or $SO = 734 \sin 17°30'$

Solving manually, the force required is 220.7 lb. The force of the stone against the incline is represented by the line SB, or

$SB = SG \cos 17°30'$ or $SB = 734 \cos 17°30'$

The manual solution is 700 lb; Flowchart 8-3 details the series of computing steps needed. The program statements follow:

```
C PROGRAM THAT COMPUTES FORCES EXERTED BY A HEAVY OBJECT
      REAL MIN
      READ(5,100)DEG,MIN,WGT
C DEG = DEGREES OF ANGLE, MIN = MINUTES OF ANGLE, WGT = WEIGHT
      THETA = .0174528*DEG + .0002909*MIN
      SO = WGT * SIN(THETA)
      SB = WGT * COS(THETA)
      WRITE(6,200)WGT,SO,SB
100   FORMAT(2F3.0,F4.0)
200   FORMAT(@1THE FORCE REQUIRED TO PREVENT AN OBJECT WEIGHING @,
     1F6.0,@ POUNDS@/@ FROM FALLING DOWN AN INCLINE IS @,F7.1,@ POUNDS.@
     2/@ THE FORCE EXERTED AGAINST THE INCLINE IS @,F7.1,@ POUNDS.@)
      STOP
      END
```

The variable THETA in this sample again must be computed to use the SIN and COS functions because their arguments must be expressed in radians. The constants in the assignment are derived from the same conversion formulas, $1° = \pi/180$ rad and $1' = 1°/60 = 0.0174528/60$ rad.

Using the weight of the stone and the angle in degrees and minutes as input data, the output from the program is

FUNCTIONS AND SUBPROGRAMS

```
17 30 734
```

```
THE FORCE REQUIRED TO PREVENT AN OBJECT WEIGHING    734. POUNDS
FROM FALLING DOWN AN INCLINE IS    220.7 POUNDS.
THE FORCE EXERTED AGAINST THE INCLINE IS    700.0 POUNDS.
```

This sample serves only to illustrate the use of the SIN and COS functions. In many cases, the program here would be but one small part of a larger routine.

8-4 Statement Functions

The same computation performed with different data values at various locations within a program can be incorporated as a statement function. A statement function specifies an operation to be executed whenever the function is called within another statement in the same program. It functions similarly to the FORTRAN-supplied subprogram; however, it is limited in scope to one statement. The general form of the statement is

name$(a_1, a_2, \ldots, a_n)$ = [expression or formula]

where a statement label is not permitted, "name" is the statement-function name, a_1, a_2, . . . , a_n are unsubscripted variables

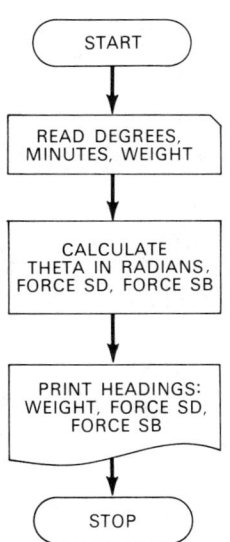

Flowchart 8-3 Force exerted—Trigonometric functions.

employed as dummy arguments, and the expression or formula is any valid FORTRAN expression, excluding subscripted variables. All statement-function definitions must appear at the beginning of a program, preceding the first executable statement and following the DIMENSION statement.

An example, prior to defining the rules applying to the instruction, will help clarify its use. Consider the statement

SUM(A,B,C) = A + B*2. + C*4.

which defines the statement-function definition SUM with SUM as the function name and A, B, and C as the dummy arguments. The formula to the right of the equals sign specifies the operations to be performed when the function is referenced in an assignment statement. For example, the function could be referenced by the statement

X = SUM(1.0, 2.0, 3.0)

The dummy arguments A, B, and C are replaced by the actual arguments 1.0, 2.0, and 3.0, respectively, in the calling statement. Thus, X is assigned the value 17.0 (1.+2.0*2.+3.0*4.). The variables A, B, and C are called *dummy arguments* in the statement function because they are not assigned a value in the definition. The arguments are assigned values in the calling statements, at which time the arguments are no longer dummy variables but valid ones that are used in the actual computation.

The rules applying to the statement function are summarized as

1. The type (mode) may be assigned by the predefined convention or by an explicit specification statement.

2. The name may consist of from one to six alphanumeric characters, the first of which must be alphabetic. Embedded blanks are ignored.

3. The dummy arguments must be unsubscripted and there must be at least one in the argument list. Constants are not permitted. However, in the calling statement, subscripted variables and constants are valid.

4. The number of dummy arguments and actual arguments in the calling reference must be the same, of the same type (mode), and of the same order.

FUNCTIONS AND SUBPROGRAMS

5 Recursive definition is not permitted, meaning the expression defining the function must not contain a reference to the function.

Figures 8-3 and 8-4 contain examples of user-created statement functions.

Statement Function Exercises

1 Given that X, Y, and Z have values of 5.5, 6.5, and 1.5, respectively, evaluate the following statements:

  (a) XBAR(A,B) = (A + B*(A + B))/50.
.
.
.
      ZB = XBAR(X, Y)

  (b) FUN(B,A,C) = A*C*B/50.
.
.
.
      FAB = FUN(X,Y,Z)

  (c) AREA(X,Y,Z) = SQRT((X−5.)*(Y−4.)*Z)
.
.
.
      BAREA = AREA(X,Z,Y)

  (d) PATS(X,A,B) = EXP((X*(B−A)**2)+5.)
.
.
.
      TAPS = PATS(3.5,X,Y)

  (e) SAPT(A,C,E,F) = A +C*2. +E*3. +F*4.
.
.
.
      BAP = SAPT(2.5,X,3.5,Y)

2 Write the statement-function definitions and appropriate function references that equate to the following verbal descriptions:

  (a) The roots of the quadratic equation $ax^2 + bx + c = 0$ are

$$x = \frac{-b \pm \sqrt{b^2 - 4ac}}{2a}$$

when the equation is not factorable. Supply a statement-function definition for x.

  (b) The law of cosines is

Figure 8-3 Examples of statement functions.

	Program Statements	Description
	FUNX(X) = 10.*(X−2.)+14.5	A statement function FUNX establishes a defined expression with one argument X. The function is used twice to assign values to the variables A1 and A2. In statement labeled 281, the 3.5 is substituted for X in FUNX, and A1 is assigned a value of 29.5. Likewise, A2 is assigned a value of 39.5.
281	A1 = FUNX(3.5)	
184	A2 = FUNX(4.5)	
	PROD(A,B) = 5.*A+B**2+.33	A statement function PROD establishes a defined expression with two dummy arguments A and B. The function statement is used to assign values to PDD and PD1. In the first use of PROD, the constants 6.0 and 5.0 are substituted for A and B. As a result, PDD is assigned a value of 55.33. Likewise, PD1 is assigned a value of 3058.39.
	PDD = PROD(6.0,5.0)	
	PD1 = PROD(PDD,PDD)	
	XTA(A,B) = A*B/(A−B*2.)	The statement function XTA, with two dummy arguments A and B, is referenced twice in label 578. As illustrated here, any valid expression is permitted as the actual argument in the calling statement, including a function reference.
578	T = XTA(X,XTA(4.3,6.2))	
	THE(X,Y) = .0002909*X + .0174528*Y	Although subscripted variables are not permitted in the statement-function definition, they are legal as actual arguments in the function reference. Thus X(1) and X(2) are substituted for X and Y.
	THETA = THE(X(1),X(2))	
	SUM(X,Y,I) = (X+Y+AB)**I	Four variables are contained in the statement function SUM, but only three are arguments X, Y, and I. To use the function, the variable AB must be assigned a value prior to the function use in label 10. Note also that two of the arguments are real mode and one integer mode. Thus, the value of SQ is dependent on the substitution of 1. for X, 3. for Y, and 2 for I. The result of the substitutions gives SQ a value of 64.0. RHO is assigned a value of 81.0 minus 17424.0 or −17343.0.
	AB = 4.	
10	SQ = SUM(1.,3.,2)	
	RHO = SUM(2.,3.,2) − SUM(SQ,SQ,2)	

FUNCTIONS AND SUBPROGRAMS   235

Figure 8-4 Common errors that occur with statement functions.

	Program Statements	Description
	XTRA(3,I(1)) = I(1)*3+I(1)**3 . . .	The arguments in the statement function can contain only variables. Constants and subscripted variables are not permitted. A correct entry would be XTRA(I,I1) = I1*I+I1**I
  754	BEA(X,A,K) = X*A+((X−A)**K) . . . B = BEA(2,2)	The number and mode of the arguments must agree in both the statement function and its reference within the program at label 754. The first two arguments in the function definition are real mode and the third integer. Therefore, the call must conform as shown by the correction B = BEA(2.,2.,2)

48
76
 	
	A = 7.25
	 B = 8.25
	 AREA(X,Y) = A*B**2+X*Y**2
	 .
	 .
	 B5 = AREA(5.2,6.1)
		There are two errors in this sample. First, the statement function can not be labeled, and second, it must precede all the executable statements in a program. AREA defines a function and thus must precede all the other statements. Correct entries would be
		     AREA(X,Y) = A*B**2 + X*Y**2
		     A = 7.25
		 48 B = 8.25
		     .
		     .
		     .
		     B5 = AREA(5.2,6.1)

	BASE = X*Y*Z**2
	 .
	 .
	 .
	 READ(5,100)X,Y,Z
	 WRITE(6,200) BASE
		Two errors are contained in this sample. First, there must always be at least one dummy argument in a statement-function definition. Second, the function can not be referenced in a WRITE statement. Correct entries would be
		     BASE(X,Y,Z) = X*Y*Z**2
		     .
		     .
		     .
		     READ(5,100)X,Y,Z
		     B = BASE(X,Y,Z)
		     WRITE(6,200) B

$$a^2 = b^2 + c^2 - 2bc \cos A$$

Supply a statement-function definition for a.

(c) The area of a triangle with sides a, b, and c is

$$A = \sqrt{s(s-a)(s-b)(s-c)} \qquad \text{where } s = \tfrac{1}{2}(a+b+c)$$

Supply a statement-function definition for A.

(d) The variance of the hypergeometric distribution is

$$\text{var} = \frac{nab(a+b-n)}{(a+b)^2(a+b-1)}$$

Supply a satement-function definition for var. Avoid a mixed-mode expression.

(e) The t-test for certain populations is

$$t = \frac{\bar{x}_1 - \bar{x}_2 - \sigma}{\sqrt{\left[\dfrac{(n_1-1)s_1^2 + (n_2-1)s_2^2}{n+n_2-2}\right]}\sqrt{\dfrac{1}{n_1} + \dfrac{1}{n_2}}}$$

Supply a statement-function definition for t.

3 Identify and correct errors in the following statements:

(a)   ISTX(M,N) = (M+5)*(N+4)

                    .
                    .
                    .

                    S = ISTA(13,72) − ISTA(4,78)

(b)   107   ITSP(K,L,M) = (K*2)/(L+M+5)

                    .
                    .
                    .

                    IX = ITSP(A,B,C)

(c)   PRB(5,X,Y) = X**5 + (Y*X)/X**5
(d)   RECUR(Z,B) = Z+B*RECUR(6.7,.025)
(e)   GAM(B,C,D,E(I)) = B/C+C/D+B*C/E(I)
(f)   SEMB(H,P,Q,R) = 5.23*(H−P+Q)/R+Q

                    .
                    .
                    .

                    EM = SEMB(10.2,SEMB(A,B,C,D),X)

8-5 Program Sample STATISTICS

In Sec. 8-2, the standard deviation was computed for each group in the STATISTICS problem. In the definition of the problem, what additional steps would be required to compute a standard deviation for all groups combined? Overall totals for the sum of the values, the squared values, and the number of

FUNCTIONS AND SUBPROGRAMS

observations would be necessary. With these three totals, a standard deviation can be computed that is indicative of all the values. Flowchart 8-4 identifies the logic steps necessary. As indicated in the flowchart, a statement-function definition is employed to compute the standard deviation for each group and for the total of all groups. The statements reflecting the flowchart logic are

```
C PROGRAM STATISTICS-22
C THIS PROGRAM COMPUTES THE AVERAGE FOR A VARIABLE NUMBER OF VALUES
C IN MULTIPLE GROUPS OF DATA. THE STANDARD DEVIATION IS ALSO COMPUTED.
      SD(A,B,C) = SQRT(A/C - B**2)
      DATA OSUM,OSUMSQ,OXN/3*0.0/
      WRITE(6,300)
      READ(5,201)NOG
      DO 2 I = 1, NOG
      SUM = 0.
      SUMSQ = 0.
      READ(5,201)NOV
      DO 1 J = 1, NOV
      READ(5,200)VALUE
      SUM = SUM + VALUE
      SUMSQ = SUMSQ + VALUE**2
1     CONTINUE
      XN = FLOAT(NOV)
      AVG = SUM/XN
      STD = SD(SUMSQ,AVG,XN)
      WRITE(6,301)NOV,SUM,AVG,STD
      OSUM = OSUM + SUM
      OSUMSQ = OSUMSQ + SUMSQ
      OXN = OXN + XN
2     CONTINUE
      OAVG = OSUM/OXN
      OSD = SD(OSUMSQ,OAVG,OXN)
      K = IFIX(OXN)
      WRITE(6,302)K,OSUM,OAVG,OSD
200   FORMAT(F5.1)
201   FORMAT(I3)
300   FORMAT(@1NUMBER OF VALUES    SUM     AVERAGE    STANDARD DEVIATION@/)
301   FORMAT(9X,I3,4X,F8.1,1X,F8.1,3X,F10.3/)
302   FORMAT(@ SUMMARY @,I3,4X,F8.1,1X,F8.1,3X,F10.3/)
      STOP
      END
```

In the program, three new counters, OSUM, OSUMSQ, and OXN, are established to store the totals for the calculation of the overall standard deviation. Also, the computation of the standard deviation is performed at two locations by a statement function. In the first location, the arguments SUMSQ, AVG, and XN replace the dummy arguments A, B, and C, respectively, and the calculation performed. In the second location, the

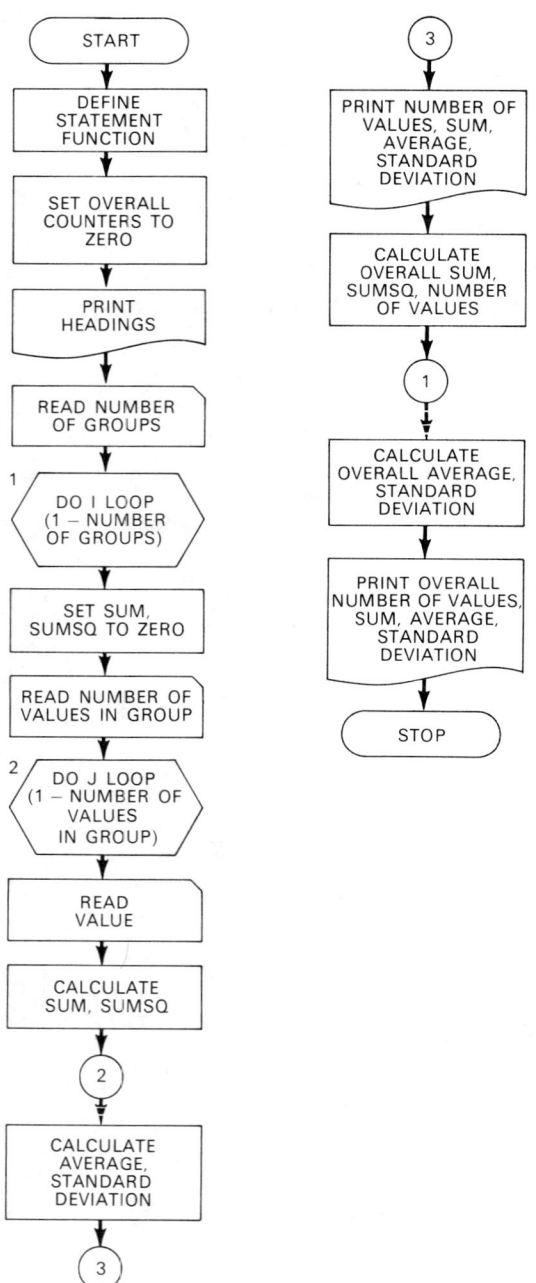

Flowchart 8-4 STATISTICS—Statement-function definition.

FUNCTIONS AND SUBPROGRAMS

arguments OSUMSQ, OAVG, and OXN replace the dummy arguments A, B, and C. A new WRITE is also added to print the overall totals and standard deviation. Data and output from STATISTICS-22 are

```
    2
  004
   98.9
   82.2
   69.5
   71.9
  005
   79.9
   87.3
   82.6
   92.5
   87.8
```

NUMBER OF VALUES	SUM	AVERAGE	STANDARD DEVIATION
4	322.5	80.6	11.580
5	430.1	86.0	4.383
SUMMARY 9	752.6	83.6	8.801

Although not essential, the statement-function definition does reduce the amount of repetitious coding. However, it is advantageous only if it is referenced at least twice in the program. The same complicated expression that is referenced often should suggest the use of statement-function definitions in a program.

8-6 Miscellaneous Program Sample

Two statement-function definitions will be included in the following sample program. Consider a problem that requests the largest area of three triangles to be printed by a program, given the three sides of each triangle. To determine the largest, the area of each triangle must be computed. Since the three sides of the triangle are given, the formula

$$\text{Area} = \sqrt{s(s-a)(s-b)(s-c)} \qquad \text{where } s = \tfrac{1}{2}(a+b+c)$$

can be used. Once the area for each triangle is computed, IF statements can be used to determine the largest. The logic is outlined in Flowchart 8-5. The statements, including two function definitions, follow:

```
C AREA OF TRIANGLES
      S(A,B,C) = 0.5*(A+B+C)
      AREA(A,B,C,X) = SQRT(X*(X-A)*(X-B)*(X-C))
C A1, B1, ....,C3 ARE THE SIDES OF THE TRIANGLES
5     READ(5,100,END=9)A1,B1,C1,A2,B2,C2,A3,B3,C3
      S1 = S(A1,B1,C1)
      AREA1 = AREA(A1,B1,C1,S1)
      S2 = S(A2,B2,C2)
      AREA2 = AREA(A2,B2,C2,S2)
      S3 = S(A3,B3,C3)
      AREA3 = AREA(A3,B3,C3,S3)
C FIND THE LARGEST TRIANGLE
      IF(AREA1.GT.AREA2)GO TO 6
      IF(AREA2.LT.AREA3)GO TO 7
      WRITE(6,200)A2,B2,C2,AREA2
      GO TO 5
6     IF(AREA1.GT.AREA3)GO TO 8
7     WRITE(6,200)A3,B3,C3,AREA3
      GO TO 5
8     WRITE(6,200)A1,B1,C1,AREA1
      GO TO 5
100   FORMAT(9F5.1)
200   FORMAT(@0THE TRIANGLE WITH SIDES@,3F6.1,@ HAS THE LARGEST AREA@,
     1F8.1)
9     STOP
      END
```

The function S is referenced three times, once for each of the triangles, as is the function AREA. The sides of the triangles are used as the actual arguments, replacing the dummy arguments A, B, and C in both functions. The dummy argument X in the AREA function is replaced by the values of S1, S2, and S3, calculated by the S function. The use of the functions in this program reduces somewhat the amount of coding that must be done by the programmer. The number of statements could be reduced, also, by combining the calculation of S1 into the AREA1 statement as

AREA1 = AREA(A1,B1,C1,S(A1,B1,C1))

where the variable S1 is replaced by the function reference S. The same idea also applies to S2 and S3. However, it is simpler to analyze the program with the separate statements. Three sets of data plus the output from the program are listed.

```
3.0   4.0   5.0   6.0   4.5   4.5   7.0   8.5   7.5
10.0  15.0  20.0  14.0  15.0  16.0  14.0  10.0  10.0
2.5   3.3   2.1   5.4   5.7   5.8   3.0   2.9   2.4
```

FUNCTIONS AND SUBPROGRAMS   241

```
THE TRIANGLE WITH SIDES    7.0    8.5    7.5 HAS THE LARGEST AREA    24.9
THE TRIANGLE WITH SIDES   14.0   15.0   16.0 HAS THE LARGEST AREA    96.6
THE TRIANGLE WITH SIDES    5.4    5.7    5.8 HAS THE LARGEST AREA    13.7
```

In this program, if two triangles have equal areas, only one is printed. However, revised IF and added WRITE statements could provide the capability of printing equal areas if so desired. However, here the emphasis is placed on the use of the statement functions.

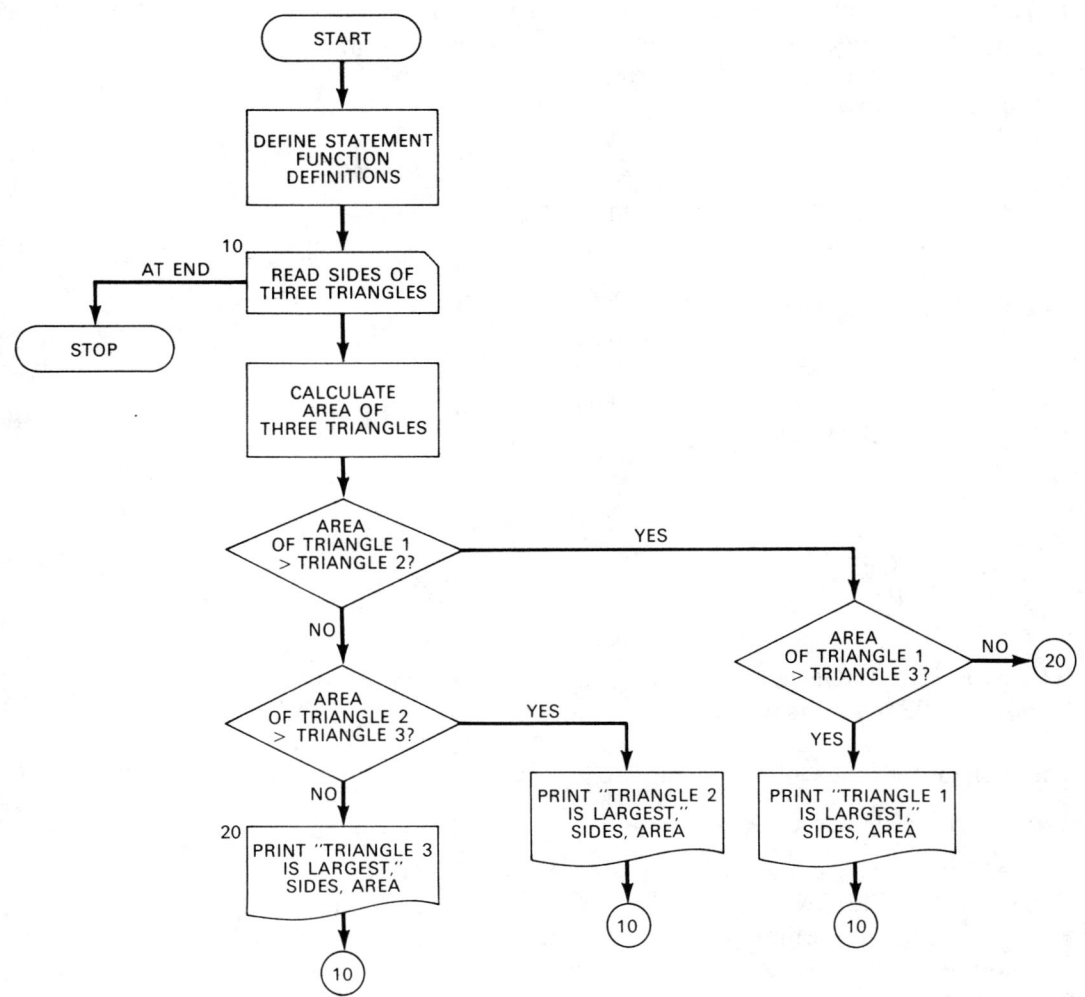

Flowchart 8-5   Area of triangles—Statement-function definitions.

A limitation of statement functions is that the definition can consist of only one statement. However, certain applications require a series of statements to arrive at a particular answer. When the same series of statements appear at various locations within a program and the statements yield one result, a FUNCTION subprogram can be used to simplify the program.

8-7 FUNCTION Subprograms

A FUNCTION subprogram is a routine that consists of a FUNCTION statement followed by other FORTRAN instructions, including at least one RETURN statement, and terminated physically by an END command. It is a separate program that is executed whenever it is referenced in another program. Shown schematically, a main program and a FUNCTION subprogram follow:

Main Program	FUNCTION Subprogram
.	FUNCTION SUM(G,H)
.	.
.	.
2 X = SUM(A,B)	.
.	SUM = G+H
.	RETURN
.	END
3 Y = SUM(C,D)	
.	
.	
.	
STOP	
END	

where the FUNCTION subprogram is called twice, by statement labels 2 and 3, by a main program.

The general form of the statement is

Type FUNCTION name $(a_1, a_2, \ldots, a_n)$

where "type" is omitted or may be INTEGER, REAL, or DOUBLE PRECISION, "name" is the function name, and $a_1, a_2, \ldots, a_n$ are dummy arguments. When the name of the function with a list of arguments appears in an expression within a main program, the reference causes the computations to be performed as directed by the function definition. The

FUNCTIONS AND SUBPROGRAMS

resultant quantity is assigned to the function name. Before listing the rules that apply to a FUNCTION subprogram, consider the example

Main Program		FUNCTION Subprogram
	DIMENSION A(100),AA(100)	FUNCTION SUM(Y,N,X)
	.	DIMENSION X(100)
	.	SUM = 0.
	.	DO 1 I = 1,N
5	X = SUM(B,M,A)	SUM = SUM+X(I)
	.	1 CONTINUE
	.	SUM = SUM*Y
	.	RETURN
6	Y = SUM(BB,MM,AA)	END
	.	
	.	
	.	
	STOP	
	END	

The name of the real FUNCTION subprogram is SUM, with dummy arguments of Y, N, and array X. The effect of the statements up to the RETURN is to (1) accumulate the sum of N elements found in array X and (2) multiply the sum by the variable Y. The resultant quantity is assigned to the function name SUM.

In the main program, the function is referenced twice. At label 5, the array A replaces the dummy array X, and the variables B and M replace the dummy variables Y and N. Thus, M elements of array A are accumulated and the sum multiplied by B. The result is assigned to the variable X in the main program. At label 6, array AA and variables BB and MM replace the dummy variables X, Y, and N, respectively. The result of the function evaluation is assigned to the variable Y in the main program.

Without the subprogram, the FUNCTION statements would be duplicated with different parameters at two locations in the main program. The rules that apply to the usage of FUNCTION subprograms are similar to those of statement-function definitions. They are

1. The type (mode) may be assigned by the predefined convention, by an explicit specification in the FUNCTION statement, or by an explicit specification statement located within the subprogram.
2. The name may consist of one to six alphanumeric characters.
3. The dummy arguments must be unsubscripted (although array names are permitted), and there must be at least one in the argument list. Constants are not permitted. However, in the calling statement, subscripted variables and constants are permitted.
4. The dummy arguments and the actual arguments must agree in type (mode), number, and order.
5. Because the FUNCTION subprogram is a separate program, its variable names and statement labels may be the same as those appearing in a main program.
6. The FUNCTION statement must appear as the first statement in the subprogram.
7. The name of the function must be assigned a value at least once in the subprogram.
8. The last statement of the subprogram must be an END instruction, specifying for the compiler the physical end. At least one RETURN statement, with an optional label, must be included. Multiple RETURNS are valid within the subprogram. The form of the RETURN statement is simply

    sl   RETURN

    where sl is an optional statement label.

A description of FUNCTION subprograms and the common errors that occur in its use are shown in Figs. 8-5 and 8-6. Normally, it is assumed that FUNCTION subprograms return only one value, via the function name, to the calling program. It is possible, however, to return several by assigning values to the dummy arguments within the subprogram.

Figure 8-5 Examples of FUNCTION subprograms.

	Program Statements	
Main Program	FUNCTION Subprogram	Description
DIMENSION Z(100) REAL MIN	REAL FUNCTION MIN(X,N) DIMENSION X(100)	The real FUNCTION subprogram MIN, with dummy

FUNCTIONS AND SUBPROGRAMS

Program Statements

Main Program	FUNCTION Subprogram	Description
· · SMALL=MIN(Z,10) · · · STOP END	MIN=X(1) DO 1 I = 2,N IF (X(I).LT.MIN)MIN=X(I) CONTINUE 1 RETURN END	arguments array X and variable N, is called by the main program. When it is referenced, X is replaced by the actual argument Z and N is replaced by 10. Effectively, then, the subprogram searches the first 10 locations of Table Z and assigns the minimum value to MIN. In the main program, SMALL is assigned the value of MIN.
· · PROD1=FUNC(E,F,G) PROD2=FUNC(X,Y,Z) · · STOP END	FUNCTION FUNC(A,B,C) X=A*B*C+7.25*(A*B) FUNC=.05*X+A/B RETURN END	A main program specifies the use of a FUNCTION subprogram. The name of the function is FUNC, and it is called twice in this example. The value of FUNC is determined by the actual arguments assigned to the dummy arguments A, B, and C and the remaining statements in the function. Only the final value of FUNC is returned to the main program. Since FUNC implies real mode, real values are assigned to PROD1 (dependent on the values of E, F, and G) and PROD2 (dependent on the values of X, Y, and Z).
INTEGER XS INT1=XS(I,K,M) INT2=XS(J,K,L)−XS(M,N,N1) · · 2 STOP END 1	FUNCTION XS(I1,I2,I3) INTEGER XS XS=(I1+I2+I3)*3 IF(XS)1,2,1 XS=100 RETURN XS=XS+10/I3 RETURN END	This sample shows the integer FUNCTION XS being called three times by the main program. It is called the first time passing the three arguments I, K, and M. The second time it is referenced J, K, and L are the three arguments passed to the function. The third time it is referenced the arguments M, N, and N1 are

Figure 8-5 Examples of FUNCTION subprograms *(cont'd)*.

Program Statements		
Main Program	FUNCTION Subprogram	Description
		processed in the FUNCTION subprogram. The variable INT1 is assigned the value of XS directly, and the variable INT2 is assigned the difference of XS, with J, K, and L as arguments and XS with M, N, and N1 as arguments. The sample also illustrates that multiple RETURN are permitted within the subprogram.

Figure 8-6 Common errors that occur with FUNCTION subprograms.

Program Statements		
Main Program	FUNCTION Subprogram	Description
. . X = MSQ(A,B) . STOP END	FUNCTION MSQ(A,B) . MSQ = ((A*B)/15.5)**2 . RETURN END	The FUNCTION subprogram MSQ is integer mode by default. However, the calculations involve real variables and constants. Therefore, the function name should be real mode also. REAL specification statements in both the main and subprogram are required as REAL MSQ

.
.
PIX = FUNX
.
.
STOP
END
	FUNCTION FUNX
	.
	.
	FUNX = A*B + 3.213
	RETURN
	END
		The FUNCTION subprogram FUNX must have at least one argument in the argument list. A correct entry for the main would be
		    PIX = FUNX(A,B)
		and in the subprogram:
		    FUNCTION FUNX(A,B)

. . RHO = RHOD(A,B) . STOP END	FUNCTION RHOD(C,A(I),3) . . RHOD = C*A(I)**3 RETURN END	Two errors are contained in this sample, with both occurring in the FUNCTION statement. The arguments in the list must be unsubscripted variables or array names. Constants and subscripted

FUNCTIONS AND SUBPROGRAMS

Program Statements

Main Program	FUNCTION Subprogram	Description

		variables are not permitted. Correct entries would be
		    FUNCTION RHOD(X,Y)
		        .
		    RHOD = X*Y**3

DIMENSION X(25)
.
SIGX = SIG(H,A,X,P)
.
.
STOP
END
	DIMENSION E(25)
	FUNCTION SIG(C,D,E,F)
	C = D*E + F
	F = C/2.546
	RETURN
	END
		The FUNCTION statement must appear first in the routine, and the name SIG must be assigned a value at least once in the subprogram. Although the arguments are used in the subprogram, the function name is not. Correct entries are
		    FUNCTION SIG(C,D,E,F)
		    DIMENSION E(25)
		        .
		    SIG = C/2.546

.
.
DELX = DELT(P1,P2,I)
.
STOP
END
	FUNCTION DELT(A,B,C,D)
	.
	.
	RETURN
	END
		Two types of errors are illustrated by this set. The mode and the number of arguments in the calling statement and the subprogram must agree. In this case, the calling statement has only three, one integer mode, and the FUNCTION subprogram contains four real arguments. Two correct entries are plausible:
		    DELX = DELT(P1,P2,P3,P4)
		        or
		    FUNCTION DELT(A,B,IN)

FUNCTION Subprogram Exercises

1 Write FUNCTION subprograms and the appropriate statements that, if placed in a main program, would call the subprogram for the following descriptions:
   (a) Compute the average of n elements in a one-dimensional array.
   (b) Compute the average of $n \times n$ elements in a two-dimensional array.
   (c) Compute the greatest common divisor of two positive integers.
   (d) Compute the third side of a triangle, given two sides and the

included angle in degrees and minutes. Use the formula
$$a^2 = b^2 + c^2 - 2bc \cos A$$
where the angle A must be converted to radians (see Sec. 8-3).

(e) For principal P, a bank pays r interest compounded annually How much is on deposit at the end of n years? Use the formula
$$\text{New deposit} = P \frac{(1+r)^n - 1}{r}$$

(f) Sort the n elements of array X in descending order. Return the sorted array via the dummy array name. If the smallest value in the sorted table is negative, zero, or positive, return a -1, 0, or 1, respectively, via the FUNCTION subprogram name.

2 In samples (a) to (d), what values are assigned to X and Y in the main program?

	Main Program	Subprogram
(a)	INTEGER TAP, X, Y . . . X = TAP(3,5) Y = TAP(4,6)	INTEGER FUNCTION TAP(I,J) K = I*J − (I+J+10) TAP = IABS(K)*I RETURN END
(b)	. . . X = TAP(3.2,4.2) Y = TAP(4.2,4.3) .	FUNCTION TAP(A,B) X = A*B − (A+B+10.) TAP = ABS(X)*A RETURN END
(c)	. . A = 4.8 B = 9.6 X = PG(3.2/A,3.2/B) Y = PG(A*3.2,B*3.2)	FUNCTION PG(X,Y) IF(X.GT.Y)GO TO 5 PG = X−Y**2+X*Y RETURN 5 PG = X+Y**2−X*Y RETURN END

FUNCTIONS AND SUBPROGRAMS

(d)
```
            X = 1.                          FUNCTION XG(C,F)
            Y = 2.                          XG = 72.15*(C−F)+900.
            A = XG(X,Y)                     C = XG*2.
            WRITE(6,200)A,X,Y               F = XG*3.
     200    FORMAT(3F10.2)                  RETURN
                                            END
```

(Note: In this sample, what are the three values printed by the WRITE statement?)

3   Correct errors, if any, in statements (a) to (d):

Main Program	Subprogram
(a) ·	FUNCTION LET(X,Y)
·	·
·	·
LEM = LET(A,B)	·
	LET = X*Y+35.
	RETURN
	END
(b) ·	FUNCTION BAR(X,Y)
·	·
·	·
BAR = BAP(X,Y)	·
	BAR = X−Y*(X+Y)
	RETURN
	END
(c) REAL LAST	REAL LAST
·	FUNCTION LAST(F,H,X)
·	·
·	·
Z = LAST(3.,4.)	·
	LAST = F−H/X
	RETURN
	END
(d) ·	FUNCTION TPA(A,I,B,5)
·	·
·	·
ZBAR = TPA(2,4.5,3.1)	·

8-8 Program Sample STATISTICS

To illustrate the use of a FUNCTION subprogram, the definition of the STATISTICS problem is expanded here to include the parameters: (1) in addition to printing the sum, average, and standard deviation, print also the highest value in each group; and (2) print the highest standard deviation, considering all groups.

The solution presented in STATISTICS-22 is the basis for the answer here. Flowchart 8-6 identifies the changes necessary to print the answers for the expanded problem. The important differences in the flowchart concern the added subprogram. It is referenced in two locations in the logical flow: with the Table VALUE and NOV as arguments and with the Table STD and NOG as arguments. STATISTICS-23 contains the necesary program statements:

```
C PROGRAM STATISTICS-23
C THIS PROGRAM COMPUTES THE AVERAGE FOR A VARIABLE NUMBER OF VALUES
C IN MULTIPLE GROUPS OF DATA. THE STANDARD DEVIATION IS ALSO COMPUTED.
      DIMENSION STD(100),VALUE(100)
      DATA OSUM,OSUMSQ,OXN/3*0.0/
      SD(A,B,C) = SQRT(A/C - B**2)
      WRITE(6,300)
      READ(5,201)NOG
      DO 2 I = 1, NOG
      SUM = 0.
      SUMSQ = 0.
      READ(5,201)NOV
      DO 1 J = 1, NOV
      READ(5,200)VALUE(J)
      SUM = SUM + VALUE(J)
      SUMSQ = SUMSQ + VALUE(J)**2
1     CONTINUE
      XN = FLOAT(NOV)
      AVG = SUM/XN
      STD(I) = SD(SUMSQ,AVG,XN)
      HS = HI(VALUE,NOV)
      WRITE(6,301)I,NOV,SUM,AVG,STD(I),HS
      OSUM = OSUM + SUM
      OSUMSQ = OSUMSQ + SUMSQ
      OXN = OXN + XN
2     CONTINUE
      OAVG = OSUM/OXN
      OSD = SD(OSUMSQ,OAVG,OXN)
      K = IFIX(OXN)
      OHS = HI(STD,NOG)
      WRITE(6,302)K,OSUM,OAVG,OSD,OHS
200   FORMAT(F5.1)
201   FORMAT(I3)
300   FORMAT(@1GROUP NUMBER   NUMBER IN GROUP    SUM     AVERAGE STANDARD DE
     1VIATION HIGHEST VALUE@/)
301   FORMAT(5X,I3,13X,I3,5X,F8.1,1X,F8.1,7X,F10.3,2X,F10.1/)
302   FORMAT(5X,@SUMMARY@,9X,I3,5X,F8.1,1X,F8.1,7X,F10.3,2X,F10.3/ )
      STOP
      END
C
      FUNCTION HI(X,N)
      DIMENSION X(100)
      HI = X(1)
      DO 1 I = 1, N
      IF(HI.LT.X(I)) HI = X(I)
```

FUNCTIONS AND SUBPROGRAMS

```
1       CONTINUE
        RETURN
        END
```

The FUNCTION subprogram HI, because it is an independent routine, is placed after the END statement in the main program. In the next section it will be shown that it can be placed in front of the main program also. The statements in the subprogram are similar to the first example found in Fig. 8-5. In this case, the first N elements of array X are examined, with the highest value assigned to the name HI. The dummy arguments N and X are replaced by actual arguments in the calling program.

To use the subprogram as it is written, all the individual values and the standard deviation for each group must be placed in tables. Hence, the DIMENSION statement is required. To store the individual values in each group, the index J of the inner loop determines the proper location. But to store the individual standard-deviation values, the index I of the outer loop is required because its value identifies the appropriate standard-deviation group number. Three groups of data plus the output from the program follow:

```
  3
003
 69.9
 75.8
 61.0
004
 98.9
 82.2
 69.5
 71.9
005
 79.9
 87.7
 82.5
 67.7
 89.2
```

GROUP NUMBER	NUMBER IN GROUP	SUM	AVERAGE	STANDARD DEVIATION	HIGHEST VALUE
1	3	206.7	68.9	6.083	75.8
2	4	322.5	80.6	11.580	98.9
3	5	407.0	81.4	7.638	89.2
SUMMARY	12	936.2	78.0	10.299	11.580

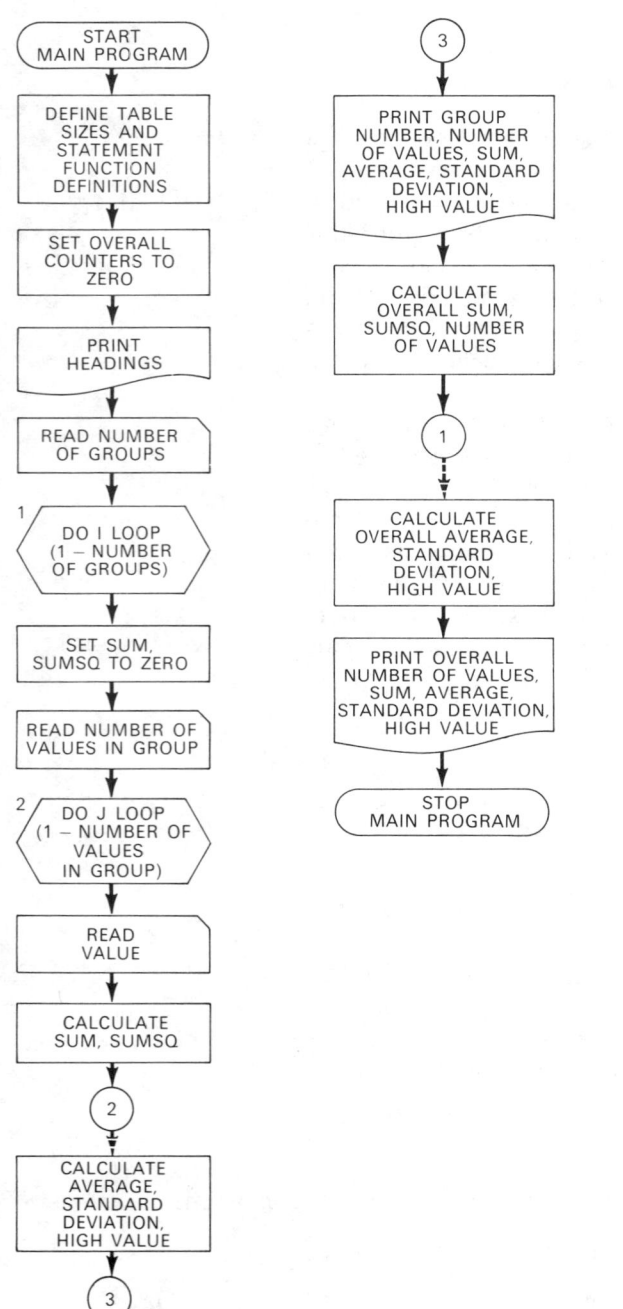

Flowchart 8-6 STATISTICS—FUNCTION subprogram.

FUNCTIONS AND SUBPROGRAMS   253

The output listed under the column heading HIGHEST VALUE contains two types of data. For the individual groups, the number represents the largest value; for the summary line, the number represents the largest standard deviation.

With limited data, as in this example, the determination of the high values could be accomplished manually. However, with a large volume of data, the technique shown is worthwhile.

In statistical applications, permutations and combinations are often computed. A permutation is a particular arrangement of certain objects. For instance, the three numbers 123 can be arranged in six particular ways:

8-9 Miscellaneous Program Sample

    123   213   321   132   231   312

The number of permutations of the three numbers 123, then, is six.

In combinations, the order of the objects is not important. Thus, the number of combinations of the three numbers 123 is just one. A more rigid definition for computing the number of permutations of r objects selected from a set of n items is $n(n-1)(n-2) \cdots (n-r+1)$ or $n!/(n-r)!$, where $n!$ is called n factorial. For the three numbers $123(n)$, taken three (r) at a time, the number of permutations is $3!/(3-3)!$, or $3 \cdot 2 \cdot 1/0!$, or $6/0!$ (where $0!$ is defined as 1) or 6. For the five numbers $12345(n)$, taken three (r) at a time, the number of permutations is $5!/(5-3)!$, or $5 \cdot 4 \cdot 3 \cdot 2 \cdot 1/2 \cdot 1$, or 60. A more rigid definition for computing the number of combinations of r objects selected from a set of n items is $n!/r!(n-r)!$. For the three numbers $123(n)$, taken three (r) at a time, the number of combinations is $3!/3!(3-3)!$, or $6/6$, or 1. For the five numbers $12345(n)$, taken three (r) at a time, the number of combinations is $5!/3!(5-3)!$, or $5 \cdot 4 \cdot 3 \cdot 2 \cdot 1/3 \cdot 2 \cdot 1(2 \cdot 1)$, or 10.

Flowchart 8-7 details the steps necessary to read values for n and r, calculate values for the number of permutations and combinations, and print the computed values. The program statements needed are

```
      FUNCTION FACT(N)
      INTEGER FACT
      FACT = 1
      IF (N.LE.1) GO TO 51
      DO 50 I = 2,N
50    FACT = FACT*I
51    RETURN
      END
C
C PERMUTATIONS AND COMBINATIONS
      INTEGER FACT,R
      WRITE(6,200)
5     READ(5,100,END=10)N,R
      NN = FACT(N)
      NR = FACT(N-R)
      NPERM = NN/NR
      NCOMB = NN/(FACT(R)*NR)
      WRITE(6,201)R,N,NPERM,NCOMB
      GO TO 5
100   FORMAT(2I3)
200   FORMAT(@1R OBJECTS    N ITEMS    NO OF PERM    NO OF COMB@/)
201   FORMAT(1X,I5,7X,I6,2(5X,I8))
10    STOP
      END
```

A FUNCTION subprogram has been incorporated in the solution. Because it is a separate routine it can be placed in front or in back of the main program. Here it is placed in front. Its purpose is to compute $n!$, where the dummy argument N is replaced in the main by the actual arguments N, R, and the expression $N-R$. The main program is simplified greatly by employing the subprogram; otherwise, the factorial routine would be repeated three times in the main. Sample data plus output from the program are

```
  3   3
  5   3
  8   2
 12   9
  7   5
```

R OBJECTS	N ITEMS	NO OF PERM	NO OF COMB
3	3	6	1
3	5	60	10
2	8	56	28
9	12	79833600	220
5	7	2520	21

FUNCTIONS AND SUBPROGRAMS

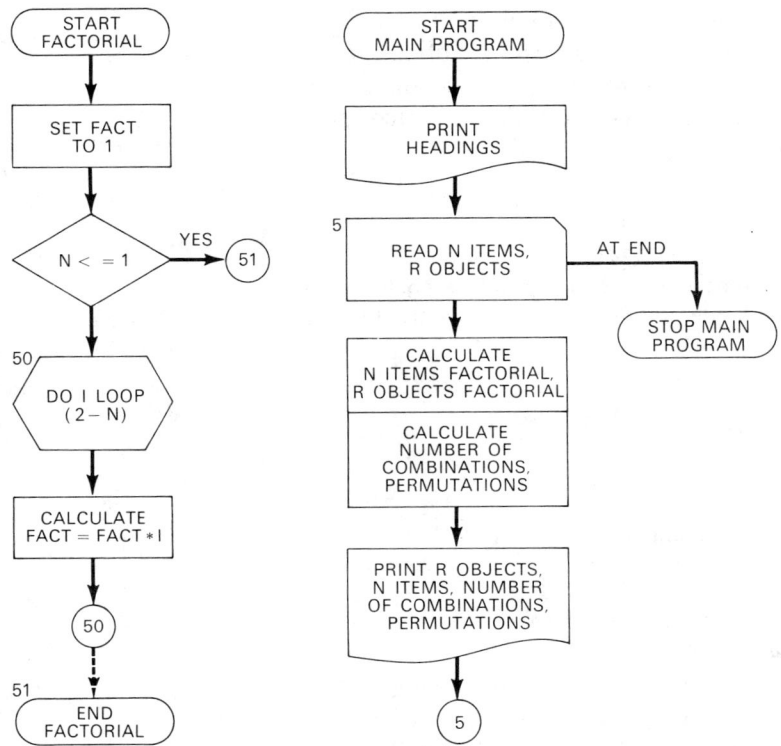

Flowchart 8-7 Permutations and combinations—FUNCTION subprogram.

When using a factorial function, one point to remember is the largest number the computer can manipulate. Try to run this program with N = 100 and R = 50. What are the results?

A variety of mathematical and service routines are provided for by a group of FORTRAN-supplied subprograms. These subprograms simplify the task of writing programs that require certain operations, such as the sine or cosine functions. Besides the FORTRAN-supplied subprograms, one-statement expressions that are used frequently throughout a program may be incorporated as statement functions. Once defined, the function can be referenced as many times as needed. A FUNCTION subprogram is a separate routine that consists of a group of statements. When its name is referred to in another program, the statements in the subprogram are executed and a

8-10 Summary

value assigned to the function name. The subprogram can be referenced as often as required. The purpose of subprograms, as with many of the program commands, is to reduce and simplify the number of statements required to solve programming problems.

Questions

To write the programs for Questions 1 to 5, the following formulas plus those discussed in the chapter are required. The area of a triangle can be computed by

$$\text{Area} = \tfrac{1}{2} bc \sin A$$

$$\text{Area} = \sqrt{s(s-a)(s-b)(s-c)} \qquad \text{where } s = \tfrac{1}{2}(a+b+c)$$

$$\text{Area} = \frac{a^2 \sin B \sin C}{2 \sin A}$$

The third side of a triangle can be computed by

$$a = \sqrt{b^2 + c^2 - 2bc \cos A}$$

The third angle of a triangle can be computed by

$$A = 180° - B - C$$

1. Two straight roads intersect at an angle of 50°0′. Car A is 400 yd from the intersection; car B is 500 yd away from the crossing. What is the distance between the two? When A is 350 yd and B 450 yd from the intersection, what is the distance? When A is 250 yd and B is 280 yd, what is the distance?

2. A motorboat heads N12°45′W on a river that flows due east. The speed of the boat is 950 fpm, traveling N7°45′E. What is the speed of the river current and the speed of the boat in still water? What if the boat travels at 1,050 fpm? 1,250 fpm?

3. One diagonal of a parallelogram makes angles of 31°30′ and 41°40′ with the sides. If the length of the diagonal is 29.5 in., find the length of the sides. If the diagonal is 31.5 in.? 28.5 in.?

4. Divide the parallelograms in Question 3 into two equal triangles. By computing the area of one triangle, find the area of each of the parallelograms.

5. In a right triangle with sides of 70 and 100 ft, find the hypotenuse and the area of the triangle. What are they if the sides are 65 and 85 ft? If the sides are 60 and 65 ft?

6. Using the subprograms written in Sec. 8-7, Exercise 1, complete programs that will
    (a) Find the average of the values found in Tables A to C:

FUNCTIONS AND SUBPROGRAMS

A	728
	9214
	1682
	2786

B	1.238
	2.674
	22.116
	143.347
	6.205
	7.717

C	89.879
	6.815
	7.216
	18.225
	6.154

(b) Find the average of the values found in arrays A to C:

A	1238	8176
	6783	2769

B	2.14	3.768	8.22	6.174
	4.187	1.081	1.882	4.716
	3.316	6.141	8.67	8.195
	6.134	5.511	6.22	5.678

C	74.65	56.47	82.81
	93.24	29.23	43.67
	39.67	14.17	48.75

7 The equation for a straight line is

$$Y = a + bx$$

The values for a and b can be found by employing the formulas

$$b = \frac{n(\Sigma XY) - (\Sigma X)(\Sigma Y)}{n(\Sigma X^2) - (\Sigma X)^2} \quad \text{and} \quad a = \frac{\Sigma Y}{n} - b\frac{\Sigma X}{n}$$

Given the data

YEAR	PRODUCTION (X)	COSTS (Y)	X^2	XY
1971	3100	2700	—	—
1972	3000	2600	—	—
1973	2800	2400	—	—
1974	2500	1600	—	—
	ΣX	ΣY	ΣX^2	ΣXY

compute the values for ΣX, ΣY, X^2, ΣX^2, XY, ΣXY, a, and b, and predict the Y values for the years 1975 to 1978 when production is planned at 2,450, 2,400, 2,350, and 2,300, respectively.

8 Modify Question 7 by supplying your own X and Y values for the years 1975 to 1978. Predict the years 1979 to 1982 with production planned at 2,300, 2,290, 2,280, and 2,250—first, with only the data from 1971 to 1974 and second, with the data from 1971 to 1978.

9 The formula for computing the binomial probability distribution is

$$P(r) = \frac{n!}{r!(n-r)!}(p)^r(q)^{n-r}$$

The formula for $P(r)$ yields the probability of r successes in n trials, where p is the probability of success and $q = 1 - p$. Write a program that will compute and print the probability of producing one

(r) defect in a production run of 10 units (n). The known probability (p) of a defect is 8 percent. What is the probability of two defects? Three? Four?

10 The values for e^x and sin x can be computed by the formulas

$$e^x = 1 + \frac{x}{1!} + \frac{x^2}{2!} + \frac{x^3}{3!} + \frac{x^4}{4!} + \frac{x^5}{5!} + \cdots$$

$$\sin x = x - \frac{x^3}{3!} + \frac{x^5}{5!} - \frac{x^7}{7!} + \frac{x^9}{9!} - \frac{x^{11}}{11!} + \cdots$$

Write a program that will compute the values of e^x and sin x when x has values of 0, $\frac{1}{2}$, 1, and $\frac{3}{2}$. Compare the computed values with the results obtained by using the FORTRAN-supplied subprograms.

11 The formula

$$D = \frac{2C}{N}\left(1 - \frac{2}{N}\right)^{n-1}$$

can be used to find the amount depreciated during the nth year for an item that is depreciated using the *double declining balance* method. If office furniture worth $30,000 ($C$) fits this category and has a life of 15 years (N), what is the amount of depreciation in each of the first five years (n)?

SUBROUTINE SUBPROGRAMS 9

Another category of subprograms, called *subroutines*, is introduced in this chapter. SUBROUTINE subprograms differ from the FUNCTION statements and FUNCTION subprograms discussed in the preceding sections. Subroutines are independent programs that may transmit many values to a main program or none at all. In contrast, the FUNCTION statements and FUNCTION subprograms generally return only one value when referenced in a main program.

9-1 Subroutines with Arguments

A SUBROUTINE subprogram is very similar in form to a FUNCTION subprogram. A SUBROUTINE subprogram consists of a SUBROUTINE statement followed by other FORTRAN instructions, including at least one RETURN statement, and terminated physically by an END command. It is a separate program that is executed whenever it is referenced by a CALL statement in another program. The following shows schematically a main program and a SUBROUTINE subprogram:

Main Program	SUBROUTINE Subprogram
.	SUBROUTINE SUB(R,T)
.	.
.	.
CALL SUB(A,B)	.

Main Program	SUBROUTINE Subprogram
1 .	RETURN
.	END
.	
CALL SUB(X,Y)	
2 .	
.	
.	
STOP	
END	

where the subroutine is called twice by the main program. After the subprogram has been referenced and executed, the RETURN statement passes control to the statement immediately following the CALL instruction. After the first CALL, control is transmitted to label 1. After the second CALL, control is transferred to label 2.

The general form of the statement required to establish a SUBROUTINE subprogram is

SUBROUTINE name$(a_1, a_2, \ldots, a_n)$

where name is the subprogram name and $a_1, a_2, \ldots, a_n$ are dummy arguments. To reference the subroutine in a main program, the statement used is

CALL name$(aa_1, aa_2, \ldots, aa_n)$

where name is the specific subroutine name and aa_1, aa_2, ..., aa_n are actual arguments supplied to the subprogram. When the subprogram is called within a main program, the reference causes the statements listed in the subprogram to be performed. The statements may be any valid FORTRAN instructions, such as READ, WRITE, and IF commands. The two exceptions that must be excluded from subprograms are another SUBROUTINE statement and a FUNCTION statement.

Values are transmitted back and forth between the main and subprogram by the list of arguments following the subprogram name and CALL statements. Before detailing the rules that apply, evaluate the following sample:

SUBROUTINE SUBPROGRAMS

Main Program		SUBROUTINE Subprogram
DIMENSION A(100), B(100)		SUBROUTINE SUM(X,K,S)
.		DIMENSION X(100)
.		S = 0.0
.		DO 10 I = 1, K
CALL SUM(A,N,SUMA)		S = S + X(I)
.	10	CONTINUE
.		K = K*2
.		RETURN
CALL SUM(B,M,SUMB)		END
.		
.		
.		
STOP		
END		

The name of the SUBROUTINE subprogram in this example is SUM, with dummy arguments X, K, and S. The effect of the statements up to the RETURN is to accumulate the sum of K elements in array X and multiply the value of K by 2.

In the main program, the subroutine is referenced twice. The first CALL statement causes the dummy arguments X and K to be replaced by the actual values of A and N. Thus, the first N elements of array A are summed. The summation is transmitted back to the main program via the dummy argument S. The variable SUMA in the main is assigned the value. Likewise, since K is multiplied by 2 in the subroutine, the variable N in the main is assigned a new value that is double its original quantity, after the CALL has been executed.

In the second CALL instruction, the dummy arguments are replaced by the values of B and M. The first M elements of array B are summed and stored in the variable location S. This value is transmitted back to the variable SUMB in the main. Similarly, the variable M in the main is assigned a new value twice its original assignment, after the second CALL has been executed.

If a subprogram were not employed, the SUBROUTINE statements would necessarily be repeated with different parameters at two locations in the main program. A summary of the rules that are pertinent to the use of SUBROUTINE subprograms is

1. The name may consist of one to six alphanumeric characters, the first of which must be alphabetic.
2. The type (mode) of a subroutine name is meaningless because values are transmitted back and forth via the argument list or by the implicit arguments in a COMMON statement (discussed in Sec. 9-4).
3. The dummy arguments must be unsubscripted variables, array names, or the dummy names of other SUBROUTINE or FUNCTION subprograms. Constants are not permitted. Additionally, there need not be any arguments in the SUBROUTINE or CALL statements (also discussed in Sec. 9-4).
4. The dummy and actual arguments listed must agree in type (mode), number, and order.
5. A SUBROUTINE subprogram is a separate program. Thus, its variable names and statement labels may be the same as those found in a calling program.
6. The SUBROUTINE statement must appear as the first statement in the subprogram. The name of the subprogram can not appear in any other statement within the routine.
7. The last statement of the subprogram must be an END instruction. At least one RETURN command, with an optional statement label, must be included. Multiple RETURN statements are permitted within the routine. The form of the RETURN is the same as that used with FUNCTION subprograms:

    sl   RETURN

    where sl is an optional statement label.

A description of SUBROUTINE subprograms is listed in Fig. 9-1. Figure 9-2 lists the common errors that occur in their use.

SUBROUTINE SUBPROGRAMS

Figure 9-1 Examples of SUBROUTINE subprograms.

Program Statements

Main Program	SUBROUTINE Subprogram	Description
DIMENSION X(10), 1 Y(10),Z(10) . . CALL DIFF(X,Y,Z) . . STOP END	SUBROUTINE DIFF (A,B,C) DIMENSION A(10),B(10), 1 C(10) DO 1 I = 1, 10 C(I) = A(I) − B(I) 1 CONTINUE RETURN END	In this sample, the elements in Tables X and Y from the main program replace the dummy arguments A and B in the subprogram. The difference between the elements in A and B is stored in the elements of Table C. The answers are transmitted to Table Z in the main via Table C in the argument list.
READ(5,10)A,B,C CALL TEST(A,B,C,D) READ(5,10)X,Y CALL TEST(X,Y,D,E) WRITE(6,55)D,E . STOP END	SUBROUTINE TEST(G,H,T,S) S = G*H*T IF(S.LE.G/T) GO TO 7 WRITE(6,50)S,G,T 50 FORMAT(3F10.3) 7 RETURN END	The main program references subroutine TEST twice in this example. The values of A, B, and C replace the dummy arguments G, H, and T, respectively. The value of S is calculated in the subprogram and returned to the main via the argument D. The subprogram also includes a logical IF test. If the test fails, three values are printed by the subprogram. Otherwise, control is returned to the main. In the second CALL, X, Y, and D replace G, H, and T, respectively. The calculated value of S is returned to the main via the argument E.
READ(5,100)N,X,Y CALL NXY(N,X,Y,BAL) WRITE(6,20)BAL M = N*2 − 5 READ(5,101)T,S CALL NXY(M,T,S,SSL) WRITE(6,20)SSL CALL NXY(M,BAL−SSL, 1 BAL, TOT) WRITE(6,20)TOT . . STOP END	SUBROUTINE NXY(I,A,B,C) C = (A + B)/ 2.33 I = I/2 + 1 RETURN END	In this sample, the main program references the subroutine NXY three times. In the first call, the values of N, X, and Y replace the dummy arguments I, A, and B in the subprogram. As illustrated here, two new values are passed back to the main, the value of C and a new value assigned to the argument I. These two are assigned to the variables N and BAL in the main. Likewise, in the second CALL, M, T, and S replace the dummy arguments I, A, and B. New values are assigned to M and SSL in the

Figure 9-1 Examples of SUBROUTINE subprograms *(cont'd).*

	Program Statements	
Main Program	SUBROUTINE Subprogram	Description
		main. In the third CALL, M and BAL replace the arguments I and B. The value of the expression BAL−SSL is used for A. The new values are returned to M and TOT.
DOUBLE PRECISION Y · CALL AVER(5.2,Y) WRITE(6,10) Y · X = 6.555 CALL AVER(X,Y) · STOP END	SUBROUTINE AVER(A,B) DOUBLE PRECISION B · · RETURN END	In this sample, the main program statements are performed in order by the computer: 1 The main is processed until the first CALL is encountered, where control is passed to the subroutine. Note that the constant 5.2 is permitted as an actual argument. 2 The subroutine is executed until the RETURN is reached. 3 The statements in the main are then processed, beginning with the WRITE, until the second CALL is executed. 4 The subroutine is performed a second time. 5 Finally, the main is processed until terminated by the STOP statement. Observe also that the variable Y is specified as DOUBLE PRECISION in the main. Likewise, B must be specified as DOUBLE PRECISION in the subprogram.
· · CALL SUBA(A,B,C) · CALL SUBA(H,R,T) · CALL SUBB(IX,JX) · CALL SUBB(LX,KX) · STOP	SUBROUTINE SUBA(X,Y,Z) · · RETURN END SUBROUTINE SUBB(I,J) · · RETURN END	In this sample, a main program and two subroutines SUBA and SUBB are included. The statements are performed in the following order: 1 The main is processed up to the first CALL. 2 SUBA is processed until the RETURN is reached. 3 Control is passed back to the main until the second CALL is executed. 4 SUBA is processed again.

Program Statements		
Main Program	SUBROUTINE Subprogram	Description
END		5 The main regains control a third time until the CALL for SUBB is reached.
		6 SUBB is processed until the RETURN is encountered.
		7 The main regains control a fourth time.
		8 SUBB is performed a second time.
		9 The main is executed again until terminated by the STOP statement.
.	SUBROUTINE SUB(A,B,C)	The statements shown here reflect the use of nested subroutines. One subroutine is called from within another. Control follows this sequence:
.	.	
CALL SUB(X,TOT,Y)	.	
.	CALL NESTED(P,R,TO)	
CALL SUB(X,TX,TB)	.	
.	RETURN	1 The main is executed up to the first CALL.
STOP	END	
END		2 SUB is processed until the CALL NESTED is reached.
	SUBROUTINE NESTED(S,G,Q)	
	.	3 The subroutine NESTED is executed up to the RETURN, where control is passed back to SUB.
	.	
	RETURN	
	END	4 SUB is processed until control is transferred back to the main.
		5 The main is processed until the second CALL SUB is encountered, when steps (2) through (4) are repeated.
		6 Finally, the main program is processed until terminated by the STOP.

Figure 9-2 Common errors that occur with SUBROUTINE subprograms.

Program Statements		
Main Program	SUBROUTINE Subprogram	Description
.	SUBROUTINE SUBRTN	When arguments are specified in either the CALL or SUBROUTINE statements, the order, number, and type must be the same in the
SUM = AVG	.	
CALL SUBRTN(SUM,KM)	.	
.	RETURN	

Figure 9-2 Common errors that occur with SUBROUTINE subprograms *(cont'd).*

Program Statements

Main Program	SUBROUTINE Subprogram	Description
STOP END	END	other. A correct entry would be SUBROUTINE SUBRTN(X,K)

.
SUM = AVG
CALL (SUM,X(I),Y(I))
.
.
STOP
END
	SUBROUTINE (S,X(I),Y(I))
	.
	.
	.
	RETURN
	END
		Two errors are contained in this sample. First, the name of the subprogram must be identified in both the CALL and SUBROUTINE statements. Second, only unsubscripted variable names may be placed as dummy arguments in the SUBROUTINE instruction. Correct entries for the sample are
		    CALL SX(SUM,X(I),Y(I))
		        and
		    SUBROUTINE SX(S,X,Y)

INTEGER X X = 5 CALL AVG(X,Y) . . .	SUBROUTINE AVG(X,Y) . . RETURN END	Two errors are listed here. One, the main program consists of all the entries to the left. The main must be terminated by STOP and END statements because it is entirely separate from the subprogram. Two, since X is specified as INTEGER mode in the main, the dummy argument X must also be specified as integer mode. The statement INTEGER X must be inserted immediately after the SUBROUTINE statement.
DIMENSION Z(20,20), 1 Y(20,20) . . CALL BET(M,N,Z,Y) . STOP END	SUBROUTINE 1 BET(A,B,C,D) . . . STOP END	Three errors are contained in this short example: (1) The actual and dummy arguments must agree in type; the first two actual arguments M and N do not agree in mode with the dummy arguments A and B. (2) Because Z and Y are dimensioned in the main, they must also be dimensioned in the subprogram. (3) A STOP is used in place of a RETURN in the subprogram. The STOP terminates the

SUBROUTINE SUBPROGRAMS 267

Program Statements		
Main Program	SUBROUTINE Subprogram	Description

		processing instead of returning control to the main program. Correct entries would be
		
		    SUBROUTINE BET(I,J,C,D)
		    DIMENSION C(20,20),D(20,20)
		    .
		    .
		    .
		    RETURN
		    END

Subroutines with Arguments—Exercises

1 Supply the CALL, SUBROUTINE, and specification statements that will satisfy the following criteria. Create your own variable names for use as actual arguments in the calling statements.

    (a) Following labels 1 and 2, jump to a subprogram SBG that has dummy arguments I, M, and P.

    (b) Following labels 7 and 12, pass control to subroutine BGXT. It has dummy arguments X, Y, M, N, and O. The variables X and Y are both 10×10 arrays.

    (c) Subprogram ZEP lists dummy arguments Z, E, P, !, and J. The variables P and I are double-precision 10-element tables. The subroutine is called three times in the main program.

    (d) Subroutine TANY lists dummy arguments T, A, N, and Y, with variables A and N as real 100-element tables. The subprogram is referenced at three locations in the main.

2 What values are printed by the following main programs and subprograms?

```
(a)            B = 5.                   SUBROUTINE A(G,H,T)
               CALL A(2.,B,X)           H = H*2.
               WRITE(6,200)X            T = G*H − 3.5
               CALL A(X,B,Y)            RETURN
               WRITE(6,200)B,Y          END
       200     FORMAT(2F10.2)
               STOP
               END

(b)            INTEGER A,X,Y            SUBROUTINE B(I,J,K)
               A = 5                    J = J/2
               CALL B(1,A,X)            K = I + J + 2
               WRITE(6,200)A,X          WRITE(6,1)I
```

```
                CALL B(A,X,Y)              1      FORMAT(I6)
                WRITE(6,200)X,Y                   RETURN
       200      FORMAT(2I6)                       END
                STOP
                END
   (c)          C = 2.*4.                         SUBROUTINE X(R,S)
                CALL X(C,D)                       S = R*5.
                CALL X(C+5.,E)                    R = S / 10.
                WRITE(6,200)C,D,E                 RETURN
       200      FORMAT(3F10.3)                    END
                STOP
                END
```

3 Identify and correct errors that occur in the following statements:
   (a)   READ(5,100)A,B   SUBROUTINE SUM(T,V)
         X = SUM(A,B)   .
         Y = SUM(A**2,B**2)   .
         WRITE(6,200)A,B,X,Y   .
            .   RETURN
            .   END
            .
         STOP
         END
   (b)   DIMENSION K(70), J(70)   SUBROUTINE TOTK(A,B)
            .   B = 0.
            .   DO 10 I = 1, 70
            .   10   B = B + A(I)
         CALL TOTK(K,X)   RETURN
         CALL TOTK(J,Y)   END
            .
            .
            .
         STOP
         END
   (c)   REAL X(100), K(100)   REAL IN(100)
            .   SUBROUTINE XBAR(N,IN)
            .   .
            .   .
         CALL XBAR(N,X)   .
            .   RETURN
            .   END
            .
         CALL YBAR(M,K)
            .
            .
            .

SUBROUTINE SUBPROGRAMS

```
            STOP
            END
(d)         DOUBLE PRECISION A,B              SUBROUTINE XLEST(A,B,X(I))
              .                                Z = A + B
              .                                X(I) = A + Z/B
              .                                A = X(I) + Z*A
            CALL (XLEST,A,B)                   RETURN
              .                                END
              .
              .
            STOP
            END
```

When is it efficient or effective to utilize SUBROUTINE subprograms? Whenever a group of similar statements is found at two or more locations in a program, often the statements can be formed into a subprogram. Program STATISTICS-22 is an example where similar statements are used to (1) compute the average and standard deviation plus writing the output for each individual group and (2) compute the two statistics and write the output for all groups combined. The statements required to perform these operations can be segregated from the remaining statements and incorporated as a subroutine. Flowchart 9-1 (page 273) indicates the revisions in the flow of logic needed to introduce the subprogram. In the flowchart, observe the use of the symbol ⌷, which dictates to the reader that a separate routine is referenced. Also, the flowchart symbols for the subprogram are set apart from the main program.

9-2 Program Sample STATISTICS

The statements constituting program STATISTICS-24 are

```
C     PROGRAM STATISTICS-24
C     THIS PROGRAM COMPUTES THE AVERAGE FOR A VARIABLE NUMBER OF VALUES
C     IN MULTIPLE GROUPS OF DATA. THE STANDARD DEVIATION IS ALSO COMPUTED.
      DATA OSUM,OSUMSQ,LNOV/2*0.0,0/
      WRITE(6,300)
      READ(5,201)NOG
      DO 2 I = 1, NOG
      SUM = 0.
      SUMSQ = 0.
      READ(5,201)NOV
      DO 1 J = 1, NOV
      READ(5,200)VALUE
      SUM = SUM + VALUE
      SUMSQ = SUMSQ + VALUE**2
1     CONTINUE
```

```
        CALL STAT(SUMSQ,SUM,NOV)
        OSUM = OSUM + SUM
        OSUMSQ = OSUMSQ + SUMSQ
        LNOV = LNOV + NOV
2       CONTINUE
        WRITE(6,301)
        CALL STAT(OSUMSQ,OSUM,LNOV)
200     FORMAT(F5.1)
201     FORMAT(I3)
300     FORMAT(@1NUMBER OF VALUES    SUM    AVERAGE    STANDARD DEVIATION@/)
301     FORMAT(@ SUMMARY DATA@/)
        STOP
        END
C
        SUBROUTINE STAT(X,Y,K)
        Z = FLOAT(K)
        AVG = Y/Z
        SD = SQRT(X/Z - AVG**2)
        WRITE(6,301)K,Y,AVG,SD
301     FORMAT(9X,I3,4X,F8.1,1X,F8.1,3X,F10.3/)
        RETURN
        END
```

Although the subprogram here is placed after the main program, the next section will show that it is permitted in front of the main program as well. The important programming points worth mentioning concern the two CALL statements. The first CALL is used to calculate and print the average and standard deviation for each individual group. The actual arguments, thus, are SUMSQ, SUM, and NOV, replacing the dummy arguments X, Y, and K, respectively, in the subroutine. In the second CALL, the arguments representing the overall totals for the sums of the squared values, the values, and the number of values are OSUMSQ, OSUM, and LNOV. They too replace the dummy arguments X, Y, and K in the subroutine. The same operations are performed twice in the main program, with one set of subroutine instructions, by using different arguments in the CALL statements. This utilization is the primary purpose of SUBROUTINE subprograms. Data for three groups of numbers plus the output from STATISTICS-24 are

```
   3
 003
 67.6
 58.7
 80.2
 004
 98.9
 82.2
 69.5
 71.7
```

```
004
 65.5
 56.8
 74.8
 84.1
```

NUMBER OF VALUES	SUM	AVERAGE	STANDARD DEVIATION
3	206.5	68.8	8.821
4	322.3	80.6	11.618
4	281.2	70.3	10.198

SUMMARY DATA

11	810.0	73.6	11.660

Even though this version of the program differs from the corresponding program STATISTICS-22, the output from it is essentially the same.

9-3 Miscellaneous Program Sample

Examine the position of a classroom instructor who has two sections of the same course, one at night and one during the day. His students have taken a test; a sampling of the results is

DAY		NIGHT	
TGM	74	TGA	64
RSB	72	SLR	76
MMN	81	DLF	83
NQB	79	GSN	49
BPT	68		

Assume that the instructor desires a program that provides a (1) listing of the day class, in order from the highest grade to the lowest; (2) listing of the night class, in order from the highest to the lowest; and (3) combined listing of both classes, in order from the highest to the lowest. No averages or totals are required, only the rearranged sequences. Once a program has been developed to handle this sample data, the instructor will furnish data for the remaining students. Thus, the program must be flexible to solve a variable number of students. Flowchart 9-2 details the sorting technique incorporated as a subroutine required to solve the defined problem. The program statements satisfying the task are

```
      SUBROUTINE SORT(N,M,NM,GR,L)
      INTEGER NM(100),GR(100),TEMP
      N1 = M - 1
      DO 1 I = N, N1
      K = I + 1
      DO 1 J = K, M
      IF(GR(I).GE.GR(J))GO TO 1
      TEMP = GR(I)
      GR(I) = GR(J)
      GR(J) = TEMP
      TEMP = NM(I)
      NM(I) = NM(J)
      NM(J) = TEMP
1     CONTINUE
      WRITE(6,200)L
      DO 2 I = N,M
2     WRITE(6,201)NM(I),GR(I)
200   FORMAT(@1SORTED VALUES FOR GROUP@,I4,/@CINITIALS@,3X,@GRADE@/)
201   FORMAT(3X,A4,4X,I4)
      RETURN
      END
C
C SORTING STUDENT GRADES
      INTEGER NAME(100), GRADE(100)
      N = 1
      READ(5,100)NODAY
      DO 1 I = 1, NODAY
1     READ(5,101)NAME(I),GRADE(I)
C CALL SUBROUTINE TO SORT GROUP ONE
      CALL SORT(N,NODAY,NAME,GRADE,1)
      READ(5,100)NONGT
      DO 2 I = 1, NONGT
      N2 = NODAY + I
2     READ(5,101)NAME(N2), GRADE(N2)
C CALL SUBROUTINE TO SORT GROUP TWO
      CALL SORT(NODAY+1,N2,NAME,GRADE,2)
C CALL SUBROUTINE TO SORT BOTH GROUPS COMBINED
      CALL SORT(N,N2,NAME,GRADE,3)
100   FORMAT(I3)
101   FORMAT(A4,I3)
      STOP
      END
```

In this program, only the student's initials, which can be stored in one variable location, are processed along with the grade. An integer table NAME is specified for storing the student's initials because the sorting technique requires switching. If a real table were specified, unpredictable results would appear after the switching because the computer method for storing integer and real values is different.

The subprogram SORT is referenced three times by the main program. The arguments or parameters differ in each case, con-

SUBROUTINE SUBPROGRAMS

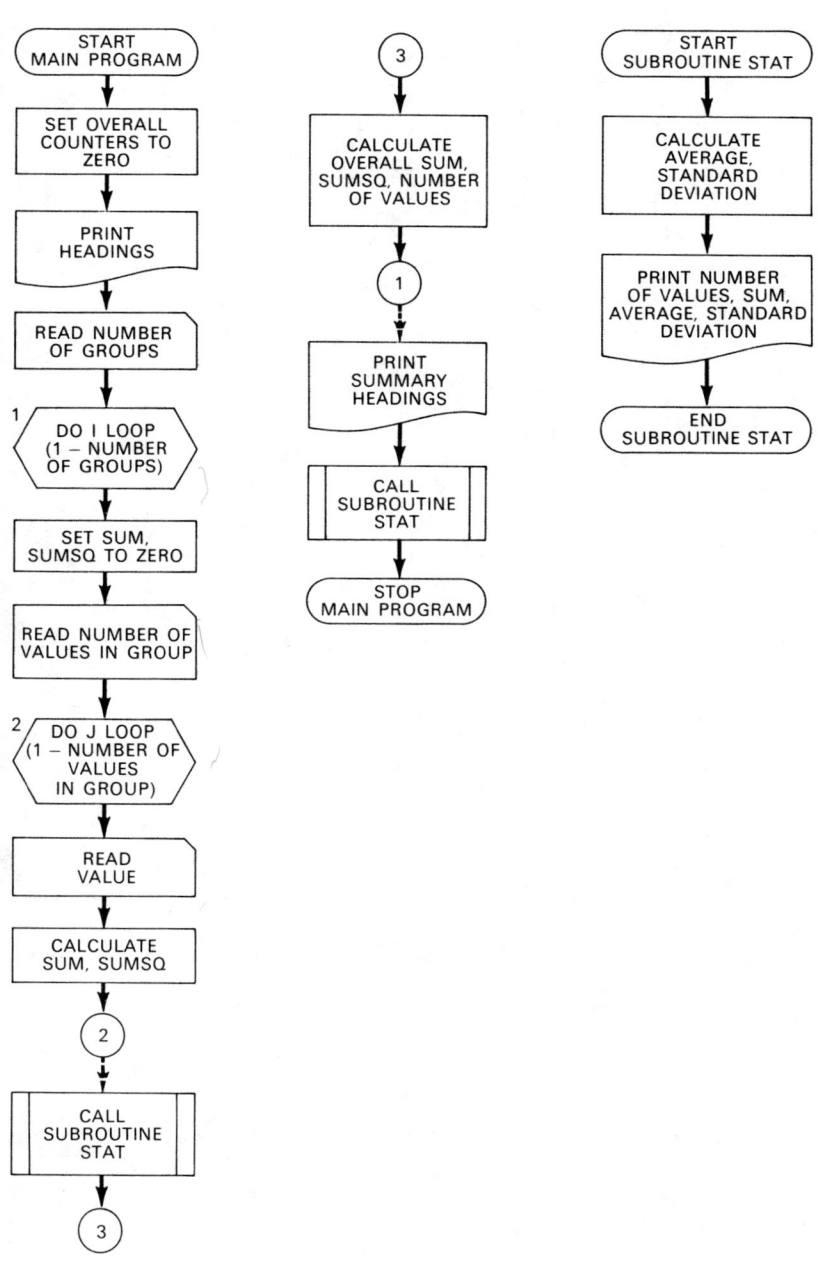

Flowchart 9-1 STATISTICS—SUBROUTINE subprogram.

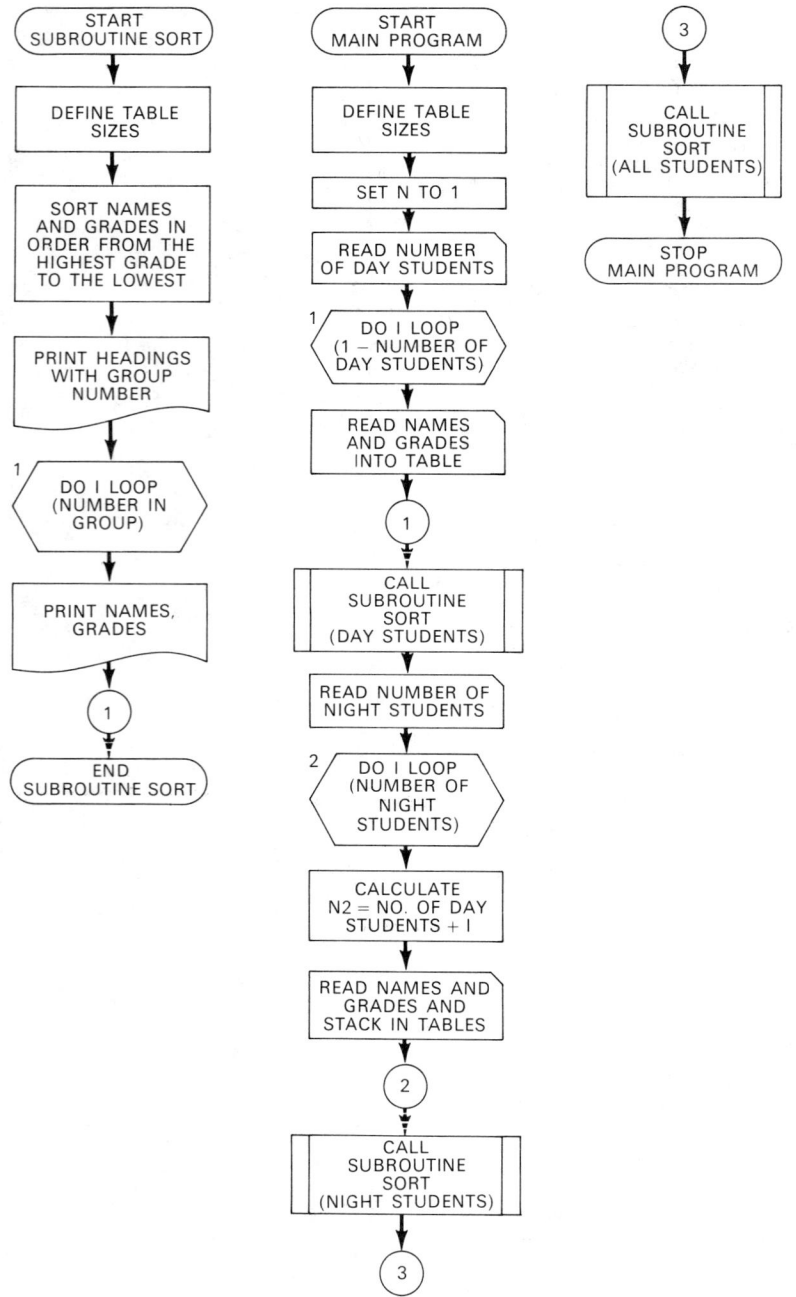

Flowchart 9-2 Student sorting—SUBROUTINE subprogram.

SUBROUTINE SUBPROGRAMS

trolling the operations performed. Before the first CALL is issued, the two tables would appear in memory as

	NAME	GRADE
(1)	TGM	74
(2)	RSM	72
(3)	MMN	81
(4)	NQB	79
(5)	BPT	68

In the first CALL, the arguments N and NODAY control how many table values are to be sorted. The N indicates the beginning location, and NODAY denotes the last location in the table to be sorted in this execution of the subroutine. The variables NAME and GRADE contain the data to be sorted; the 1 indicates the class number. The second group of data is read into the program by the DO-2 loop. The data is "stacked" in the tables NAME and GRADE by the use of the index N2. The value of N2 takes into account how many students were in group one and places the new data in successive locations in the tables. In memory before the second CALL, the tables would appear as

	NAME	GRADE
(1)	MMN	81
(2)	NQB	79
(3)	TGM	74
(4)	RSB	72
(5)	BPT	68
(6)	TGA	64
(7)	SLR	76
(8)	DLF	83
(9)	GSN	49

The first five locations are in order because they have been sorted by the subroutine and the rearranged values passed back to the main via the argument list. To sort the second group of data found in locations 6 to 9 is the next requirement of the problem. The CALL statement, with NODAY+1 and N2 as arguments, control the table locations to be processed. The value of NODAY+1 is six, the first location of the table to be examined at this stage, and the value of N2 is nine, the last location in the table. As before, the data is contained in NAME and GRADE, while the argument 2 specifies the second class. Thus, the values of the arguments dictate the exact locations in the table that are to be sorted by the subprogram.

The final requirement of the problem is to sort all the values in the tables. The arguments N and N2 indicate the first and last locations of the entire table; the argument 3 indicates the third group. Using the data from the previous pages, the output from the program is

```
005
TGM    74
RSB    72
MMN    81
NQB    79
BPT    68
004
TGA    64
SLR    76
DLF    83
GSN    49
```

SORTED VALUES FOR GROUP   1

INITIALS   GRADE

```
    MMN       81
    NQB       79
    TGM       74
    RSB       72
    BPT       68
```

SORTED VALUES FOR GROUP   2

INITIALS   GRADE

```
    DLF       83
    SLR       76
    TGA       64
    GSN       49
```

SORTED VALUES FOR GROUP   3

INITIALS   GRADE

```
    DLF       83
    MMN       81
```

NQB	79
SLR	76
TGM	74
RSB	72
BPT	68
TGA	64
GSN	49

Although only nine students have been processed by this program, the use of variables ensures its value as a flexible program when more input data is available. A different approach to the solution for the third part of the problem would be to merge the two sorted groups together, as opposed to re-sorting the entire list. However, this task is left for the student to solve in the questions at the end of the chapter.

In each of the samples covering FUNCTION subprograms and SUBROUTINE subprograms thus far, whenever a DIMENSION statement appeared in the main program, a DIMENSION statement of the same size has been incorporated in the subprogram. However, to be flexible enough so other programmers can use the same subprogram, it would be advantageous if the size of the DIMENSION in the subprogram were declared at execution time. This can be accomplished by passing an argument to the subprogram, where the argument is used to specify the size of the table or array. Consider the following sample:

Main Program	*SUBROUTINE Subprogram*
DIMENSION A(100), B(100)	SUBROUTINE SUM(J,X,K,S)
.	DIMENSION X(J)
.	S = 0.0
.	DO 10 I = 1,K
CALL SUM(100,A,N,SUMA)	S = S + X(I)
. 10	CONTINUE
.	K = K*2
.	RETURN
CALL SUM(100,B,M,SUMB)	END
.	
.	
.	
STOP	
END	

The size of arrays A and B is 100; thus, the size of X in the subprogram must be set to 100. This is accomplished by the actual argument 100 in the two calling statements. The value 100 is assigned to J in the subprogram, which sets the size of X properly. Thus, to dimension an array in a subprogram at execution time the main program must pass an argument to the subprogram, where the argument is used to establish the array size. A few rules apply when following this procedure:

1 A statement of the form

DIMENSION X(J)

can *only* appear in a subprogram. The form can never be used in a main program.

2 For both FUNCTION and SUBROUTINE subprograms, dimension sizes can be assigned at execution time.

3 Arrays that are listed in the FUNCTION and SUBROUTINE statements are the only ones that may have variable dimension sizes. If the arrays are not in the parameter list, they can't be dimensioned at run time.

4 The variable used to indicate the size of the array in the subprogram should not be assigned a new value during execution of the routine.

To illustrate its use, assume that two instructors wish to use the student sorting subprogram. However, one has a class size of 100 students, and the second has 200. But why not simply change the array sizes each time they want to use the program? Often, subprograms are stored in a library and made available for general use. By revising the sorting subprogram to permit variable dimensioning, the routine can be stored on the computer system and made available to any instructor who wishes to use it. The changes required to the subprogram to permit variable dimensioning are

```
      SUBROUTINE SORT(IS,N,M,NM,GR,L)
      INTEGER NM(IS),GR(IS),TEMP
      N1 = M - 1
      DO 1 I = N, N1
      K = I + 1
      DO 1 J = K, M
      IF(GR(I).GE.GR(J))GO TO 1
      TEMP = GR(I)
      GR(I) = GR(J)
      GR(J) = TEMP
      TEMP = NM(I)
```

```
              NM(I) = NM(J)
              NM(J) = TEMP
       1      CONTINUE
              WRITE(6,200)L
              DO 2 I = N,M
       2      WRITE(6,201)NM(I),GR(I)
       200    FORMAT(@1SORTED VALUES FOR GROUP@,I4,/@0INITIALS@,3X,@GRADE@/)
       201    FORMAT(3X,A4,4X,I4)
              RETURN
              END
```

The variable IS has been added in the SUBROUTINE statement. It is used to establish the size of the arrays NM and GR. This revision creates the desired flexibility. The first instructor, with a class size of 100, must supply the following main program, with revised CALL statements to specify the size of the arrays:

```
C SORTING STUDENT GRADES
         INTEGER NAME(100), GRADE(100)
         N = 1
         READ(5,100)NODAY
         DO 1 I = 1, NODAY
 1       READ(5,101)NAME(I),GRADE(I)
C CALL SUBROUTINE TO SORT GROUP ONE
         CALL SORT(100,N,NODAY,NAME,GRADE,1)
         READ(5,100)NONGT
         DO 2 I = 1, NONGT
         N2 = NODAY + I
 2       READ(5,101)NAME(N2), GRADE(N2)
C CALL SUBROUTINE TO SORT GROUP TWO
         CALL SORT(100,NODAY+1,N2,NAME,GRADE,2)
C CALL SUBROUTINE TO SORT BOTH GROUPS COMBINED
         CALL SORT(100,N,N2,NAME,GRADE,3)
 100     FORMAT(I3)
 101     FORMAT(A4,I3)
         STOP
         END
```

The second instructor, with a class size of 200, must supply the following main program, with revised CALL statements:

```
C SORTING STUDENT GRADES
         INTEGER NAME(200), GRADE(200)
         N = 1
         READ(5,100,NODAY
         DO 1 I = 1, NODAY
 1       READ(5,101)NAME(I),GRADE(I)
C CALL SUBROUTINE TO SORT GROUP ONE
         CALL SORT(200,N,NODAY,NAME,GRADE,1)
         READ(5,100)NONGT
```

```
      DO 2 I = 1, NONGT
      N2 = NODAY + I
2     READ(5,101)NAME(N2), GRADE(N2)
C CALL SUBROUTINE TO SORT GROUP TWO
      CALL SORT(200,NODAY+1,N2,NAME,GRADE,2)
C CALL SUBROUTINE TO SORT BOTH GROUPS COMBINED
      CALL SORT(200,N,N2,NAME,GRADE,3)
100   FORMAT(I3)
101   FORMAT(A4,I3)
      STOP
      END
```

For both programs, the output would be similar in form to that shown in the original version.

Besides this type of application, variable size dimensioning also plays an important role when the programmer requires the use of subroutines supplied by the computer manufacturer or another source. In these cases it may be impossible or impractical to revise the subroutine so that execution time dimensioning is mandatory.

9-4 Subroutines with COMMON Statements

In Sec. 9-1, in the listing of the rules that apply to subroutines, it was stated that arguments may be omitted from the CALL and SUBROUTINE statements. When dummy and actual arguments are omitted, data values are passed back and forth between the main and subprogram by use of the COMMON statement. A previous discussion of the COMMON statement disclosed its use in establishing the size of arrays. However, its deployment here is much more important.

The COMMON statement is listed in a main program and a subprogram to define a storage area that can be referenced by both. Therefore, variables, tables, or arrays that appear in a calling program or subprogram share, if listed in appropriate COMMON statements, the same physical storage locations with variables, tables, or arrays found in other subprograms. Implicitly then, arguments can be passed between a calling program and a subprogram via a common area. Examine the following sample:

Main Program	*SUBROUTINE Subprogram*
COMMON A(10), B(10)	SUBROUTINE DUP
.	COMMON A(10), B(10)

Main Program	SUBROUTINE Subprogram
.	DO 1 I = 1, 10
.	A(I) = B(I)*2.
CALL DUP	1 CONTINUE
WRITE(6,20)A,B	RETURN
.	END
.	
.	
STOP	
END	

In this case, the subprogram DUP has no dummy arguments. Values are transmitted to DUP via the COMMON declaration found in both routines. Tables A and B in the main share the same area as the Tables A and B listed in the subprogram. After the subprogram has been executed, the new values for A, which are twice the contents of each of the values of B, are transmitted back to the main implicitly through the common area.

Arguments passed in a COMMON statement are subject to the same rules as arguments passed in an argument list. That is, the type (mode), order, and number of variables must agree. If there is more than one COMMON statement, the entries are cumulative. For examples, the two sets of statements listed are equivalent:

COMMON X,Y,Z(100)   COMMON X,Y,Z(100),N
COMMON N,P(10,4),K   and   COMMON P(10,4),K

In the program example above, both COMMON statements listed Tables A and B. Because there is a direct one-to-one correspondence the variable names need not be the same. For example, the statements could be written as

COMMON X(10), Y(10)   and   COMMON H(10), G(10)

where it is concluded that the 10 elements of X (in the main program) share the exact same 10 physical locations as Table H (in the subprogram). Likewise, the 10 elements of Y and G share the same common block area. A final rule states that the same variable can not be entered in both an argument list and a common area.

Figure 9-3 contains examples of subroutines that employ

COMMON statements which implicitly transfer arguments. The errors that occur using COMMON statements are listed separately in Fig. 9-4. As implied by these samples, the rules for constructing SUBROUTINE subprograms are exactly the same whether using an argument list or a common area to transmit values from a main program.

Figure 9-3 More examples of SUBROUTINE subprograms.

Program Statements		
Main Program	SUBROUTINE Subprogram	Description
COMMON XB,YB,Z(100) INTEGER Z . . CALL SB . . STOP END	SUBROUTINE SB COMMON A,B,C(100) INTEGER C . . RETURN END	The COMMON statements in the main and subprogram eliminate the need for arguments in the CALL and SUBROUTINE statements. The COMMON statements specify that the variables XB, YB, and the Table Z share the same computer memory area as the variables A, B, and the Table C.
DIMENSION Z(100) COMMON XB,YB,Z INTEGER Z . . CALL SB . . STOP END	SUBROUTINE SB DIMENSION C(100) COMMON A,B,C INTEGER C . . RETURN END	This example is equivalent to the one above; the difference is that a DIMENSION statement has been used to establish the size of the two Tables Z and C. Because the table size has been established in both the main and subprogram prior to the COMMON statement, it would be redundant and wrong to duplicate the size of the tables in the COMMON statements. It is required, however, to list the table names Z and C in the COMMON instructions for them to share the same memory area.
DIMENSION X(10), 1 Y(10),Z(10) COMMON X,Y,Z . . CALL DIFF . STOP END	SUBROUTINE DIFF DIMENSION A(10),B(10), 1 C(10) COMMON A,B,C DO 1 I = 1, 10 C(I) = A(I) − B(I) 1 CONTINUE RETURN END	In this sample, the COMMON specifies that the three tables X, Y, and Z in the main share the same physical locations as Tables A, B, and C in the subprogram. The values of C calculated in the subroutine are implicitly transmitted to Z in the main by the use of the common area.

SUBROUTINE SUBPROGRAMS

Program Statements

Main Program	SUBROUTINE Subprogram	Description
COMMON X(50),Y(50), 1 Z(50) . . CALL DIFF(N) . STOP END	SUBROUTINE DIFF(L) COMMON A(50),B(50), 1 C(50) DO 1 I = 1, L C(I) = A(I) − B(I) 1 CONTINUE RETURN END	As in the prior example, a common area is specified so that the Tables X, Y, and Z share the same storage area as Tables A, B, and C. The significant difference is, however, that an argument is contained in the CALL and SUBROUTINE statements. As shown here, it is possible to combine the use of the COMMON statement and an argument list to pass values between a main program and a subprogram.
COMMON B(10),C(10) COMMON D(5,2),K DOUBLE PRECISION K . CALL MULT . STOP END	SUBROUTINE MULT COMMON X(10),Y(10), 1 Z(5,2),L DOUBLE PRECISION L . . RETURN END	When more than one COMMON statement appears in a main program or subprogram, the effect is cumulative. Thus, the two COMMON statements in the main are exactly equivalent to the one in the subroutine.

Figure 9-4 More common errors that occur with SUBROUTINE subprograms.

Program Statements

Main Program	SUBROUTINE Subprogram	Description

COMMON A,B,C
.
.
CALL MAP(A)
.
STOP
END
	SUBROUTINE MAP(X)
	COMMON X,Y,Z
	.
	.
	RETURN
	END
		The same variable can not be placed in both the common area and an argument list. In this case, A in the main and X in the subprogram violate this rule. Correct entries would exclude the two variables from either the COMMON statement or the argument list, such as
		    CALL MAP
		    and
		    SUBROUTINE MAP

DIMENSION X(3,4) COMMON K,X(3,4) .	SUBROUTINE BASE DIMENSION A(3,4) COMMON A(3,4),N	Two elementary errors are listed here. First, the size of a table or an array can not be specified in both

Figure 9-4 More common errors that occur with SUBROUTINE subprograms *(cont'd)*.

Program Statements		
Main Program	*SUBROUTINE Subprogram*	*Description*

CALL BASE
·
·
STOP
END
	·
	·
	RETURN
	END
		DIMENSION and COMMON statements. The size can be described in only one. Second, the order of the variables in the COMMON specification must agree. In the main, the integer K is followed by array X, and the order is reversed in the subprogram. A correct entry for the main would be
		    COMMON K,X
		A correct entry for the subprogram would be
		    COMMON N,A

COMMON X,Y,I
·
·
CALL ONE
·
·
STOP
END
	SUBROUTINE ONE
	COMMON A,B,J
	·
	SUBROUTINE TWO
	COMMON R,S,M
	·
	·
	RETURN
	END
		In a SUBROUTINE subprogram, only one SUBROUTINE statement can be listed. In this example, two are listed. Each subprogram must be established independently with separate CALL, RETURN, and END statements. A correct set of entries would be
		  SUBROUTINE ONE
		  COMMON A,B,J
		  ·
		  ·
		  CALL TWO
		  RETURN
		  END
		  SUBROUTINE TWO
		  COMMON R,S,M
		  ·
		  ·
		  RETURN
		  END

COMMON M,N,Z(13,5) COMMON S,T(5,5) REAL N DOUBLE PRECISION S · CALL KMT	SUBROUTINE KMT COMMON A,B,C(13,5),R,S(6,10) · · RETURN END	Three errors are contained in the use of the COMMON statements listed. The effect of the two COMMON statements in the main is cumulative, so the variables M, N, Z, S, and T are in-

Program Statements

Main Program	SUBROUTINE Subprogram	Description

.
STOP
END
		tended to share the same locations as the variables A, B, C, R, and S in the subprogram. A conflict in the mode occurs between the M and A because the first is integer mode and the second is real. REAL N and B plus arrays Z and C align properly. However, a conflict occurs between S and R because S is defined as double-precision mode. Finally, the arrays T and S must agree in size. Entries in the subprogram required to correct these errors would be
		    SUBROUTINE KMT
		    COMMON A,B,C(13,5),R,S(5,5)
		    INTEGER A
		    DOUBLE PRECISION R

DOUBLE PRECISION C COMMON A,B,C . . CALL X . STOP END	SUBROUTINE X DOUBLE PRECISION T COMMON R,T . . RETURN END	Three variables—two real, A and B, and one double-precision, C—are specified as COMMON in the main program. In the subroutine, only two are listed, corresponding to A and C in the main. An error occurs because the number of variables in the two COMMON statements do not agree. Hence, a correct entry in the subroutine would be COMMON R,DUMMYV,T where DUMMYV is a dummy variable that forces A and R plus C and T to share the same common area. Note: This type of error usually occurs when more than one subprogram with common areas are involved.

FORTRAN IV PROGRAMMING AND APPLICATIONS

Subroutines with COMMON Statements—Exercises

1 What values are printed by main programs (a) to (d)?

(a)
```
          COMMON A,B,C                          SUBROUTINE ZIP
          A = 2.                                COMMON A,B,X
          B = A*2.                              A = A/2.
          CALL ZIP                              B = B + 2.
          B = C*2.                              X = A*B
          CALL ZIP                              RETURN
          WRITE (6,200) A,B,C                   END
    200   FORMAT (3F10.5)
          STOP
          END
```

(b)
```
          COMMON X(5), Y(5), Z(5)               SUBROUTINE TABLE
          INTEGER X,Y,Z                         COMMON I(5), J(5), K(5)
          DO 1 I = 1,5                          DO 1 M = 1,5
          X(I) = I+2                      1     K(M) = I(M)*J(M) – J(M)
      1   Y(I) = I**2                           RETURN
          CALL TABLE                            END
          WRITE (6,200) Z
    200   FORMAT(5I6)
          STOP
          END
```

(c)
```
          COMMON M(100), N(100)                 SUBROUTINE SUB(I)
          DO 1 I = 1,50                         COMMON M(100), N(100)
      1   M(I) = I*I                            DO 1 L = I,100
          K = 51                          1     M(L) = M(L-50) – 1
          CALL SUB(K)                           I = 10
          WRITE(6,200)(M(I),I=1,50,K)           RETURN
          STOP                                  END
          END
```

(d)
```
          COMMON M(100), N(100)                 SUBROUTINE SUB(I)
          DATA M,N/200*0/                       COMMON M(100), N(100)
          CALL SUB(7)                           DO 1 L = 1, I, 4
          CALL SUB(10)                          M(L) = L + M(L)
          CALL SUB(15)                    1     N(L+5) = L+5+N(L+5)
          WRITE(6,200)(M(I),I=1,15)             RETURN
          WRITE(6,200)(N(I),I=1,15)             END
    200   FORMAT(1X,(10I6))
          STOP
          END
```

2 Supply the COMMON and specification statements in the main program and subprogram required to satisfy the criteria stated:
   (a) The variables X, Y, I, and T in the main program are intended to share the same common area as B, X, I, and S in a subprogram.

(b) In the main program, variables B, C, and D are common to the variables I, J, and K in a subprogram. All the variables are double-precision mode.
(c) Tables AB and XY in a main program each contain 10 elements. In a subprogram, A and X are 10-element tables that are synonymous with AB and XY.
(d) Arrays Z and ZB are 3 × 5 matrices in a main program. In a subprogram, A and B are 3 × 5 matrices that are synonymous with Z and ZB. Array ZB is integer mode.
(e) The variables M, N, O, and P in the main program are intended to share the same common area as the variables R, S, T, and U. In the main program, M is real mode; P is double-precision.

3 Identify and correct errors located in samples (a) to (d):

(a)
```
COMMON ZX,AI                SUBROUTINE THT
    .                       COMMON I, J
    .                           .
    .                           .
CALL THT                        .
    .                       RETURN
    .                       END
    .
STOP
END
```

(b)
```
DIMENSION M(5)              SUBROUTINE MTMT
COMMON A, B, M              COMMON X, Y, Z
    .                           .
    .                           .
    .                           .
CALL MTMT                   MTMT = 1
    .                       RETURN
    .                       END
    .
STOP
END
```

(c)
```
COMMON X(5),Y,K             SUBROUTINE STEPA
DOUBLE PRECISION Y          COMMON A(5),Y,K
REAL K                          .
    .                           .
    .                           .
    .                       A(6) = K
CALL STEPA                  RETURN
    .                       END
    .
    .
RETURN
END
```

(d)
```
      COMMON X,A,P,T              SUBROUTINE DIM(A)
      COMMON G(5),H(5)            COMMON TX,TA,TP
          .                       COMMON TG(5),TH(5)
          .                           .
          .                           .
                                      .
      CALL DIM(T)
          .                       RETURN
          .                       END
          .
      STOP
      END
```

9-5 Miscellaneous Student Sorting Sample

The same student sorting problem discussed previously will be solved in this section by introducing a common area to pass certain of the values back and forth between the main and the subprogram. In Sec. 9-3, the solution to the problem contained CALL statements, with five arguments listed. In each of the three CALLs, the Tables NAME and GRADE were included as the third and fourth arguments. The table names can be removed from the argument list and placed in a common area. Flowchart 9-3 outlines the general logic flow specifying a common area, and the necessary statements are

```
            SUBROUTINE SORT(N,M,L)
            INTEGER NM(100),GR(100),TEMP
            COMMON NM,GR
            N1 = M - 1
            DO 1 I = N, N1
            K = I + 1
            DO 1 J = K, M
            IF(GR(I).GE.GR(J))GO TO 1
            TEMP = GR(I)
            GR(I) = GR(J)
            GR(J) = TEMP
            TEMP = NM(I)
            NM(I) = NM(J)
            NM(J) = TEMP
      1     CONTINUE
            WRITE(6,200)L
            DO 2 I = N,M
      2     WRITE(6,201)NM(I),GR(I)
      200   FORMAT(@1SORTED VALUES FOR GROUP@,I4,/@0INITIALS@,3X,@GRADE@/)
      201   FORMAT(3X,A4,4X,I4)
            RETURN
            END
      C
      C SORTING STUDENT GRADES
            INTEGER NAME(100), GRADE(100)
```

SUBROUTINE SUBPROGRAMS

```
      COMMON NAME, GRADE
      N = 1
      READ(5,100)NODAY
      DO 1 I = 1, NODAY
1     READ(5,101)NAME(I),GRADE(I)
C CALL SUBROUTINE TO SORT GROUP ONE
      CALL SORT(N,NODAY,1)
      READ(5,100)NONGT
      DO 2 I = 1, NONGT
      N2 = NODAY + I
2     READ(5,101)NAME(N2), GRADE(N2)
C CALL SUBROUTINE TO SORT GROUP TWO
      CALL SORT(NODAY+1,N2,2)
C CALL SUBROUTINE TO SORT BOTH GROUPS COMBINED
      CALL SORT(N,N2,3)
100   FORMAT(I3)
101   FORMAT(A4,I3)
      STOP
      END
```

The new statements here include two COMMON specifications, one in the main and the other in the subprogram. The variables NM and NAME plus GR and GRADE share the same common area as a result. Thus, it is unnecessary to place NAME and GRADE in the argument list of the CALL statements. For the same data used earlier, the output is identical:

```
005
TGM   74
RSB   72
MMN   81
NQB   79
BPT   68
004
TGA   64
SLR   76
DLF   83
GSN   49
```

SORTED VALUES FOR GROUP   1

INITIALS   GRADE

```
   MMN       81
   NQB       79
   TGM       74
   RSB       72
   BPT       68
```

SORTED VALUES FOR GROUP   2

INITIALS   GRADE

```
DLF         83
SLR         76
TGA         64
GSN         49
```

SORTED VALUES FOR GROUP   3

INITIALS   GRADE

```
DLF         83
MMN         81
NQB         79
SLR         76
TGM         74
RSB         72
BPT         68
TGA         64
GSN         49
```

As the samples indicate, the choice of inserting a common area or passing values through an argument list is a personal preference of the programmer because the effect is the same. A second sample elaborates on the use of a common area.

9-6 Miscellaneous Payroll Sample

The general definition of the problem revolves around a simple payroll task. For the employees of a small firm, net pay is calculated by employing the parameters:

1. Given the hours worked and the hourly rate.
2. Gross pay is equal to the hourly rate times hours worked up to 40 hours, plus double time for all hours over 40.
3. The tax paid is equal to 10 percent of the gross pay.
4. Net pay is equal to the gross pay minus the tax paid.

However, one of the employees is singled out each week and paid a new hourly rate that represents a bonus. The new rate is determined by calculating the average pay per employee and dividing the average by 20. To determine the bonus rate, it is necessary to first process all the employees. At this point the pay for the lucky employee can be recomputed and printed. Because the instructions for calculating the net pay of the

SUBROUTINE SUBPROGRAMS

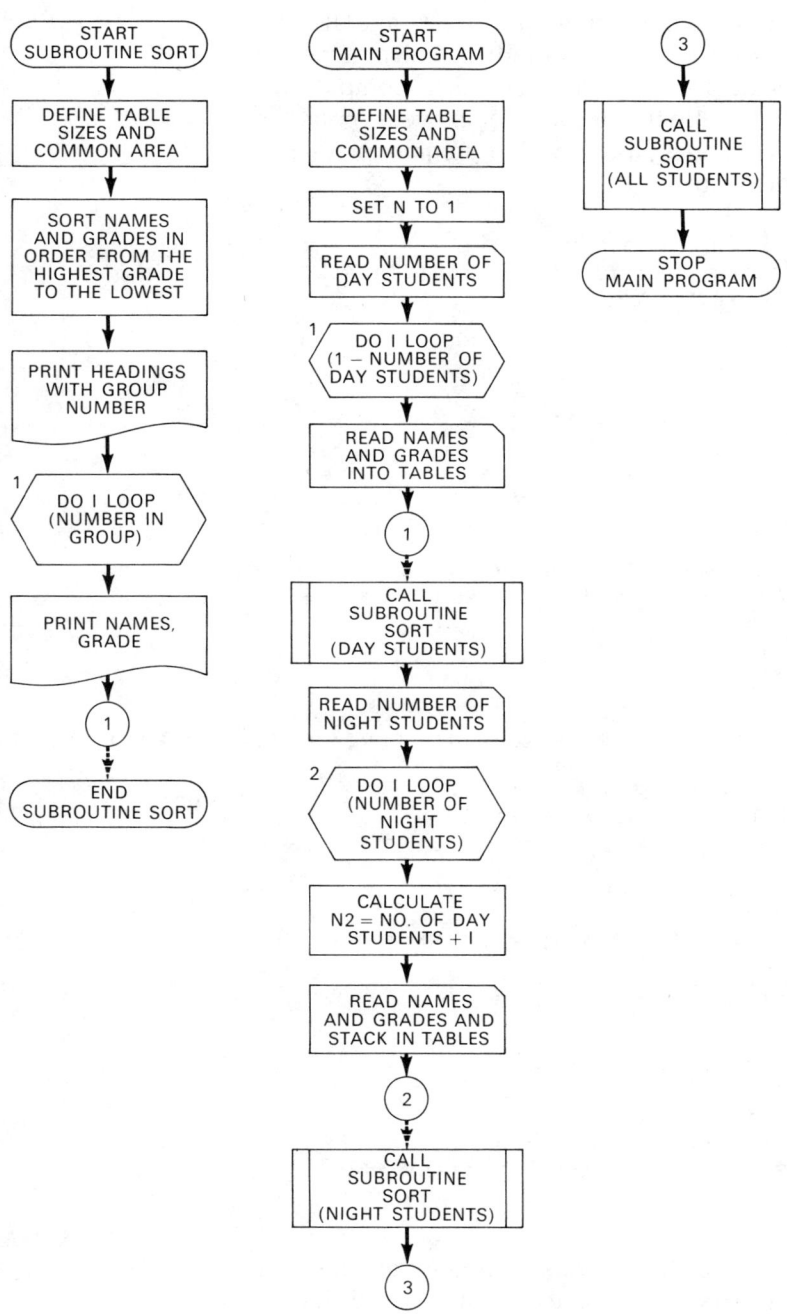

Flowchart 9-3 Student sorting—SUBROUTINE subprogram with COMMON.

employees are required at two different locations, a SUBROUTINE subprogram is an efficient method for solving the problem. Flowchart 9-4 details the steps needed to compute the items above plus the total net pay for all employees, considering the new pay of the lucky person. The program statements to solve the problem are

```
C SPECIAL EMPLOYEE PAYROLL PROGRAM
      DIMENSION NAME(100),HRW(100),RATE(100),PAY(100)
      COMMON NAME,HRW,RATE,PAY
      WRITE(6,200)
      READ(5,100)NOE
      TOTPAY = 0.0
      DO 1 I = 1, NOE
      READ(5,101)NAME(I),HRW(I),RATE(I)
      CALL PAYROL(I)
      TOTPAY = TOTPAY + PAY(I)
1     CONTINUE
      WRITE(6,201)
      READ(5,100)LUCK
      RATE(LUCK) = (TOTPAY/FLOAT(NOE))/20.
      TOTPAY = TOTPAY - PAY(LUCK)
      CALL PAYROL(LUCK)
      TOTPAY = TOTPAY + PAY(LUCK)
      WRITE(6,202)TOTPAY
100   FORMAT(I4)
101   FORMAT(A4,2F5.2)
200   FORMAT(@1EMPLOYEE NAME   HOURS WORKED   HOURLY RATE   TAX PAID   NET P
     1AY@/)
201   FORMAT(@0TODAYS LUCKY EMPLOYEE IS ...@/)
202   FORMAT(@0TOTAL NET PAY@,37X,F9.2)
      STOP
      END
C
      SUBROUTINE PAYROL(I)
      DIMENSION N(100),H(100),R(100),PAY(100)
      COMMON N,H,R,PAY
      IF(H(I).GT.40.)GO TO 15
      G = H(I)*R(I)
      GO TO 10
15    G = (H(I)-40.)*R(I)*2.+ 40.*R(I)
10    TAX = .10*G
      PAY(I) = G - TAX
      WRITE(6,200)N(I),H(I),R(I),TAX,PAY(I)
200   FORMAT(6X,A4,6X,F10.2,4X,F9.2,4X,F7.2,1X,F9.2)
      RETURN
      END
```

For each employee, the initials, hours worked, hourly rate, and the calculated net pay are retained in tables that are part of the common area. The variables NAME and N, HRW and H, RATE and R, plus PAY and PAY share the same storage locations as

SUBROUTINE SUBPROGRAMS

293

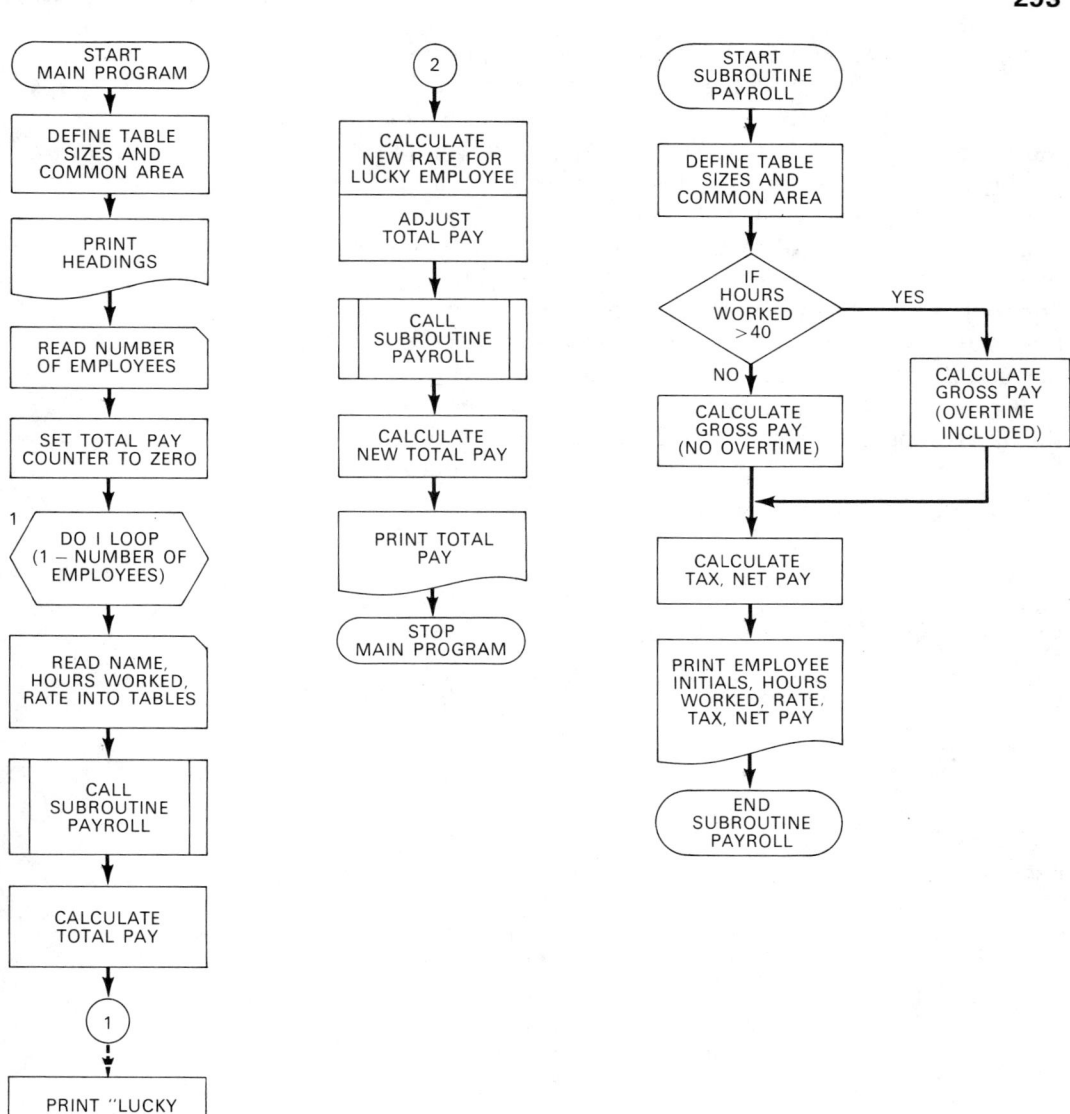

Flowchart 9-4 Payroll—SUBROUTINE subprogram with COMMON.

a result of the two COMMON statements. The information stored in this area is available in either the main or subprogram as a result. The first CALL statement inside the DO loop calls the subprogram, which processes the employee and prints the pertinent data. When this DO loop is completed, a number is read, represented by the variable LUCK, to determine the lucky employee. The value of LUCK is used as an index pointing to the location of the lucky person for the week. (Only the boss knows how the lucky employee is selected.) Once the bonus rate is computed, the second CALL recomputes and prints the net pay for the lucky person. The total net pay is adjusted by subtracting the original pay of the lucky employee and adding the new net pay. If the adjustment were omitted, the total would inaccurately reflect too large a sum. Data and output for seven employees follow :

```
0007
CJS 40.00 2.85
BMJ 41.50 3.15
NPT 39.75 3.03
KBX 43.25 2.75
RSL 40.00 3.25
WHS 36.00 3.62
JST 47.75 3.10
0004
```

EMPLOYEE NAME	HOURS WORKED	HOURLY RATE	TAX PAID	NET PAY
CJS	40.00	2.85	11.40	102.60
BMJ	41.50	3.15	13.55	121.90
NPT	39.75	3.03	12.04	108.40
KBX	43.25	2.75	12.79	115.09
RSL	40.00	3.25	13.00	117.00
WHS	36.00	3.62	13.03	117.29
JST	47.75	3.10	17.21	154.85

TODAYS LUCKY EMPLOYEE IS ...

KBX	43.25	5.98	27.80	250.24

TOTAL NET PAY   972.28

Note that the fourth employee was singled out as the special employee of the week. In this sample, the SUBROUTINE statements effectively reduce the size of the main program because otherwise the instructions would necessarily be listed twice.

SUBROUTINE SUBPROGRAMS

SUBROUTINE subprograms can appreciably shorten the length of a main program when the programmer groups together similar statements, found at various locations, and forms one separate routine. Other advantages also accrue. A large program can be separated into small segments (subroutines) that are easier to write, debug (remove errors), and document. The same idea also allows several programmers to write different segments of a very large project, reducing the time required to complete the task. These advantages are possible because statement labels and variables are local to each subprogram.

Information can be transmitted back and forth between a main program and the separate subprograms by means of an argument list, a common area, or a combination of the two as shown in the samples in the chapter. Programmer preference dictates the use of argument lists, common areas, or a combination of the two.

9-7 Summary

Questions

1. Solve Question 8 of Chap. 8 by using a SUBROUTINE subprogram.
2. Solve Question 9 of Chap. 8 by using a SUBROUTINE subprogram.
3. Modify the student sorting problem found in Sec. 9-3 so that three groups of students can be sorted separately and also in total.
4. Once again modify the original student sorting problem found in Sec. 9-3 so that the instructor would be able to input up to eight characters for each student name rather than just the initials.
5. Two Tables IA and IB are arranged in order from the smallest to the largest:

IA		IB	
(1)	−5	(1)	−2
(2)	3	(2)	−1
(3)	8	(3)	6
(4)	12	(4)	9
(5)	19		

Write a program that will merge the two tables, resulting in a new Table IC with a total of nine values in order from smallest to largest.

(Note: Do not place the values in one table and sort, but begin by comparing each of the locations in both tables and proceeding from there.)

6. For product ZEM, profit is equal to

P = units sold (unit price − unit cost) − fixed cost

Using the formula for P, write a program that will calculate and print a report according to the following layout:

PRODUCT ZEM

DAY	UNITS SOLD	UNIT PRICE	UNIT COST	FIXED COST	PROFIT
MON	785	217.38	196.16	485.00	X
TUES	695	217.38	201.03	485.00	X
WED	672	217.38	202.40	485.00	X
THUR	1286	217.38	191.64	485.00	X
FRI	942	217.38	184.47	485.00	X
TOTALS	X				X

Use the data shown as input.

7. Modify Question 6, repeating the cycle for a 2-week period (supply your own data for the second week). Calculate weekly and overall totals.

8. Using the program and data from Question 7, supply the statements required to print the daily average for units sold, unit cost, and profit.

9. The trapezoidal rule for approximating the value of an integral is

$$A = \frac{1}{2} dx \, (y_0 + 2y_1 + 2y_2 + \cdots + 2y_{n-1} + y_n)$$

Given the function $y = \sqrt{(1 + x^3)}$, $n = 8$, $a = 0$, and $b = 2$, write a program to find the value of A when $a \leq x \leq b$. The quantity of dx is equal to $(b - a)/n$. What is the value of A if $n = 16$ and the remaining items hold constant? The value of A if $n = 25$?

10. The cube root of a number can be approximated using the Newton-Raphson method noted below. Given x, the cube root of x can be obtained by the formula $y_2 = \frac{1}{3}[x_2/(y_1 + 2y_1)]$, where y_1 is an approximation of the cube root. The value of y_2 is then used again so that $y_3 = \frac{1}{3}[x_2/(y_2 + 2y_2)]$. This sequence is repeated until the absolute difference between y_{i+1} and y_i is less than a given degree of accuracy $e(|y_{i+1} - y_i| < e)$. Given x as 100.01, the first approximation of y_1 as 5.0, and the degree of accuracy e as 0.1E−6, write a program to find the cube root (a) by the Newton-Raphson method and (b) by raising 100.01 to the $\frac{1}{3}$ power. Which is more accurate? As a second part of the problem, use 0.1D−12 for e and double-precision variables to obtain a more precise answer.

11 Generalize the program in Question 10 to (a) accept a code where, if a 1 is entered, y is computed to single-precision accuracy and, if a 2 is entered, y is computed to double-precision accuracy; (b) accept a value for x; and (c) approximate y by dividing x by 3. The program should be able to find the cube root of as many values entered.

12 In an inventory control application for MAUMY Co. the number of days of stock on hand is made up of four elements, namely, (a) stock-in-process, (b) safety stock, (c) transit time, and (d) allowance for shipping frequency. The optimum inventory level is the total of the optimum level for each of the four items above plus or minus 10 percent. For seven products, the following data is available:

PRODUCT	IN-PROCESS	SAFETY	TRANSIT	ALLOWANCE	ON-HAND
AX	1.6	3.2	5.0	5.0	13.5
BX	1.8	4.5	4.5	5.0	14.0
CX	.5	2.5	6.0	2.0	11.5
BYG	2.3	6.9	12.0	10.0	25.0
BYH	.3	1.2	4.2	4.2	11.5
BYO	1.5	3.0	3.0	5.5	14.5
BYM	2.2	4.4	8.6	5.0	18.0

The data reveals that the exact optimum is not on hand for any of the items. The problem is to write a program that will calculate the total of the four elements [(a) to (d) representing the optimum] and compare the on-hand quantity to ±10 percent of the optimum. Within the program, generate two separate listings: one listing containing the product name, total stock on hand, and optimum level for the products that fall within the ±10 percent category; the other listing containing the product name, total stock on hand, optimum level, difference between the on hand and the optimum, and percent difference for the items that fall outside the tolerance range. Label the first report IN-TOLERANCE ITEMS and the second OUT-OF-TOLERANCE ACTION NEEDED. Supply additional data once the original problem is solved.

WATFOR AND WATFIV EXTENSIONS TO FORTRAN IV *A*

A fast FORTRAN IV compiler program, called WATFOR for WATerloo FORtran, was developed at the University of Waterloo, Ontario, Canada. A subsequent revision to the first program was named WATFIV, for WATerloo Fortran IV. These two compilers are used at many colleges and universities to satisfy certain educational and research requirements. Three basic advantages of the compilers are as follows. First, short programs are compiled and executed rapidly. With a large volume of student problems, a significant savings in computer time can be realized because the WATFOR and WATFIV jobs can be grouped together as a batch. Second, a comprehensive set of error diagnostics is included in the programs. Many errors and warnings generated by the WATFOR and WATFIV compilers are not listed when compiling under a manufacturer's operating system. These diagnostics facilitate the debugging process in many large and complicated research projects as well as in student problems. Third, a number of extensions and modifications to standard FORTRAN IV have been built into the compilers. These extensions will be discussed further after the limitations of WATFOR and WATFIV are detailed.

One of the primary drawbacks of the two compilers is that of limited program size. Larger programs can be executed when using the manufacturer's operating system as opposed to

WATFOR or WATFIV. However, this limitation usually affects only research projects and does not hamper processing of most student jobs.

A second disadvantage concerns subroutines stored on the system library, subroutines written in assembly language, and object program decks. None of these three program segments or routines can be included or referenced in a WATFOR or WATFIV batch deck.

The third limiting factor of WATFOR and WATFIV involves the extensions built into the compilers. If the student intends to continue working with FORTRAN, once outside the university atmosphere he must restrict himself only to the options and instructions available with the particular system being used. Normally, this environment at present excludes the use of WATFOR and WATFIV extensions.

Assignment Statement Extensions

When operating under WATFOR or WATFIV, multiple assignment statements are permitted, the effect of which is to assign the result of one expression or constant to a number of variables. The general form of the statement is

sl   [variable-1] = [variable-2] = $\cdots$ = [variable-n] = [expression]

where sl represents an optional statement label, variable-1, variable-2, ... , variable-n are valid FORTRAN variable names, and the expression is any valid FORTRAN expression, variable, or constant. Values are assigned from right to left in the assignment process. For example, the statements

```
5157   I = J = K = 0
       A = B = C = D = E = 6.3*5.1*3.3
```

assign the value of zero to K, J, and I, in order. Likewise, E, D, C, B, and A are assigned the value of 106.029 in the order specified.

Also permitted with the WATFOR and WATFIV compilers are the standard assignment statements. Thus, statements of the forms

sl   [real variable] = [integer expression]

and

sI [integer variable] = [real expression]

are valid. Examples of the first case are

```
10      A = 1
11      XN = N
12      B = I*J
```

where statement label 10 is executed properly with accurate results. The variable A is assigned the value of 1.0. However, a loss of accuracy may occur in the next two statements. If the value of N or I*J is greater than or accurate to more than seven digits in length, only the seven most significant digits are retained in the real variables XN and B. For example, if N is equal to 210666735, XN is assigned the real value 0.2106667E+9. This loss of accuracy is attributed to the method in which real and integer variables are stored within the memory unit of the computer.

Examples of the second general form are

```
100     I = 1.
101     J = 15.6
102     K = A*B
```

where statement label 100 is executed properly with the predictable result of I being set equal to the integer one. In label 101, however, the constant 15.6 is truncated and the resultant 15 assigned to J. Another type of problem can occur with the last statement listed. On the IBM 360, for example, the largest integer value that can be stored is 2147483647, and the largest real value is approximately 10^{75}. Therefore, if A*B is equal to 0.234E+25 or another similarly large value, a proper conversion to K can not be made because the magnitude of A*B is too large.

Consider another innocent-looking multiple assignment:

M = A = N = 761249875

In this example, because the computer assigns the values right to left, three different constants are assigned to the variables: N is assigned the value 761249875; A the value 0.7612498E+9; and M the value 761249800. By writing the statement as

A = M = N = 761249875

M and N are assigned the same values.

Another option permitted is statements of the form

1   AB = 2 + B*A +5
2   L = 2*A + Z*6

where mixed-mode expressions are contained to the right of the equals sign. Although the computer executes these statements properly, an internal conversion is required first. The statements revised below execute much faster than the mixed-mode versions:

3   AB = 2.0 + B*A +5.0
4   L = 2.0*A + Z*6.0

The time-consuming statements 1 and 2 should be avoided and replaced by statements of the form identified by 3 and 4.

I/O Extensions

What may be considered the most advantageous extension built into the WATFOR and WATFIV compilers is the format-free input/output instructions. Format-free I/O permits the programmer to process input and output without reference to a specific FORMAT statement. The two general statements used are

sl   READ, [list of variables, separated by commas]

and

sl   PRINT, [list of variables, separated by commas]

where sl is an optional statement label, references to a device and a FORMAT statement are omitted, and the list of variables is any valid FORTRAN variable names. The card reader and the line printer are the input and output devices by default when using these statements. Examples of the READ statement are

473   READ, A,B,I,J
         READ, M,X,Y

where the first reads two real constants followed by two integer constants, and the second reads one integer value followed by two real values. To supply input for the first READ, the data can be punched in two forms: the four values can be entered in the proper order (two real, two integer) on one card separated by commas and/or one or more blanks; or one value can be punched per input card (the long way).

Note that the data must not begin in column 1 but may begin in any other column. For the second READ, input data may be punched in either of the forms discussed as long as there is a one-to-one correspondence in number, type, and order.

Two rules that apply when reading data under control of WATFOR, WATFIV, or other compilers are (1) each time a READ statement is executed, a new input card is processed; and (2) when required, additional input data cards are read until all the variables in the list have been assigned values.

To avoid repetitive punching of the same input constant, a duplication factor (*) can be inserted in the data. For example, if A, B, and C in the READ below are to be assigned one value, that is, 13.51,

81   READ, A,B,C

the data could be punched as 3*13.51. As another example, the statements

DIMENSION NUMBER(100)
READ, NUMBER

can be processed so that all the locations of NUMBER are set to zero by supplying within the data the duplication factor in the form 100*0.

Examples of the format-free PRINT statement are

1005   PRINT, A,B,I,J
        PRINT, M,X,Y
        PRINT, DP

where the first prints two real values using a 2E16.7 format specification followed by the printing of two integer values using a 2I12 format specification. When printing real values, an E16.7 format code is used by default. When printing integer values, an I12 format code is used by default. A format code of D28.16 is used to print declared double-precision variables. Thus, the second PRINT causes one integer to be printed followed by two real values on the same line. Assuming that the variable DP is double-precision mode, the third PRINT causes the value to be generated according to a format code of D28.16.

When necessary, the output is continued on a second line of print. The statement

PRINT, A,B,C,D,E,F,G,H,X,Y

requires 160 columns (10 × E16.7); therefore, two lines of output are generated by the one free-format statement.

Another version of the free-format print permits programmers to include expressions in the statement. The statements permitted are of the form

783   PRINT, 5.24*8.33*6.417, A*B/C**2
        PRINT, 1,2,3

where the first evaluates the two calculations and prints the two results using the E16.7 format code. The second generates the integer values of 1, 2, and 3 on one line of output. The second form is useful as a debugging technique when tracing the logic path of a particularly difficult program that is not working properly.

Expressions or calculations can also be inserted in the WRITE statement. Instead of using the free I/O instruction, the previous PRINT statements could be written as

783   WRITE(6,100) 5.25*8.33*6.417, A*B/C**2
        WRITE(6,200) 1,2,3

where the output device is data set number 6 and FORMAT labels 100 and 200 control the form of the output.

The final print option permits character information to be included as part of the free-format instruction. This option has been implemented in the WATFIV compiler but it is not available when using WATFOR.

784   PRINT, 'COLUMN A   COLUMN B'
        PRINT, 'NO OF OBS', NOB, 'LEVEL', L

where the first generates two column headings and the second prints on one line the message NO OF OBS followed by the numeric value of NOB and the message LEVEL followed by the numeric value of L.

Additionally, there are a few minor extensions not listed here.

However, their importance is minimal in relation to the language capabilities.

Given the formula $r^2 = x^2 + y^2$, the value for r can easily be computed if values for x and y are known. Assuming that x is 1.23 and y is 3.832, a short program[1] using the extensions discussed in this section can be developed:

WATFIV Program Samples

```
PRINT,@THE VALUE OF R IS@, SQRT(1.23**2 + 3.832**2)
END
```

Output from this program would appear on one line as

```
THE VALUE OF R IS    0.4024563E 01
```

Note that the expression can be calculated within the PRINT statement. Also, data could be read into the program instead of using fixed constants for x and y, by using the free-format READ:

```
READ, X,Y
PRINT,@THE VALUE OF R IS@, SQRT(X**2 + Y**2)
END
```

The result would be the same as before if the input data card were punched as

1.23 3.832

or

1.23, 3.832

or

      1.23, 3.832

or

1.23
3.832

all of which are valid data entries. In all four cases, X would be assigned the value 1.23 and Y the value 3.832.

---

[1] The STOP statement can be omitted from a WATFOR or WATFIV program; however, an execution error is printed noting the omission.

To generate a more flexible solution handling a number of x's and y's, the following statements are more efficient:

```
10      READ, X,Y
        IF(X.LT.0.0)STOP
        PRINT,@THE VALUE OF R IS@, SQRT(X**2 + Y**2)
        GO TO 10
        END
```

where this program terminates when a negative value is supplied for X.

As a final example, to illustrate the use of the multiple assignment statement, assume that a test has been given to 100 students and the grades range from 17 to 95. Assume that most of the scores lie between 60 and 90. The instructor wants two averages to be computed: one representing all the grades and the second representing only the grades with a score above 50. One reason for requesting the second average is that two or three extremely low grades might bias the overall average downward. Consider the statements

```
C       THIS PROGRAM COMPUTES TWO AVERAGES - AN OVERALL AVERAGE
C       AND A SELECTIVE AVERAGE. STATEMENTS LABELED 1000 OR HIGHER
C       CONTAIN MIXED-MODE EXPRESSIONS
1000    ALL=OVER50=NOV50=0
        DO 1 I = 1,100
        READ, GRADE
        ALL = ALL + GRADE
1001    IF(GRADE.LE.50)GO TO 1
        OVER50 = OVER50 + GRADE
        NOV50 = NOV50 + 1
1       CONTINUE
1002    PRINT,@TOTAL FOR 100@,ALL, @AVERAGE FOR 100@,ALL/100
        PRINT,@TOTAL FOR GRADES OVER 50@,OVER50
        PRINT,@NO OF STUDENTS OVER 50@,NOV50
1003    PRINT,@AVERAGE FOR GRADES OVER 50@,OVER50/NOV50
        STOP
        END
```

With this program, 100 data cards must be punched using real constants, one per card. Also, a number of mixed-mode expressions are included. Although the correct answers would be generated by these statements, the following statements represent a more efficient solution that avoids mixed-mode expressions:

```
C        THIS PROGRAM COMPUTES TWO AVERAGES - AN OVERALL AVERAGE
C        AND A SELECTIVE AVERAGE
         INTEGER GRADE(100), ALL, OVER50
         ALL = OVER50 = NOV50 = 0
         READ, GRADE
         DO 1 I = 1,100
         ALL = ALL + GRADE(I)
         IF(GRADE(I).LE.50)GO TO 1
         OVER50 = OVER50 + GRADE(I)
         NOV50 = NOV50 + 1
1        CONTINUE
         PRINT,@TOTAL FOR 100@,ALL, @AVERAGE FOR 100@,FLOAT(ALL)/100.
         PRINT,@TOTAL FOR GRADES OVER 50@,OVER50
         PRINT,@NO. OF STUDENTS OVER 50@,NOV50
         PRINT,@AVERAGE FOR GRADES OVER 50@,FLOAT(OVER50)/FLOAT(NOV50)
         STOP
         END
```

With this program, as many grades as can be punched on one data card are permitted. Also, the grades can be punched in integer form. Hence, fewer input cards are required by this version. Mixed-mode expressions have been removed also. As a result of these revisions, the computer would execute and print the same results faster.

Note that the programs listed in this appendix can be compiled and executed only by using a WATFIV compiler. To run them under WATFOR, the character information must be omitted from the PRINT statements. However, to run them under control of a different compiler would require substantial modifications.

Summary

WATFOR and WATFIV are compiler programs developed at the University of Waterloo, Ontario, Canada. They are fast FORTRAN IV modified compilers aimed directly at serving the educational and research needs of colleges and universities. In addition to fast processing, a complete and descriptive set of error diagnostics and a number of extensions have been incorporated into the compilers to aid in the development of programs. The format-free I/O instructions are among the most important of the attributes included because their use normally allows the students to begin writing programs at the earliest possible moment.

USING THE CARD PUNCH TO PREPARE PROGRAM AND DATA CARDS B

To enter program instructions and data information into many computer systems, it is first necessary to card punch or *keypunch* the instructions and the data on 80-column cards (Fig. B-1). Card punching, or as it is commonly referred to, *keypunching*, is the process of preparing these 80-column cards for use as input to the computer. One of the most popular keypunch machines used today is the IBM Model 029 card punch (Fig. B-2). It is used to punch decimal numbers, alphabetic characters, a limited set of special characters, and finally, other combinations achieved by the use of the multiple punch-key capability. Four particular card-punching functions—(1) the punching of one or more cards, (2) the duplication of one or more cards, (3) the correction of keypunch errors, and (4) the multiple punching of card columns—will be discussed in detail after listing a general description of the control switches and special keys required to operate the machine.

Control Switches and Special Keys

The MAIN-LINE switch turns the power on. It is located below and to the right of the keyboard on the front panel (shown in Fig. B-2). Also shown in Fig. B-2 are the COLUMN INDICATOR and the BACKSPACE keys. The COLUMN INDICATOR points to the column in the card that will be punched with the next striking of one of the keys, and depressing the

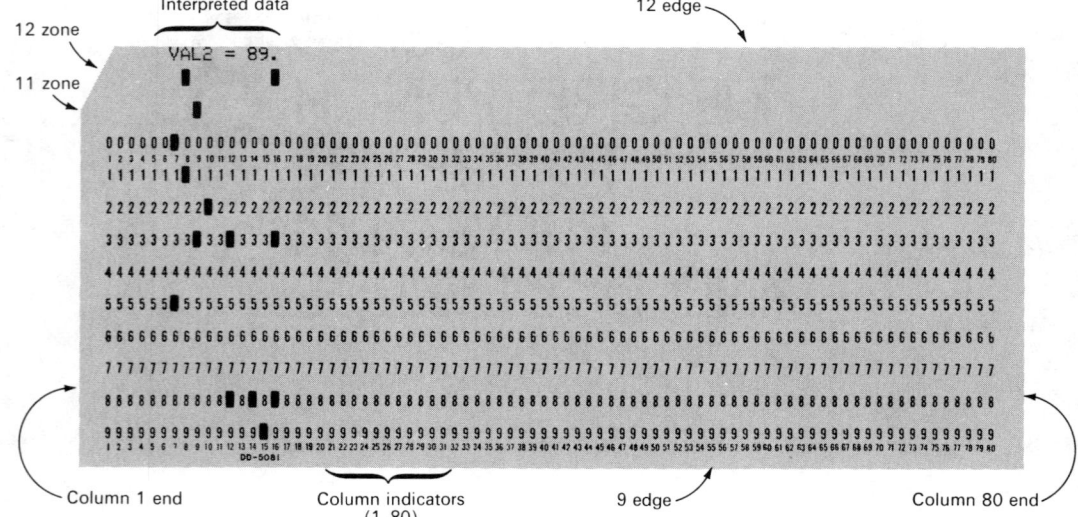

Figure B-1 Standard 80-column card.

BACKSPACE key causes the card to return to the right one space per depression. For the simple tasks outlined in this appendix, the PROGRAM CONTROL lever should be placed in the OFF position (i.e., turned to the right); this control is used primarily in larger-scale keypunching jobs. Figures B-3 and B-4 present the layout of the keyboard and control switches.

The FEED key advances a card from the card hopper to the punch station. The card can not be punched, however, until it is properly aligned in the punch station, which is accomplished by depressing the REG key.

The REG key properly aligns cards in the punch and read stations. It must be depressed before a card can be punched or read. The REL key releases a card and advances it to the next station. When it is depressed, a card will advance from the punch to the read station or from the read station to the card stacker.

The DUP key serves to duplicate entire cards or portions. When a previously punched card is placed in the read station and a blank card in the punch station, the DUP key will transfer and punch information column by column. By holding the key

USING THE CARD PUNCH TO PREPARE PROGRAM AND DATA CARDS

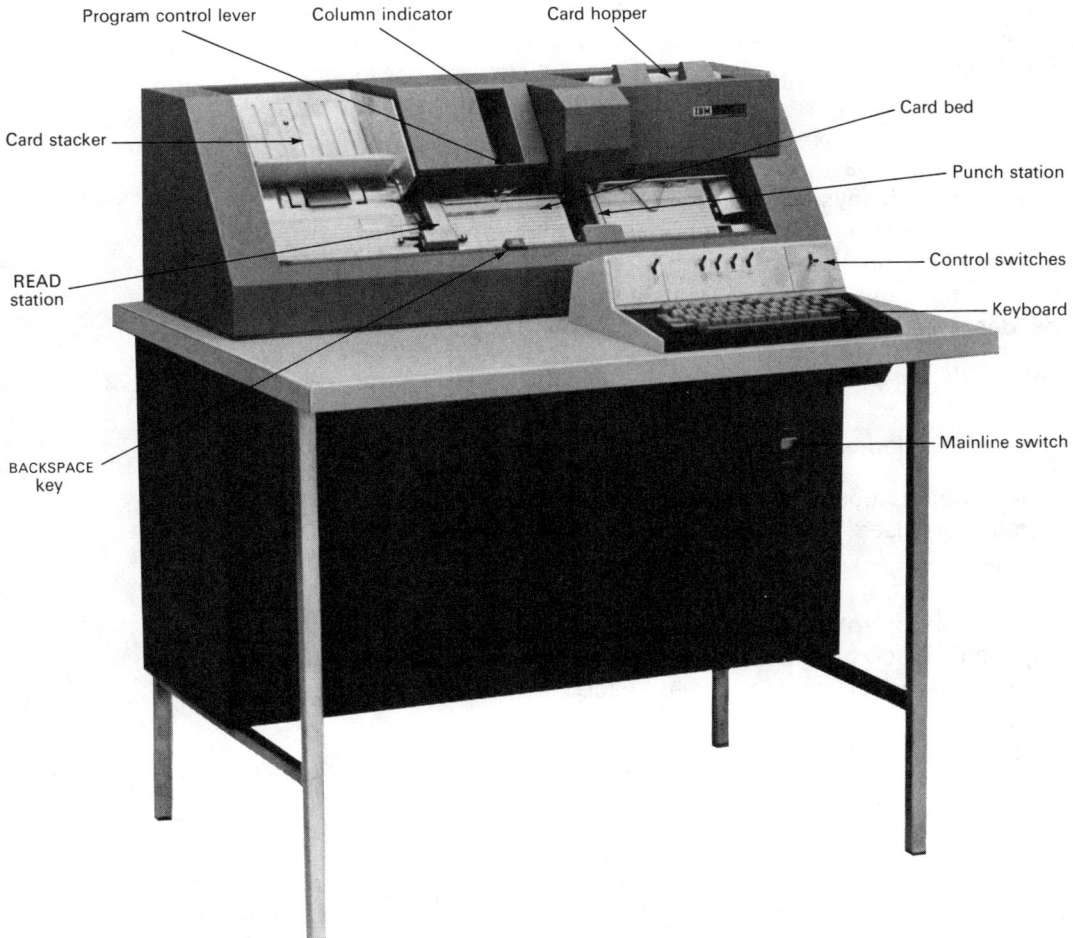

Figure B-2 IBM Model 029 card punch. (*Reprinted by permission of IBM Corporation.*)

down, the entire contents of the card at the read station are reproduced into the card at the punch station.

The MULT PCH key permits any combination of characters or bits to be punched in any one column. As long as the MULT PCH key is depressed, the card is prevented from advancing to the next column and successive punches appear in the same column.

The ERROR RESET key is depressed to release the keyboard when it is locked. It may become accidentally locked for several reasons, such as the power being turned off during a punch operation.

The keyboard has two characters indicated on most of the keys. Two shift keys, NUMERIC and ALPHA, determine whether the upper or lower half of the key is punched. To punch the lower half, simply depress the desired key. However, to punch the top half, the NUMERIC shift and the applicable key must be depressed at the same time. For example, to punch a U, simply depress the key labeled $\left(\frac{1}{U}\right)$. However, to punch the number 1, depress the NUMERIC shift and the $\left(\frac{1}{U}\right)$ key together. For most student jobs, the ALPHA key can be ignored. It is used, however, when the program control unit is activated.

Of the six control switches that are located at the top of the keyboard panel, only three are important for the tasks outlined here. The PRINT switch, when placed in the ON position,

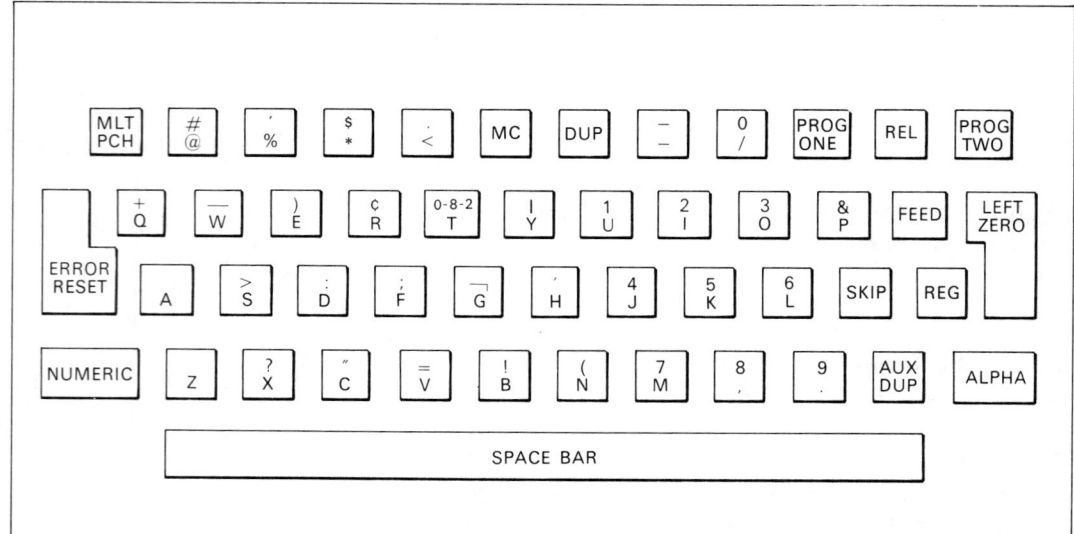

Figure B-3   IBM Model 029 keyboard layout.

USING THE CARD PUNCH TO PREPARE PROGRAM AND DATA CARDS

Figure B-4 IBM Model 029 control switches. (*Reprinted by permission of IBM Corporation.*)

causes each character punched to be printed at the top of the appropriate card column simultaneously. When placed in the OFF position, characters punched in the card are not printed.

The AUTO FEED switch, when placed in the ON position, causes cards to be automatically fed from the card hopper, registered, and stacked in the card stacker. It should be placed ON when a number of cards are to be punched. When punching only one or two cards, the switch is normally placed in the OFF position.

The CLEAR switch, when held in an upward position, removes cards contained in the read and punch stations and places them in the card stacker. An internal spring returns it to the OFF position when it is released by the operator.

The remaining three switches are used for more complicated jobs than those discussed here. When placed in the OFF position they can be ignored.

To Punch One or More Cards

The following steps can be used to punch one card at a time:

1 Turn the MAIN-LINE and PRINT switches ON. The remaining control switches should be in the OFF position.
2 Place blank cards in the card hopper, with the face of the card forward and the 9 edge (the edge with the row of 9's along the bottom) down.
3 Depress the FEED and REG keys to feed and register a card in the punch station.
4 Begin keypunching the desired data. Remember that the lower half of each key is punched in the card unless the NUMERIC key is depressed. When the NUMERIC shift key is depressed, the upper half of the key is punched.
5 When finished punching the desired data or if column 80 has been reached, remove the card from the card bed by lifting upward the CLEAR switch. (Note: In substitution for the CLEAR switch, the operator can punch the keys REL, REG, and REL in the sequence listed to remove the card from the card bed.)

The procedure required to punch more than one card is similar to the previous steps:

1 Besides turning the MAIN-LINE and PRINT switches on, also place the AUTO FEED switch on.
2 Same as above.
3 Strike the FEED key twice. This places one card in the punch station and another card adjacent to it, ready to be punched after the first has been completed.
4 Same as above.
5 When finished punching, depress the REL key. Because the AUTO FEED switch is ON (*a*) the first card is released from the punch to the read station; (*b*) the adjacent card is registered in the punch station; and (*c*) a new card is fed from the card hopper. If column 80 is reached, steps 5(*a*) to (*c*) are performed automatically.

USING THE CARD PUNCH TO PREPARE PROGRAM AND DATA CARDS 315

6   Punch the remaining cards, repeating step 5 when each card is completed. After the last card has been completed, lift the CLEAR switch to the ON position to remove the last cards from the card bed. The sequence REL, REG, and REL can also be used to remove cards from the card hopper (after turning the AUTO FEED switch to OFF).

If a card jam should occur accidentally during the operation of the keypunch, consult the computer center operating personnel who are most experienced at locating the problem.

To Duplicate One or More Cards

Occasionally a card or a number of cards is required in duplicate. Perhaps the same program statement or data card is needed for two different tasks or jobs. Rather than punching the card twice, it is faster and more efficient to punch it once and reproduce it. The following steps are used to duplicate one card:

1   Turn the MAIN-LINE and PRINT switches ON and place blank cards in the card hopper.

2   Manually insert at the read station the card to be reproduced. (Be sure to place the card under the machine guides.)

3   Depress the FEED and REG keys to properly align the two cards at the read and punch stations.

4   Depress the DUP key until all the columns have been punched.

5   Lift the CLEAR switch to remove the cards.

The procedure above works fine when reproducing one card. However, to duplicate a deck of cards, the following steps are more efficient:

1   Turn the MAIN-LINE, PRINT, and AUTO FEED switches ON.

2   Interweave the deck of cards to be duplicated with blank cards (e.g., place an original card first followed by a blank, original, blank, and so forth). Place the interwoven cards in the card hopper.

3   Strike the FEED key twice, placing the first original in the punch station and a blank adjacent to it.

4   Strike the REL key, which moves the first original to the read station and the first blank to the punch station.

5   Depress the DUP key until all the columns have been punched.

6   Strike the REL key twice; this removes the original and duplicate cards and places the next original and blank in the read and punch stations. (Note: If column 80 has been reached, it is necessary to strike the REL key only once.)

7   Repeat steps 5 and 6 until all the cards have been duplicated.

8   Lift the CLEAR switch to remove the last cards from the card bed.

To Correct Keypunch Errors

Keypunch errors that occur when preparing data cards or program statements must be corrected. A card with an error, for example, a 5 has been punched instead of 4, can not be used as is; it must be replaced by a new card with correct data. If a particular card contains only a few incorrect punches, it is easier to duplicate the correct columns and punch the corrections than repunch the entire card. The steps needed are

1   Turn the MAIN-LINE and PRINT switches ON and place blank cards in the card hopper.

2   Manually insert at the read station the card that contains an error (assume that column 40 contains a 1 instead of a U).

3   Depress the FEED and REG keys to properly align the cards at the read and punch stations.

4   Depress the DUP key until the COLUMN INDICATOR is pointing to 40. Keypunch the U (see assumption in step 2). Depress the DUP key again until all the columns have been punched. In general, hold the DUP key down until the error column or columns are reached, punch the correct data, and then continue with the DUP key. Any number of column corrections can be made using this procedure.

5   Lift the CLEAR switch to remove the cards.

6   Check the cards to make sure that the corrections have been made properly. Destroy the invalid card so that it is not used erroneously.

To Multiple Punch Card Columns

When using the IBM Model 029 keypunch, it is sometimes necessary to punch characters or combinations of digits not listed in Table B-1. Any combination of characters or digits can be punched by using the MULT PCH key on the keyboard panel. The steps required are

1   Turn the power on, insert a card in the card bed, and begin punching the desired data.

2   When the COLUMN INDICATOR points to the particular column where the special characters are required, depress the MULT PCH key. When this key is held down, the card will not advance. Thus, striking two or more keys causes the punches to be placed in only one column. When the special character has been punched, release the MULT PCH key and continue processing in a normal manner.

Many other tasks plus the four outlined here can be completed using the keypunch. For more detailed instructions and a discussion of certain capabilities omitted here, refer to the *IBM 029 Keypunch Reference Manual,* A24-3332-5.

Table B-1 The Standard Set of 49 Characters Acceptable in FORTRAN Statements.[1]

Alphabetic Characters	Model 029 Card Code[2]	Numeric Characters	Model 029 Card Code[2]	Special Characters	Model 029 Card Code	Model 026 Card Code
A	12-1	0	0	+	12-8-6	12
B	12-2	1	1	−	11	11
C	12-3	2	2	*	11-8-4	11-8-4
D	12-4	3	3	/	0-1	0-1
E	12-5	4	4	(	12-8-5	0-8-4
F	12-6	5	5	)	11-8-5	12-8-4
G	12-7	6	6	=	8-6	8-3
H	12-8	7	7	.	12-8-3	12-8-3
I	12-9	8	8	,	0-8-3	0-8-3
J	11-1	9	9	;	8-5	8-4
K	11-2					
L	11-3					
M	11-4					
N	11-5					
O	11-6					
P	11-7					
Q	11-8					
R	11-9					
S	0-2					
T	0-3					
U	0-4					
V	0-5					
W	0-6					
X	0-7					
Y	0-8					
Z	0-9					
$	11-8-3					

[1] Note: Additionally, any valid card code is acceptable if it is part of a Hollerith or literal field.
[2] When punching these characters, either an 029 or 026 machine can be used. However, note that the same special character may require a different card code on the 029 and 026 machines. When limited to one machine, the special card codes can be punched by using the MULT PCH feature to construct the proper codes.

FORTRAN-SUPPLIED MATHEMATICAL SUBPROGRAMS C

Listed in the following table is a summary of most of the built-in mathematical functions available with FORTRAN IV processors. It should be noted that specific installations may not make all of the functions listed available to the programmer, but other computer centers may include additional subprograms.

Subprogram Operation	Function Reference Name	Sample Assignment Statement[1]	Definition
Absolute value	ABS	A = ABS(X)	$\|X\|$
	DABS	DA = DABS(DX)	$\|DX\|$
	IABS	IA = IABS(IX)	$\|IX\|$
Arccosine	ARCOS	A = ARCOS(X)	arccos X
	DARCOS	DA = DARCOS(DX)	arccos DX
Arcsine	ARSIN	A = ARSIN(X)	arcsin X
	DARSIN	DA = DARSIN(DX)	arcsin DX
Arctangent (in radians)	ATAN	A = ATAN(X)	arctan X
	DATAN	DA = DATAN(DX)	arctan DX
Common logarithm	ALOG10	A = ALOG10(X)	$\log_{10} X$
	DLOG10	DA = DLOG10(DX)	$\log_{10} DX$

Subprogram Operation	Function Reference Name	Sample Assignment Statement[1]	Definition
Cosine	COS	A = COS(X)	cos X
	DCOS	DA = DCOS(DX)	cos DX
Cotangent	COTAN	A = COTAN(X)	cot X
	DCOTAN	DA = DCOTAN(DX)	cot DX
Exponential	DEXP	DA = DEXP(DX)	e^{DX}
	EXP	A = EXP(X)	e^X
Fixed point	IFIX	IA = IFIX(X)	Convert X from real to integer
Floating point	DFLOAT	DA = DFLOAT(IX)	Convert IX from integer to real
	FLOAT	A = FLOAT(IX)	
Hyperbolic cosine	COSH	A = COSH(X)	cosh X
	DCOSH	DA = DCOSH(DX)	cosh DX
Hyperbolic sine	DSINH	DA = DSINH(DX)	sinh DX
	SINH	A = SINH(X)	sinh X
Hyperbolic tangent	DTANH	DA = DTANH(DX)	tanh DX
	TANH	A = TANH(X)	tanh X
Largest value[2]	AMAX0	A = AMAX0(IX,IY,...)	max(IX,IY,...)
	AMAX1	A = AMAX1(X,Y)	max(X,Y,...)
	DMAX1	DA = DMAX1(DX,DY)	max(DX,DY,...)
	MAX0	IA = MAX0(IX,IY)	max(IX,IY,...)
	MAX1	IA = MAX1(X,Y)	max(X,Y,...)
Modular arithmetic	AMOD	A = AMOD(X,Y)	$X - \text{sgn}(X/Y)[\lvert X/Y \rvert]Y$
	DMOD	DA = DMOD(DX,DY)	$DX - \text{sgn}(DX/DY)[\lvert DX/DY \rvert]DY$
	MOD	IA = MOD(IX,IY)	$IX - \text{sgn}(IX/IY)[\lvert IX/IY \rvert]IY$
Natural logarithm	ALOG	A = ALOG(X)	$\log_e X$
	DLOG	DA = DLOG(DX)	$\log_e DX$
Sine	DSIN	DA = DSIN(DX)	sin DX
	SIN	A = SIN(X)	sin X
Smallest value[2]	AMIN0	A = AMIN0(IX,IY)	min(IX,IY,...)
	AMIN1	A = AMIN1(X,Y)	min(X,Y,...)
	DMIN1	DA = DMIN1(DX,DY)	min(DX,DY,...)
	MIN0	IA = MIN0(IX,IY)	min(IX,IY,...)
	MIN1	IA = MIN1(X,Y)	min(X,Y,...)
Square root	DSQRT	DA = DSQRT(DX)	$DX^{1/2}$
	SQRT	A = SQRT(X)	$X^{1/2}$

FORTRAN-SUPPLIED MATHEMATICAL SUBPROGRAMS

Subprogram Operation	Function Reference Name	Sample Assignment Statement[1]	Definition
Tangent	DTAN	DA = DTAN(DX)	tan DX
	TAN	A = TAN(X)	tan X
Truncation	AINT	A = AINT(X)	Sign of argument times the absolute value of largest integer argument
	IDINT	IA = IDINT(DX)	
	INT	IA = INT(X)	

[1] The variables X, Y, and A are real mode; IX, IY, and IA are integer mode; and DX, DY, and DA are double-precision mode in this group of assignment statements. Also, when using the double-precision operations, the function reference name must appear in a DOUBLE PRECISION specification statement.

[2] More than two arguments within parentheses may be used with these functions.

ERROR MESSAGES D

Included in this appendix is a summary and general description of program and statement errors[1] that lead to diagnostic messages generated by the computer system, more specifically by the compiler program. The errors are stated in general terms and a more detailed explanation can be obtained by referring to the specific systems manual being used.

Error Message	Description
Statement label error	A required statement label is missing. For example, a statement following either an arithmetic IF, STOP, RETURN, or a GO TO statement is not labeled as it should be, or the label on a FORMAT statement is omitted.
Illegal statement label error	A statement label has been used erroneously in one of the instructions. For example, referring to a FORMAT label within a GO TO or IF statement is invalid. Listing a label in either a READ or WRITE that is not the label of a FORMAT statement is illegal also.
Duplicate statement label error	The same label has been listed at least twice (appears in columns 1 to 5 more than once) within one program. A label can be defined and appear in columns 1 to 5 only once in a particular program.

[1] Note that unfortunately the system can not identify the programmer's logic errors, but only errors that occur in the use of the language.

Undefined statement label error	A label referenced in the program is omitted. This usually occurs as a result of a keypunch or syntax error and not the actual omission. For example, a GO TO 10 statement where the statement labeled 10 has been erroneously punched with a label of 100 will cause this error.
Length of variable name	A variable name consists of more than six characters or two variable names appear in succession without proper delimitation, as in an arithmetic expression where the operator symbol has been omitted or in a READ or WRITE where the comma has been omitted.
Undimensioned subscript error	Based on the use of a variable name in an instruction, an array is implied. However, the variable name does not appear in a DIMENSION or another array specification statement.
Comma error	A specific comma required in an instruction has been omitted, as in the DO statement where commas delimit the parameters.
Type or ID conflict	A variable name or subprogram name has been listed in such a way that it is in conflict with the type or mode that was previously assigned to it. For example, an array name appears in an arithmetic assignment.
Syntax errors	A broad category that identifies statements which do not conform to the specifications established in FORTRAN IV. These errors occur often as a result of mispunching or misspelling key words such as READ or WRITE or using an alpha character in a label; or listing an illegal constant such as $1,205, where the $ and the , are not permitted.
DO loops unclosed	One or more DO loops have been started, but the terminating label or statement is not listed; or two or more loops are nested incorrectly. Note: The error may occur as a result of a syntax error in the termination statement.
Number of arguments	The correct number of arguments required for a library subprogram is not listed.
No END card	The program source deck does not contain an END card as is needed.

MORE ON LOGICAL OPERATIONS E

In the discussion of the logical IF instruction in Sec. 5-4, the six relational operators were identified, and examples that illustrated their use in IF statements were given. In this appendix, additional logical operations are introduced. Note that, as with the logical IF, the operations listed here are not available in all FORTRAN compilers.

There are three *logical operators,* in addition to the six relational operators, available for use in a logical IF. The three are

.AND.
.OR.
.NOT.

Logical Operators

where the periods before and after are essential parts of each operator. Recall that in the logical IF instruction a test is made and the expression results in either a true or false condition. Using the three logical operators extends the capability of the IF instruction but still results in either a true or false condition. For example, to write an IF statement corresponding to the question "If gross sales are greater than $4,500 and returns are less than $100, set bonus pay to $50," requires the following:

```
  IF((GSALES.GT.4500.).AND.
1  (RETURNS.LT.100.))BONPAY=50.
```

The effect of this statement is to set the value of BONPAY equal to $50 only if both conditions (sales over $4,500 and returns under $100) are met or are true. If either condition is not met or is false, (i.e., either sales are less than or equal to $4,500 or returns are equal to or greater than $100), then the next statement in the program is executed without assigning $50 to bonus pay. Several further examples are

IF(A.EQ.1.5.AND.B.EQ.3.5) GO TO 50
IF((AB+BC.NE.SUM).AND.(X.LT.Y)) WRITE (6,1)SUM
IF((M−N−6.LE.22).AND.(M∗N∗6.GE.420)) GO TO 1

In the last two statements, extra sets of parentheses have been inserted for readability purposes only; however, they are not necessary. To summarize the .AND. operator, a statement is true if and only if both expressions adjoining the operator .AND. are true. If either one is false, the statement condition is false.

In contrast, the .OR. operator works as follows:

IF((A.EQ.1.5).OR.(B.EQ.3.5)) GO TO 50

If either A equals 1.5, or B equals 3.5, or both, the computer transfers control to statement 50. Only if A is not 1.5 and B is not 3.5 does the computer fall through to the next statement. Thus, only one of the conditions must be met for the statement to be true. Several additional examples are

IF((SALES.GT.4500).OR.(RETURNS.LT.100))BONPAY=50.
IF(X+Y.LT.A+B.OR.Z+8.33.LT.5.33)STOP
IF((P.LT.PX).OR.(P.GT.PXY.AND.PXZ)) GO TO 100

In the last statement, the .OR. and .AND. operators have been combined in one statement. The statement equates to the condition "if P is less than PX or if P is greater than both PXY and PXZ, the computer passes control to 100." Note once again that the parentheses are not needed, but their use facilitates interpreting the instruction.

The .NOT. is the third operator. Occasionally, it is easier to approach a problem by stating that "if A and B are not equal, transfer control to 10." The IF statement incorporating .NOT. as part of the instruction would be

IF(.NOT.(A.EQ.B)) GO TO 10

MORE ON LOGICAL OPERATIONS

In this example, if A is not equal to B, the statement is true and the GO TO is executed. Otherwise, if A is the same as B, the GO TO is not executed. Additional examples are

IF(X.NOT.75.1)WRITE(6,3)X,Y
IF((X.NOT.75.1).AND.(A.GT.B)) GO TO 51
IF((X+Y.NOT.2.2).OR.(X.LT.6.6))X=200.

In the last statements, two operators have been incorporated. When more than one operator appears, the following list provides the priority scale from highest to lowest for evaluating expressions:

Operator
**
* and /
+ and −
.EQ.,.NE.,.LT.,.LE.,.GT., and .GE.
.NOT.
.AND.
.OR.

The first three are mathematical operators; these are followed by the relational operationals, and finally, by the three logical operators.

Logical Constants and Variables

Besides integer and real constants and variables, there is also a set of logical constants and variables. Although there are numerous integer and real constants in FORTRAN, there are only two logical constants, .TRUE. and .FALSE., where the periods are essential.

The two logical constants can only be assigned to logical variables. Logical variables are designated by use of a declaration statement placed at the beginning of a program deck. For example, to declare XA and YB as logical variables requires the statement

LOGICAL XA,YB

Any valid FORTRAN variable name can be designated as logical by listing it in a LOGICAL statement. To assign one of the two constants or the results of a logical expression to a logical variable requires the general form

sl   [v] = [l]

where sl is an optional statement label, v is a declared logical variable, and l is a logical constant or logical expression.

A few examples are

```
          LOGICAL A,B,C,D,E,F
          .
          .
          .
1         A = .TRUE.
2         B = .FALSE.
3         C = K.GE.KJ
4         D = K1.GT.KJ1
5         E = C.OR.D
6         F = D.AND.E
```

In statements labeled 1 and 2, A and B are assigned the logical constants .TRUE. and .FALSE., respectively. In statements labeled 3 and 4, the values of the variables K, KJ, and K1, KJ1 determine the logical constants assigned to C and D. In 3, if K is less than KJ, .FALSE. is assigned to C; otherwise a value of .TRUE. is assigned to it. In 4, the logical variable D is set equal to .TRUE. only if the value of K1 is greater than the value of KJ1. For the variable E to be set equal to .TRUE., either C or D must be true; E is set to .FALSE. otherwise. In the last statement, both D and E must be true before F is assigned the value of .TRUE.; otherwise, if one or the other is false, then F is false also.

As indicated in the samples, logical constants and variables are not arithmetic values. Hence, they can never be used in arithmetic expressions using the arithmetic operators. They may, however, be used in logical IF tests.

To print the value of a logical variable, a new format code is needed. The format code is **Logical Format**

Lw

where L indicates a logical variable and w specifies the width of the print field. For example, the code L5 defines a logical field

MORE ON LOGICAL OPERATIONS

five positions in length. When a logical variable is printed with the L code, only a T or F appears in the rightmost position of the field. For example, if a logical variable has been assigned the value .TRUE. and is printed according to the following FORMAT statement

1001   FORMAT(1X ,L5)

the T would appear in column 5.† Likewise, if a logical variable has been assigned the constant .FALSE. and is printed according to the FORMAT listed,

1002   FORMAT(1X,L1)

the F would appear in column 1. For input, the same rules are applicable, but only a T or F must be punched in the data cards. If columns 1 to 5 of a data card are punched TFTFT, and if A, B, C, D, and E are logical variables, reading the variables according to the following FORMAT

1003   FORMAT(5L1)

results in the constant .TRUE. being assigned to A, C, and E, and the constant .FALSE. would be assigned to B and D. If a particular column in a data card is left blank, the constant .FALSE. is assigned.

As discussed in this appendix, logical constants, variables, and operators can be used effectively in FORTRAN programs when the need arises for logical-type manipulations, as contrasted with arithmetic manipulations.

---

†It is assumed in these samples that the 1X is a control character.

ANSWERS TO SELECTED EXERCISES AND QUESTIONS F

CHAPTER 1
Questions

3(a) 4.23E2
3(c) 1.12478E3
3(e) −1.00001E4
5(a) Correct.
5(c) Incorrect; because 1AVG begins with a nonalphabetic character, AVG1 could be used.
5(e) Correct.

CHAPTER 2
Arithmetic Assignment Exercises

1(a) A = 5
1(c) DELTA = 1.
1(e) DIFO1 = 9.85
3(a) 'I' would be assigned an integer value of 1 instead of the mathematical value 1.5.
3(c) In integer calculations, three divided by six is zero, not one-half. Thus, AB is assigned a value of zero.

WRITE Exercises

1(a) WRITE(6,1)
1(c) WRITE(6,1)X,XSUM,XSUMSQ
3(a) WRITE(LPD,FMT)NAME,GAME
3(c) WRITE(LPD,FMT)IMAX,IMIN,JMAX,JMIN

Questions

1 See Flowchart Q2-1.

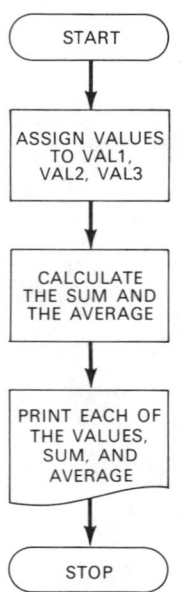

Flowchart Q2-1

3
```
      C    THIS PROGRAM PROJECTS THE ENROLLMENT AT SMT COLLEGE FOR
      C    FOUR YEARS
           WRITE(6,1)
           RATE=.042
           IYEAR=1971
           STD=6128.
           WRITE(6,3) IYEAR ,STD
           IYEAR1=IYEAR+1
           STD1=STD+STD*RATE
           WRITE(6,3) IYEAR1,STD1
           IYEAR2=IYEAR1+1
           STD2=STD1+STD1*RATE
           WRITE(6,3) IYEAR2,STD2
           IYEAR3=IYEAR2+1
           STD3=STD2+STD2*RATE
           WRITE(6,3) IYEAR3,STD3
      1    FORMAT(@1YEAR    STUDENTS@)
      3    FORMAT(I6,F10.0)
           STOP
           END
```

ANSWERS TO SELECTED EXERCISES AND QUESTIONS

CHAPTER 3
FORMAT Exercises

1(a)   5
1(c)   10.50   12.22
1(e)   A= 10.50   B= 12.22   5
3(a)   1   FORMAT(I5,F10.2)
3(c)   2   FORMAT(4E13.6)

FORMAT Extension Exercises

1(a)   0.6233000D+02 (AFTER ADVANCE OF ONE LINE)
1(c)   COND   (AFTER ADVANCE OF TWO LINES)
1(e)   0.62330D+02 0.28007D+02 (NO ADVANCE)
3(a)   1   FORMAT(I5,F7.0)
3(c)   2   FORMAT(A4,3X,F6.0,3X,A4,3X,F6.0)
              or
       2   FORMAT(2(A4,3X,F6.0,3X))

Questions

1   C   THIS PROGRAM COMPUTES THE INTEREST PAYMENT AND NEW BALANCE
         BAL=580.00
         RATE=.035
         PAY=BAL*RATE
         BALNEW=BAL+PAY
         WRITE(6,1)
         WRITE(6,3) PAY,BALNEW
    1   FORMAT(@1INTEREST PAYMENT@,5X,@NEW BALANCE@)
    3   FORMAT(F10.2,9X,F10.2)
         STOP
         END

3   C   THIS PROGRAM COMPUTES AND PRINTS THE FIRST AND LAST TERMS OF A
    C   GEOMETRIC PROGRESSION
         A=6.
         R=5.
         X=4.
         XLTERM=A*R**(X-1.)
         WRITE(6,110) A,XLTERM,R,X
    110 FORMAT(@1FIRST TERM = @,F10.2//@ LAST TERM = @,F10.2//@ R = @,
         1F10.2//@ X = @,F10.2)
         STOP
         END

CHAPTER 4
READ Exercises

1(a)   234.   23.45 23456.8

1(c)   ABCDAB −12.34567E+02 0.1234567D+01
3(a)   READ(5,100) SALE,FIXCO,VARCO
          100   FORMAT(3F8.2)

Extended I/O Exercises

1(a)   C   THIS PROGRAM COMPUTES THE RANGE OF GRAVITATIONAL PULL
               READ 8,GRAMAX,GRAMIN
          8   FORMAT(2F10.4)
               RANGE=GRAMAX−GRAMIN
               PRINT 9,RANGE
          9   FORMAT(@1THE RANGE IS @,F10.4)
               STOP
               END
3(a)   PRINT 101,BETA,GAMMA,DELTA

DATA Exercises

1(a)   X IS 3.256, Y IS 4.0007, I IS 0
1(c)   X IS .123E+03, Y IS 0.0, I IS 0
1(e)   All are set equal to zero (0).
3(a)   DATA A/2.3/
3(c)   DATA NAME/4H SUM/
3(e)   DATA SUM/2./,SUMA/3./, SUMB/4./

Questions

1   C   PROGRAM STATISTICS−7
      C   THIS PROGRAM COMPUTES THE AVERAGE OF THREE VALUES
                READ 10,MONTH,IDAY,IYEAR
                PRINT 20, MONTH,IDAY,IYEAR
                READ 30,VAL1,VAL2,VAL3
                SUM=VAL1+VAL2 VAL3
                AVG=SUM/3.
                PRINT 40,VAL1,VAL2,VAL3,SUM,AVG
          10   FORMAT(3I2)
          20   FORMAT(@1STATISTICS REPORT DATED @,I2,@/@,I2,@/@,I2)
          30   FORMAT(3F5.1)
          40   FORMAT(@01ST VALUE 2ND VALUE 3RD VALUE SUM AVERAGE@/1X,F9.1,
                12F11.1,F7.1,F9.1)
                STOP
                END
3   C   THIS PROGRAM COMPUTES THE AREA OF A TRIANGLE
                READ 8,BASE,HEIGHT
                AREA=.5*BASE*HEIGHT
                PRINT 10,AREA

	8	FORMAT(2F6.2)
	10	FORMAT(@1THE AREA OF THE TRIANGLE IS @,F8.2)
		STOP
		END

CHAPTER 5
GO TO Exercises

1(a)　　2　　GO TO 1
3(a)　　Control is passed to the WRITE statement.

IF Exercises

1(a)		IF(SIGMA.LT.21.1) GO TO 600
1(c)		IF((FCOST+VCOST).EQ.(SALES−RETURN)) GO TO 7
3(a)	174	IF(PCODE.NE.7.) GO TO 176
3(c)		IF(ECODE.EQ.1.) GO TO 221
		IF(ECODE.EQ.2.) GO TO 221
		GO TO 223
3(e)		IF((SALES−RETURN).LT.25000.) GO TO 621
		IF((SALES−RETURN).GT.70000.) GO TO 621

Computed GO TO Exercises

1(a)	57	GO TO (100,150,200,250,300),ICODE
3(a)		GO TO (7,8,6,5), IX
3(c)	256	IF(2+J**2.EQ.1) GO TO 4
3(e)		GO TO (20,30,40),KLTY

Questions

```
1    C     THIS PROGRAM COMPUTES THE NET SALES AND PAY FOR THE EMPLOYEES
     C     OF THE AJACKS COMPANY
           WRITE(6,100)
           DATA TSALES,TRETUR,TNET,TPAY/4*0.0/
     10    READ(5,110) NA,ME,SALES,RETURN
           IF(SALES.EQ.99999.99) GO TO 90
           SALEN=SALES−RETURN
           PAY=100.00+.06*SALEN
           TSALES=TSALES+SALES
           TRETUR=TRETUR+RETURN
           TNET=TNET+SALEN
           TPAY=TPAY+PAY
           WRITE(6,120) NA,ME,SALES,RETURN,SALEN,PAY
           GO TO 10
     90    WRITE(6,130) TSALES,TRETUR,TNET,TPAY
     100   FORMAT(@1NAME    SALES    RETURNS    NET SALES    PAY@/)
     110   FORMAT(2A4,F9.2,F8.2)
```

```
      120    FORMAT(1X,2A4,3X,F9.2,3X,F8.2,3X,F9.2,4X,F7.2/)
      130    FORMAT(@0TOTALS@,5X,F9.2,3X,F8.2,4X,F9.2,2X,F7.2)
             STOP
             END
3     C      THIS PROGRAM COMPUTES THE NET SALES AND PAY FOR THE EMPLOYEES
      C      OF THE AJACKS COMPANY
             WRITE(6,100)
             DATA TSALES,TRETUR,TNET,TPAY/4*0.0/
      10     READ(5,110) NA,ME,SALES,RETURN
             IF(SALES.EQ.99999.99)GO TO 90
             SALEN=SALES-RETURN
             IF(SALES.GT.15000.) GO TO 40
             IF(RETURN.LT.500.) GO TO 50
             PAY=100.00+.06*SALEN
             GO TO 70
      40     IF(RETURN.LT.500.) GO TO 60
      50     PAY=150.00+.06*SALEN
             GO TO 70
      60     PAY=200.00+.06*SALEN
      70     TSALES=TSALES+SALES
             TRETUR=TRETUR+RETURN
             TNET=TNET+SALEN
             TPAY=TPAY+PAY
             WRITE(6,120) NA,ME,SALES,RETURN,SALEN,PAY
             GO TO 10
      90     WRITE(6,130) TSALES,TRETUR,TNET,TPAY
      100    FORMAT(@1NAME     SALES     RETURNS     NET SALES     PAY@/)
      110    FORMAT(2A4,F9.2,F8.2)
      120    FORMAT(1X,2A4,3X,F9.2,3X,F8.2,3X,F9.2,4X,F7.2/)
      130    FORMAT(@0TOTALS@,5X,F9.2,3X,F8.2,4X,F9.2,2X,F7.2)
             STOP
             END
```

CHAPTER 6
DO-CONTINUE Exercises

1(a)   KB's values are 1, 2, 3, 4, and 5.
       The loop is performed five times.

1(c)   K's values are 2, 5, and 8.
       The loop is performed three times.

3(a)
```
              ITOTAL = 0
              DO 10 I = 73,123
      10      ITOTAL = ITOTAL + I
```

3(c)
```
              DATA IT1, IT2/2*0/
              DO 5 K = 10,100,2
      5       IT1 = IT1 + K
              DO 6 L = 11,100,2
      6       IT2 = IT2 + L
```

ANSWERS TO SELECTED EXERCISES AND QUESTIONS   **337**

DIMENSION Exercises

1(a)	Table Names	H	and	IHR
	Mode	Real	and	Integer
	Number of Locations	6	and	165
	Number of Rows	6	and	165
	Number of Columns	1	and	1
1(c)	Table Names	LOB	LOC	and	ALOC
	Mode	Integer	Integer	and	Real
	Number of Locations	20	16		12
	Number of Rows	5	4		3
	Number of Columns	4	4		4

3(a) X

1	1.5
2	
3	2.4
4	
5	3.3

3(c) 157

1	1000
2	1001
3	1002
4	1003
5	1004
6	1005

Implied DO Exercises

1(a) DATA((AB(I,J),J = 1,12),I = 1,3)/36*0.0/
1(c) DATA(AB(I,1),I = 1,5)/5*1.0/
1(e) DATA(AB(I,12),I = 1,5)/5*12.0/
3(a) DIMENSION X(20)
      READ(5,10)(X(I),I = 1,20,2)
3(c) DIMENSION Z(5,10)
      DATA((Z(I,J),I = 1,5),J = 1,10)/10*1.5,40*2.5/
3(e) DIMENSION SUM(4,5)
      WRITE(6,200)((SUM(I,J),I = 1,M),J = 1,N)

Questions

3   C   PROGRAM FOR MATRIX ADDITION
            DIMENSION A(4,5),B(4,5),AB(4,5)
            READ(5,100)A,B
            DO 1 I=1,4
            DO 1 J=1,5
      1   AB(I,J)=A(I,J)+B(I,J)
            WRITE(6,200)AB

```
100     FORMAT(10F5.1)
200     FORMAT(@1     THE SUM OF MATRICES A AND B IS@//4(5F8.1/))
        STOP
        END
```

CHAPTER 7
Specification Exercises

1(a)   DIMENSION X(6,5)
        INTEGER X
                or
        INTEGER X(6,5)

1(c)   DIMENSION H(3,4),I(3,4),J(3,4),HK(3,4)
        DOUBLE PRECISION H,I,J,HK
                        or
        DOUBLE PRECISION H(3,4),I(3,4),J(3,4),HK(3,4)

3(a)   INTEGER GAM,FAM

3(c)   DIMENSION X(3,5),I(2,4)
        DOUBLE PRECISION X,I

3(e)   LK and MK are declared as DOUBLE PRECISION mode. The READ statement for LK and MK references an integer-format code instead of a real-format code as required.

More Specification Exercises

1(a)   COMMON X(6,5)
        INTEGER X

1(c)   COMMON HI(6)
        DOUBLE PRECISION HI

3(a)   DIMENSION FG(12),GF(12)
        EQUIVALENCE (FG,GF)
                 or
        COMMON FG(12),GF(12)
        EQUIVALENCE(FG,GF)

Questions

```
1   C   THIS PROGRAM COMPUTES THE SUM OF THE INTEGERS BETWEEN 6 AND 26
        INTEGER SUM
        SUM=0
        DO 10 I=6,26
10      SUM=SUM+I
        WRITE(6,100) SUM
100     FORMAT(@1THE SUM IS @,I5)
        STOP
        END
```

ANSWERS TO SELECTED EXERCISES AND QUESTIONS

3
```
      C     THIS PROGRAM COMPUTES THE SUM, THE AVERAGE AND THE STANDARD
      C     DEVIATION FOR A SET OF NUMBERS
            DOUBLE PRECISION VAL,SUM,SUMSQ,STDDEV,AVG
            TOT=0.
            SUM=0.0
            SUMSQ=0.0
            READ(5,10) NUM
   10       FORMAT(I2)
            DO 20 I=1,NUM
            TOT=TOT+1.
            READ(5,30) VAL
   30       FORMAT(D20.13)
            SUM=SUM+VAL
   20       SUMSQ=SUMSQ+VAL**2.
            AVG=SUM/TOT
            STDDEV=((SUMSQ/TOT)-AVG**2.)**(1./2.)
            WRITE(6,40) SUM,AVG,STDDEV
   40       FORMAT(@1THE SUM IS @,D20.13//@ THE AVERAGE IS @,D20.13//
           1@ THE STANDARD DEVIATION IS @,D20.13)
            STOP
            END
```

CHAPTER 8

FORTRAN-supplied Subprogram Exercises

1(a)   X is assigned the value 9.375.
1(c)   Y is assigned the value 8.
1(e)   B is assigned the value 0.0.
3(a)   67842   X = FLOAT(KNT)*6.25
3(c)   Y = SIN(3.14/8.)
3(e)   S = FLOAT(10*IB)

Statement Function Exercises

1(a)   ZB is assigned the value of 1.67.
1(c)   Attempt to take the square root of a negative number.
3(a)   ISTX(M,N) = (M+5)*(N+4)
.
.
.
       IS = ISTA(13,72) − ISTA(4,78)
3(c)   PRB(X,Y) = X**5+(Y*X)/X**5
3(e)   GAM(B,C,D,E) = B/C+C/D+B*C/E

FUNCTION Subprogram Exercises

1(a)

Main Program	FUNCTION Subprogram
DIMENSION A(100) . . . Z = AVG(N,A) . . . STOP END	FUNCTION AVG(N,Y) DIMENSION Y(100) SUM=0. DO 10 I=1,N 10 SUM=SUM+Y(I) XN=FLOAT(N) AVG=SUM/XN RETURN END

3(a)

Main Program	FUNCTION Subprogram
REAL LEM,LET . . . LEM=LET(A,B)	REAL FUNCTION LET(X,Y) . . . LET=X*Y*35. RETURN END

3(c)

Main Program	FUNCTION Subprogram
REAL LAST . . . Z = LAST (3.,4.,5.) STOP END	REAL FUNCTION LAST(F,H,X) . . . LAST = F − H/X RETURN END

Questions

1
```
      C     THIS PROGRAM COMPUTES THE DISTANCE BETWEEN TWO CARS ON
      C     INTERSECTING HIGHWAYS
            WRITE(6,7)
            C=0.0
            READ(5,9) X
    5       C=C+1.
            IF(C.GT.X) GO TO 99
            READ(5,10) ACAR,BCAR,DEG
            RAD=DEG*3.14/180.
            DIST=SQRT(ACAR**2+BCAR**2−2.*ACAR*BCAR*COS(RAD))
            WRITE(6,20) DIST
            GO TO 5
    7       FORMAT(@1@)
```

ANSWERS TO SELECTED EXERCISES AND QUESTIONS

```
        9       FORMAT(F5.0)
       10       FORMAT(3F5.0)
       20       FORMAT(@0THE DISTANCE BETWEEN CAR A AND CAR B IS @,F7.2,
                1@ YARDS@)
       99       STOP
                END
3       C       THIS PROGRAM COMPUTES THE LENGTHS OF THE SIDES
        C       OF A PARALLELOGRAM
                RAD(X,Y) = X*.0174528 + Y*.0002909
                C=0.0
                READ(5,85) X
                WRITE(6,80)
                READ(5,90)ADEG,AMIN,BDEG,BMIN
                IF(AMIN+BMIN.GT.60.) GO TO 1
                CMIN = 60. - (AMIN+BMIN)
                CDEG = 179. - (ADEG+BDEG)
                GO TO 2
        1       CMIN = 120. - (AMIN+BMIN)
                CDEG = 178. - (ADEG+BDEG)
        2       C=C+1.
                IF(C.GT.X)STOP
                READ(5,100)DIAG
                RAD1=RAD(ADEG,AMIN)
                RAD2=RAD(BDEG,BMIN)
                RAD3=RAD(CDEG,CMIN)
                SIDE1=(DIAG*SIN(RAD1))/SIN(RAD3)
                SIDE2=(DIAG*SIN(RAD2))/SIN(RAD3)
                WRITE(6,110)DIAG,SIDE1,SIDE2
                GO TO 2
       80       FORMAT(@1@)
       85       FORMAT(F5.0)
       90       FORMAT(4F4.0)
      100       FORMAT(F6.2)
      110       FORMAT(@0WHEN THE LENGTH OF THE DIAGONAL IS @,F6.2,@ INCHES,
                1THE LENGTHS OF ITS SIDES ARE @,F6.2,@ AND @,F6.2,@ INCHES @)
                END
```

CHAPTER 9
Subroutines with Arguments—Exercises

```
1(a)      ·                                SUBROUTINE SBG(I,M,P)
          ·                                   ·
          ·                                   ·
          1                                   ·
                  CALL SBG(5,6,7.5)
          2
                  CALL SBG(15,16,175.0)
```

1(c)
```
           DOUBLE PRECISION X(10),L(10)          SUBROUTINE ZEP(Z,E,P,I,J)
             .                                   DOUBLE PRECISION P(10),I(10)
             .                                     .
             .                                     .
           CALL ZEP(C,D,X,L,M)                     .
             .                                   RETURN
             .                                   END
             .
           CALL ZEP(A,Y,X,L,N)
             .
             .
             .
           CALL ZEP(W,R,X,L,K)
             .
             .
             .
           STOP
           END
```

3(a)
```
           READ(5,100)A,B                        SUBROUTINE SUM(T,V,Z)
           CALL SUM(A,B,X)                         .
           CALL SUM(A**2,B**2,Y)                   .
           WRITE(6,200)A,B,X,Y                     .
             .                                   RETURN
             .                                   END
             .
           STOP
           END
```

3(c)
```
           REAL X(100),K(100)                    SUBROUTINE XBAR(N,IN)
             .                                   REAL IN(100)
             .                                     .
             .                                     .
           CALL XBAR(N,X)                          .
             .                                   RETURN
             .                                   END
             .
           CALL XBAR(M,K)
             .
             .
             .
           STOP
           END
```

Subroutines with COMMON Statements—Exercises

1(a)   .50000   14.00000   7.00000
1(c)   1,121,441,961,1681

ANSWERS TO SELECTED EXERCISES AND QUESTIONS

3(a)
```
        COMMON ZX,AI                SUBROUTINE THT
           .                        COMMON XI,YJ
           .                           .
           .                           .
        CALL THT                       .
           .                        RETURN
           .                        END
           .
        STOP
        END
```

3(c)
```
        COMMON X(5),Y,K             SUBROUTINE STEPA
        DOUBLE PRECISION Y          COMMON A(5),Y,K
        REAL K                      DOUBLE PRECISION Y
           .                        REAL K
           .                           .
           .                           .
        CALL STEPA                     .
           .                        A(5)=K
           .                        RETURN
           .                        END
        RETURN
        END
```

Questions

```
1    C    THIS PROGRAM PROJECTS COSTS FOR 1979 TO 1982
          COMMON W(12),X(12),Y(12),Z(12)
          WRITE(6,90)
          DO 10 I=1,8
          READ(5,100) X(I),Y(I)
          W(I)=X(I)**2
10        Z(I)=X(I)*Y(I)
          DO 20 J=9,12
20        READ(5,110) X(J)
          I1=1
          I4=4
          CALL PROJ(I1,I4)
          I4=8
          CALL PROJ(I1,I4)
90        FORMAT(@1@)
100       FORMAT(2F6.0)
110       FORMAT(F6.0)
          STOP
          END
          SUBROUTINE PROJ(L,M)
          COMMON W(12),X(12),Y(12),Z(12)
          L4=1970+L
```

```
              M4=1970+M
              C=0.0
              TOTW=0.0
              TOTX=0.0
              TOTY=0.0
              TOTZ=0.0
              DO 50 J=L,M
              C=C+1.
              TOTW=TOTW+W(J)
              TOTX=TOTX+X(J)
              TOTY=TOTY+Y(J)
        50    TOTZ=TOTZ+Z(J)
              B=(C*TOTZ-TOTX*TOTY)/(C*TOTW-TOTX**2)
              A=TOTY/C-B*TOTX/C
              WRITE(6,140) L4,M4
              WRITE(6,145)
              DO 60 I=9,12
              Y(I)=A+B*X(I)
              IYEAR=1970+I
        60    WRITE(6,150) IYEAR,X(I),Y(I)
        140   FORMAT(@PROJECTED COSTS BASED ON YEARS ,@I4,@ THROUGH @,I4)
        145   FORMAT(@0YEAR    PRODUCTION    COSTS@/)
        150   FORMAT(1X,I4,6X,F5.0,7X,F5.0)
              RETURN
              END
3       C     SORTING STUDENT GRADES
              INTEGER NAME(100), GRADE(100)
              N=1
              READ(5,100) NODAY
              DO 1 I=1,NODAY
        1     READ(5,101) NAME(I),GRADE(I)
        C     CALL SUBROUTINE TO SORT GROUP ONE
              CALL SORT(N,NODAY,NAME,GRADE,1)
              READ(5,100) NONGT
              DO 2 I=1,NONGT
              N2=NODAY+I
        2     READ(5,101) NAME(N2),GRADE(N2)
        C     CALL SUBROUTINE TO SORT GROUP TWO
              CALL SORT(NODAY+1,N2,NAME,GRADE,2)
              READ(5,100) NOMAR
              DO 3 I=1,NOMAR
              N5=N2+I
        3     READ(5,101) NAME(N5),GRADE(N5)
        C     CALL SUBROUTINE TO SORT GROUP THREE
              CALL SORT(N2+1,N5,NAME,GRADE,3)
        C     CALL SUBROUTINE TO SORT ALL THREE GROUPS
              CALL SORT(N,N5,NAME,GRADE,4)
```

ANSWERS TO SELECTED EXERCISES AND QUESTIONS

```
100     FORMAT(I3)
101     FORMAT(A4,I3)
        STOP
        END
        SUBROUTINE SORT(N,M,NM,GR,L)
        INTEGER NM(100),GR(100),TEMP
        N1=M-1
        DO 1 I=N,N1
        K=I+1
        DO 1 J=K,M
        IF(GR(I).GE.GR(J)) GO TO 1
        TEMP=GR(I)
        GR(I)=GR(J)
        GR(J)=TEMP
        TEMP=NM(I)
        NM(I)=NM(J)
        NM(J)=TEMP
1       CONTINUE
        WRITE(6,200) L
        DO 2 I=N,M
2       WRITE(6,201) NM(I),GR(I)
200     FORMAT(@1SORTED VALUES FOR GROUP@,I4,/@0INITIALS@,
        13X,@GRADE@/)
201     FORMAT(3X,A4,4X,I4)
        RETURN
        END
```

INDEX

A-code format, 56–58
Actual argument, 232, 260
Addition matrices, 166–169, 178–181
Algorithm, 4
.AND., 325–327
Arguments:
   actual, 232, 260
   dummy, 232, 242, 260
   implicit, 262, 280–283
Arithmetic assignments, 21–26
Arithmetic IF statements, 112
Arithmetic operators, 16–17
Arrays, 150
   one-dimensional, 152
   two-dimensional, 152–153

Built-in-error routine, 131, 166

CALL statements, 259–262
Card layout of FORTRAN coding form, 12

Card punching, 309
Central processor unit (CPU), 2
Character string constant, 47, 56–58
Closed loop, 98–99
Coding the program, 4
Column headings, 92
COMMENTS statement, 41
COMMON statement, 202–203, 280–282
Compilation, 30
Computed GO TO statement, 123–124
Computer system, 1
   components of, 1
Conditional branch instruction, 108
Conditional transfer of control statement, 108
Constants, 11, 13–14
   character string, 47, 56–58
   double-precision, 13–14
   integer, 13–14
   logical, 327–329
   real, 13–14

Continuation characters, 8, 50–51
CONTINUE statement, 136–137
Control cards, 8–9
Control character, 58
Control unit, 1–2
Counter, 107, 118, 120
Counter method loops, 120–123

D-code format, 190
D exponent, 14, 190–193
DATA statement, 87–89
Debug, 295
Declaration statements, 152, 185–215
Delimiter cards, 43
DIMENSION statement, 150–157
  execution time, 277–278
Documentation, 4
DO statement, 135–141
  implied loops, 173–175
  index of, 136
  nested loops, 138, 148, 163
  object of, 136
  parameters, 135
  range of, 136
  rules of, 138
Double-precision constant, 13–14
DOUBLE PRECISION statement, 189–190
Dummy arguments, 232, 242, 260
Dummy data values, 115–117
Dummy variable, 285
Duplication factor, 303

E-code format, 46

E exponent, 13–14, 46
END statement, 30
EQUIVALENCE statement, 203–207
Error messages, 323–324
Executable statement, 109
Execution time DIMENSIONing, 277–278
Exponentiation, 16–17
Expression, 16–17, 21

F-code format, 46
Fixed-point fields, 72
Floating decimal point field, 72
Flowchart symbols, 5–6
Flowcharts, 4
Format-free input/output, 302–305
  PRINT, 302–305
  READ, 302–305
FORMAT statement, 43
  A-code, 56–58
  D-code, 190
  E-code, 46
  F-code, 46
  H-code, 47
  I-code, 43
  L-code, 328–329
  X-code, 46–47
  use of quote ('), 58
  use of slash (/), 48–49
FORTRAN, 7
FORTRAN coding form, 8, 10
  card layout, 12
FORTRAN statements, types, 7, 8
FORTRAN-supplied subprograms, 217–218, 319–321

INDEX

FUNCTION subprograms, 242–244

GO TO statement, 97–100
   computed, 123–124

H-code format, 47
Hollerith fields, 47, 58

I-code format, 43
IF statements, 108–112
   arithmetic, 112
   logical, 108–109, 325–327
Implicit argument, 262, 280–283
Implied DO loops, 173–175
Index of DO statement, 136
Initializing of variable, 87, 118
Input unit, 1–2
Integer constant, 13–14
INTEGER statement, 185–186
I/O extensions, 80–81

Keypunch, 8
Keypunch instructions, 309–318

L-code format, 328–329
Library of FORTRAN-supplied functions, 217
Logical operations, 325–329
   constants, 327–329
   format, 328–329
   logical IF statement, 108–109, 325–327
   logical operators, 16–17, 108–109, 325–327
   LOGICAL statement, 327–329
   variables, 327–329

Loops, 97–98
   counter method, 120–123
   dummy value method, 115–117
   nested, 138, 148, 163

Mathematical operators, 16–17
   arithmetic, 16–17
   logical, 108–109, 325–327
   Priority of operations for, 17, 327
Matrices, 152–153
   addition, 166–169, 178–181
   multiplication, 168–169, 180–181
   subtraction, 168
Memory unit, 1–2
Mixed mode, 22, 302, 306–307
Multibranch conditional transfer, 123–124
Multiple assignment statements, 300–301
Multiplication matrices, 168–169, 180–181
Nested loops, 138, 148, 163
Nested subroutines, 265
Nonexecutable statement, 30, 109, 152
.NOT., 325–327

Object of DO statement, 136
One-dimensional array, 152
Operators, 16–17
   arithmetic, 16–17
   logical, 108–109, 325–327
.OR., 325–327
Out-of-data condition, 105
Out of range, 123–124

Output unit, 1–2

Parameters of DO statement, 135
Parentheses, 16–17
PRINT statement, 80
Priority of operations, 17, 327
Processor unit, 1–2
Program, 1, 3
Program loop, 97–98
Program steps, 3–4
   coding, 4
   documentation, 4
   flowcharting, 4
   method of solution, 4
   problem definition, 3

Quote format, use of, 58

Range of DO statement, 136
READ statement, 67–68, 80–81
Real constant, 13–14
REAL statement, 186–189
Recursive definition, 233
RETURN statement, 244, 259–262
Routine, 269
Rules of DO statement, 138

Service routines, 217
Single precision, 13
Slash format, use of, 48–49
Sort routine, 211
Sorting, 160–164, 271–272, 288–290
Specification statements, 185–215
   COMMON, 202–203, 280–282
   DIMENSION, 150–157

DOUBLE PRECISION, 189–190
EQUIVALENCE, 203–207
INTEGER, 185–186
LOGICAL, 327–329
REAL, 186–189
Stacked tables, 275
Standard I/O units, 80–81
Statement functions, 231–232
Statement label, 21
STOP statement, 30
Subprograms, 217
Subroutine subprograms, 259
Subroutine statements, 259–262
Subscripted variables, 150, 152
Subtraction matrices, 168

Table lookup, 171–172, 181
Tables, 150
Transfer commands, 97
Two-dimensional array, 152–153

Unconditional branch instruction, 98
Unconditional transfer of control statement, 98

Variable names, 15–16
   double-precision, 189–190
   integer, 15–16
   real, 15–16

WATFOR and WATFIV extensions, 295–307
WRITE statement, 27–29

X-code format, 46–47